Napoleon, the Jews and the Sanhedrin

THE LITTMAN LIBRARY OF JEWISH CIVILIZATION

EDITORS
David Goldstein
Louis Jacobs
Lionel Kochan

This Library is dedicated to
the memory of

JOSEPH AARON LITTMAN

Napoleon, the Jews
and the Sanhedrin

SIMON SCHWARZFUCHS

ROUTLEDGE & KEGAN PAUL
LONDON, BOSTON AND HENLEY

First published in 1979
by Routledge & Kegan Paul Ltd
39 Store Street,
London WC1E 7DD,
Broadway House,
Newtown Road,
Henley-on-Thames,
Oxon RG9 1EN and
9 Park Street,
Boston, Mass. 02108, USA
Set in Bembo 12 on 13pt
and printed and bound in Great Britain at
The Camelot Press Ltd, Southampton

British Library Cataloguing in Publication Data
Schwarzfuchs, Simon
Napoleon, the Jews and the Sanhedrin. –
(The Littman library of Jewish civilization).
1. Jews in France – History   2. Jews – Emancipation
3. Napoleon I, Emperor of the French
I. Title   II. Series
323.1'19'24044   DS135.F82   78–40812

ISBN 0 7100 8955 4

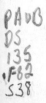

To Avrom Saltman

Contents

		page
	Foreword by Lionel Kochan	ix
	Preface	xi
I	The Revolution and the Jews of France	1
II	Napoleon's First Encounter with the Jewish Problem	22
III	The Calling of the Assembly of Notables	45
IV	The Meetings of the Assembly of Notables	64
V	The Great Sanhedrin	88
VI	The Duped	115
VII	In the Empire	143
VIII	In Non-French Europe	164
IX	The Results	179
	Bibliographical Note	195
	Notes	197
	Index	215

Foreword

The French Revolution and the Napoleonic period brought to the Jews of France, the Netherlands, Western Germany and Italy the first intimations of modernity. It brought equality before the law, an end to oppressive taxation and enforced residential restrictions, and the opportunity to participate as free men in public and political life. True to the ideals of the Enlightenment, the Revolution granted to the Jew his rights as a citizen. Article X of the Rights of Man and the Citizen declared: 'No person shall be molested for his opinions, even such as are religious provided that the manifestation of their opinions does not disturb the public order as established by the law.' It is true of course that in the reaction that followed the downfall of Napoleon, in certain areas, notably in Italy, the Jew lost his new status. Even in France itself, the early achievements of the Revolution were in part nullified by Napoleon's policy. Yet for all that, nothing can deprive the French Revolution of its rightful claim to have inaugurated a new and more hopeful era in the life of European Jewry.

But this achievement and this era were replete with ambiguities, half-lights and lurking doubts. On what grounds did certain of the revolutionaries deny their own principles and oppose emancipation? Why were the Jews of France emancipated in two stages? Most important of all: what were the new institutions that Napoleon introduced for the regulation of the religious and secular life of the Jews of France? And how did the Sanhedrin, summoned by Napoleon in 1806 in order to implement his policy, adapt Judaism to the new circumstances of its existence?

These are some of the crucial questions to which Professor Schwarzfuchs addresses himself. Now that the classical age of Jewish emancipation in the nineteenth century is concluded, a reappraisal is required that will pay due attention both to the internal Jewish aspect of emancipation and to its place in the history of Napoleonic France.

It was in Italy in 1797 and in Egypt in 1798 that Napoleon first came into contact with organised Jewish communities. But these encounters gave no real indication of the situation that confronted Napoleon, now Emperor, when he set out to reorganise Jewish life in France. Here all the ambiguities of the earlier emancipation were expressed. They found their solution in an accommodation whereby the Jews of France made a division between their public rôle as citizens and their private rôle as Jews. Whether the full implications of this enforced choice were evident at the time is by no means clear. But the decision of the Sanhedrin, skilfully guided by Rabbi David Sintzheim, certainly set the pattern for later developments in Jewish life in Western Europe. It proved possible to reconcile, even in the conditions of the modern centralised state, the continued existence of Judaism with the demands of that state.

But this clearly demanded a re-definition of Judaism – a matter to which Professor Schwarzfuchs also gives its full measure of attention. The ramifications of Napoleon's policy did not end there, for one further consequence was to create a division between the Jews of Western and those of Eastern Europe. These complex involvements of the French Revolution and Napoleon in the fate of French and European Jewry have never been examined with such closeness and clarity as in this work. Professor Schwarzfuchs has rendered great service to the history of modern Jewry and modern France alike.

Lionel Kochan

Preface

Today Napoleon has lost much of his good repute among historians. His policies are attacked no less than his so-called liberalism. Very few see in him a son of the French Revolution. Yet the legend remains.

As far as the Jews are concerned, it can hardly be doubted that Napoleon's laws regulating the life of the French-Jewish communities were a turning point in their development in modern free society. As such they have escaped the memory or stigma of their origin to become a permanent part of Jewish life. Napoleon's rôle in their establishment is a matter for historical research, but their acceptance by Western Jews is ample proof of their relevance to Jewish existence. They must be considered as the expression of an answer given to the problem of Jewish survival after emancipation. As long as the faith in this emancipation remained strong, the Napoleonic reforms were applauded. As soon as this hope began to fade, they were accused of having caused the very ills they had been intended to cure. Thus it happened that the revival of Jewish nationalism in modern times negated their usefulness and their results, even as the new state of Israel chose to apply to the Jews in Israel a system of government which recognised the rôle of the Jewish religion, while trying to determine and limit its influence within the state! There can be no doubt then that the debate is still open: the ways of Jewish survival will be discussed for a long time. Yet here is perhaps the justification for this new study of Napoleon's relations with the Jews, which would probably not have been written but for the interest shown in it by Lionel Kochan. He fostered a work which otherwise would probably not have seen the light of day.

CHAPTER I

The Revolution and the
Jews of France

In 1789, on the eve of the Revolution, there lived in France – not counting the Jews of the Comtat Venaissin, which was still a possession of the pope – about 40,000 Jews.[1] Most of these were members of the *nation allemande*,[2] and had settled either in Alsace or in Lorraine; about 20,000–25,000 lived in Alsace, and were excluded from the most important cities; another 3,500 in Metz and the surrounding townships and villages and about 4,000 in the duchy of Lorraine which had become French only about a generation before. The members of the *nation portugaise* were divided mostly between Bordeaux (2,300) and Saint Esprit, a suburb of Bayonne (1,200) which they would soon leave to settle in the city itself, when the prohibitions on local Jewish settlement had been lifted. There were also a number of smaller settlements in south-west France. The Portuguese and German nations met only in Paris, where two small communities of German and Portuguese origin coexisted. The Comtat Jews, of whom there were only about 2,500, living in their four carrières,[3] joined the mainstream of French Jewry only in 1791, after the annexation of the Comtat to France.

Amongst the Jews of north-western France, the Alsatian community was by far the most important in terms of numbers. It was also the community which gave rise to the most complex legal and economic problems. There had been a Jewish community in Alsace since the early Middle Ages. Many were put to death during the Black Death of 1349. It would seem that their number remained fairly small until the second half of the seventeenth century. It then began to increase as a result of the great increase in the westward migration of Jews from Eastern Europe. Alsace was still a patchwork of many different municipalities and principalities. The opposition between Catholics and Protestants only served to increase the confusion. The Alsatian Jewry were scattered throughout these territories and their status varied from region to region. In general they were forbidden to reside in the major cities, such as Strasbourg or Colmar, and were for the most part found living in a multitude of small rural communities. The Jewish population in any one such area might often consist of no more than a single family.

When the area came under French rule at the end of the seventeenth century, the Jews' right of residence was in practice never questioned, and their numbers rapidly grew. In 1690 there were 587 Jewish families, in 1716, 1,348, and in 1754, 2,565. In 1784, when the last census took place, there were 3,913 Jewish families, totalling 19,707 persons, in Alsace. Their number had thus increased sixfold in less than a century and this figure does not take into account the large transient population not included in the census. The Jewish communities were less numerous but more important in the Upper Rhine than in the northern part of the province. All in all, there were about 180 different communities, with the greater part of the Jewish population living in the Lower Rhine region.

Although these communities were eager to maintain their independence, the French authorities imposed on them the rule of *préposés généraux*, who represented the communities in their dealings with government officials. They were particularly active after the scandal of the 'false receipts' (to be dealt with later). The strains which appeared in Alsatian society as a result of the scandal, as well as the rumblings which heralded the outbreak of the Revolution, could not leave the authorities indifferent. They could not avoid dealing with the problem of the Jews, who were at that time very ably represented by Cerf Berr who had succeeded in receiving authorisation to reside in Strasbourg together with his numerous family.

Cerf Berr had been instrumental in securing the abolition of the poll tax which was required of any Jew wishing to spend the day in Strasbourg. Largely through his intervention a new status was given to Alsatian Jewry through Louis XVI's Letters Patent of 10 July 1784. These Letters, which governed the life of Alsatian Jewry until the Revolution, were intended to guarantee the security and stability of Jewish life in Alsace and also to limit the size of the Jewish population. They were allowed to take up different occupations but would have to continue paying their special taxes.

Only those Jews who had taken up legal residence in Alsace and had paid the customary taxes were allowed to remain in the province. All others had to depart within three months. That is why a fresh census was undertaken and a nominal list of the Alsatian Jews published, according to their village or city of residence. This would make it easy to expel all those whose names did not appear on the list. Rabbis were forbidden to officiate at weddings until they had ascertained that the bridal couple had received the indispensable authorisation to marry. Nothing was neglected to ensure that the Jewish community would not increase in size. But it must also be added that the threatened expulsions never took place.

The new economic regulations aimed to persuade the Jews to enter agriculture and handicrafts. They were still allowed to issue loans but on condition that the contracts be counter-signed by two community overseers. The authority of the rabbis and their powers as judges were reaffirmed, within the limits which had always confined their jurisdiction to religious and private problems arising among the Jews themselves. The central organisation of the Alsatian Jewish *nation* was maintained, although the *préposés généraux* were replaced by syndics.

Despite these shortcomings, especially in so far as they limited the Jewish population and its economic activities, the Jews accepted the Letters Patent, which had at least the merit of recognising officially the existence of their community. The

3

préposés were in due course elected as syndics. In fact, nothing had changed in the position of Alsatian Jewry, which continued in its old ways and had confidence in a slow improvement in its status rather than in a sudden change. The basic problem for the increasing Jewish masses settled in an impoverished border province remained economic. Most Jews were poor and could not escape from the traditional activities to which they had been confined.

The same development took place in Metz: the 4 Jewish families tolerated in 1565 had become 24 in 1603, and 420 in 1715. First concentrated in Metz, they had soon set up a number of smaller communities in the *pays messin*. Some of them also found their way into Lorraine, where their increased numbers brought about a corresponding increase in the number of their communities.[4]

The Portuguese Jews of south-western France first appeared in the second part of the sixteenth century, when so-called 'New Christian' merchants settled in Bordeaux in order to trade between France and Spain and Portugal. With every upsurge of Inquisition activity, the number of fugitives increased. Most of them probably passed through Catholic France only in order to find a safer refuge in another country. Still, many remained and joined the local secret Jewish communities of the Portuguese merchants, which is not to say that the number of those who had fled Spain and Portugal and had chosen to remain Christians was particularly small. Only in 1722 were their communities described as Jewish, although it had long been an open secret that their members were not practising Catholics. The immigration of Jewish refugees from Portugal ended, in fact, in the middle of the eighteenth century. By that time a number of Avignon Jews had already found their way to Bordeaux.[5]

The Jews of Avignon and the Comtat, who were not yet French, belonged to the oldest community with continuous existence in France. Since the sixteenth century, as a result of papal policy, they had been quartered in their four carrières – which were small and dirty ghettos – in Avignon, Carpentras, Cavaillon and l'Isle sur la Sorgue. As a result of overpopulation, the Jews of Avignon had started to leave their carrière. Some found a refuge in Bordeaux, where they constituted a separate community which had to fight the Portuguese *nation* for a long time before gaining recognition. Other Comtat Jews had settled in other southern cities (most notably in Marseilles), while others had left for Paris, where they had joined the local Portuguese community. Nevertheless, they still did not form part of the mainstream of French Jewry.[6]

These regional communities were not united in a national organisation. They were rather jealous of their independence, and coexisted as separate entities. Alsatian Jewry itself met many difficulties on its way to organisational unity, inasmuch as the province of Alsace itself was hopelessly split into many different feudal or municipal units, which were extremely reluctant to give up their rights and authority over their Jews: Alsace therefore remained divided between five or six rabbinates until the French Revolution. Nevertheless, from the middle of the eighteenth century, probably at the insistence of the provincial Intendant, there appeared a common representation of the different Alsatian communities: the *préposés généraux* represented the whole community. In 1777, the representatives of this *nation* met in Nidernai and enacted a number of *takkanot*, or ordinances, which were intended to apply to the whole of Alsatian Jewry.[7] The most important of these *préposés* or syndics was Hertz of Medelsheim, who is better known as Cerf Berr.[8] The important services he had rendered the French army, of which he had become one of the main suppliers, had brought him in contact with the French court, and he never hesitated to use his considerable influence on behalf of his Alsatian brethren.

The Jews of Metz and the surrounding county constituted a separate *nation*, which was organised independently of the Alsatian *nation*. It was dominated by the community of Metz which by virtue of its urban character differed considerably from Alsatian Jewry. The neighbouring Lorraine Jews constituted a different *nation*, with its own syndics and its own Rabbin de Lorraine.[9] Its relationship with Metz Jewry was based on personal ties, not on an organisational basis.

5

In the south-west, Bordeaux and Bayonne and a few smaller village communities were organised into the Portuguese *nation*, which looked upon itself as completely independent from the German *nations* of Alsace, Metz and Lorraine. Even in their dealings with central government, the different *nations* employed different *shtadlanim*, or representatives, who were called in French *agents de la nation*. There is no evidence that they tried before the Revolution to act together, or to co-ordinate their activities. As a matter of fact, when in 1788 the minister Malesherbes, who had just obtained official recognition of the non-Catholic Christian denominations in France, decided to deal with the problems of the Jewish religion also, and a conference of the representatives of all the Jewish *nations* was called in Paris, the split was evident. The Portuguese delegates, including Abraham Furtado who was to play a very important rôle in the Jewish assemblies which took place under Napoleon, were essentially interested in the conservation of their privileges and had no wish at all to lose their independence, or to become members of a larger French-Jewish community, to be treated on the same footing as the German *nations*. On the other hand, the delegates of the Jewish *nations* of eastern France led by Cerf Berr were mainly interested in receiving complete religious freedom, and in improving their rights of residence and commerce. They did not care about civic rights, and did not ask for them. At this conference a difference of outlook as to religious practice became evident: the rich Portuguese Jews, who by that time had become a part of the local society of Bordeaux, proved to be much more liberal than the Alsatian Jews, who had remained very attached to traditional religious practice. As Malesherbes had to leave the government by the end of the year, the conference produced no results. By that time the preparation of the États Généraux was already in full swing.[10]

The Jews were mentioned mostly in the *Cahiers de doléances* of the region they inhabited: they were considered to be more a provincial than a national problem. Most of the complaints which were raised against them had to do with their economic activities; i.e. their usury and other 'illicit dealings'. Different solutions were suggested as a means to put an end to this situation. They ranged from a demand for their expulsion from France to the enactment of very rigorous legislation to contain them and to make them change their activities. A very few of the *Cahiers de doléances* did ask for an amelioration of their status, which, it was hoped, would have a very beneficial influence on their behaviour.[11]

It would seem that the Jews had wanted to take part in the preparation of the *Cahiers de doléances* in the different provinces they lived in: after all, they belonged to a recognised corporation, and thought that they had a right to be consulted on the problems and wishes of the Third Estate. In Bordeaux they were allowed to take part in the elections, and one of them was almost elected a delegate to the Estates General. In Bayonne, or rather Saint Esprit, the local Jews, at first forgotten, were finally allowed to take part in the preparation of the *Cahiers de doléances*. Here and there, they decided not to prepare a list of their own specific demands, and not to appear as a separate body: they merged with their region as they were probably convinced that they would receive confirmation of their rights without having to fight a public war for them.[12]

The Jews of eastern France were excluded from the assemblies which prepared the *Cahiers de doléances*, and took no part in the election of delegates to the Estates General. Cerf Berr complained bitterly at these abuses, and eventually the Jews of the three eastern *nations* were allowed to submit to the Etats not a *Cahier*, but a report. The three *nations* elected a committee of six – two from each *nation* – to represent them: Rabbi David Sintzheim (Cerf Berr's brother-in-law) and Seligman Wittersheim were elected by the Jews of Alsace, the latter being soon replaced by Theodore Cerf Berr, Cerf Berr's son. Goudchaux Mayer Cahen and Louis Wolf represented Metz and Berr-Isaac Berr and Mayer Marx the communities of Lorraine. They asked for complete fiscal equality with the other citizens of France, and for the abolition of all taxes and levies which applied only to Jews. They wished to receive complete freedom of residence and commerce, and no longer to be restricted to specific areas of residence. They wanted to become citizens but insisted on being allowed 'to keep our synagogue, our rabbis and our syndics'.[13] It is evident that they did not wish to give up their autonomous organisation, and that their interest in political rights was rather weak. The important thing was to improve their conditions of existence, to put an end to various abuses, and to enjoy complete protection from violence. They did not think it was necessary to give up their specific organisation in order to attain their aims. Curiously enough, the communities of Lunéville and Sarreguemines took a different position: they wished 'to cease being a separate corporation, and remaining somehow foreign to the rest of their cities': they were therefore prepared to give up their traditional organisation. This minority opinion was not accepted by the majority.[14]

Apart from the general demands that the three German *nations* prepared for the Estates General, there were also demands of a more specific or regional nature. The Alsatian Jews asked, among others, for a relaxation of the measures which limited their right to marry, and for a severe prohibition on people in authority employing 'insulting epithets' against them.[15] The Jews of Metz were mostly worried about the Brancas tax, a yearly sum of 20,000 livres which they had had to pay to the Brancas family since 1715.[16] The Jews of Lorraine, on the other hand, wanted to be allowed to open synagogues in all the cities and villages where they lived, and to obtain the right to study freely in colleges or at the university.[17]

It soon became obvious that the forces which had already begun to shape a new France were beyond the control, and even the guidance, of the Jewish communities. In Upper Alsace, in the Sundgau, riots broke out, and the Jews who had been held responsible for all the difficulties of the impoverished peasants' lot had to flee in their hundreds, and to find a temporary refuge in Basel or Mulhouse. Abbé Gregoire, who had already won some acclaim for his prizewinning essay on the regeneration of the Jews in France and who was a delegate to the Estates General, felt that he had to draw the attention of the latter to the condition of the Jews and to ask for their protection. Nevertheless, the problem of the status of the Jews came up only with the discussion of the Declaration of the Rights of Man. On 26 August 1789, it was agreed that 'no person shall be molested for his opinions even such as are religious, provided that the manifestation of their opinions does not disturb the public order as established by the law'. This formula had the great merit of guaranteeing the stability of the Jewish communities of France, but gave no evidence of any improvement in their status.

It is worth while to note that the small community of Paris, which was well aware of the proceedings of the new National Assembly, and was in a position to play a rôle which considerably exceeded its numerical importance, had turned to the Assembly the day before, on 26 August. It had submitted a petition and asked that the Jews receive complete political equality: it offered solemnly to give up its laws, its police and its courts, and its specific leaders. It was ready to renounce its autonomy in order to allow its former members to become fully-fledged citizens of France. As such, they would keep their religion, which they had no intention of forsaking.[18]

The Jews of eastern France, who seem to have heard about the turn of events somewhat later, turned to the National Assembly on 31 August and asked again for their civil rights, but did not agree to give up their communal organisation. The Jews of Metz already suspected the great danger that complete emancipation would mean to their community: they instructed their delegates to request the enactment of a law which would forbid any and every Jew of Metz to move out of the Jewish quarter without having paid his share of the common debt: 'This necessary law will prevent disastrous emigration which would make it possible to evade one's obligations, the consequence of which would be to impose on a small number of Jews the obligations which apply today to all of those who are gathered in the same quarter.' For the first time, some of the adverse effects of emancipation were clearly delineated.[19]

The Portuguese Jews, who were also represented in Paris, did not react. Maybe they were convinced that time would work in their favour, and that it was important not to be confused with the other Jewish communities in France.

The National Assembly granted its protection to the Jews of

9

Alsace and to their property, and continued to debate the status of non-Catholic Frenchmen, that is of Christians who were not Catholics. When the problem of their eligibility came up, some members of the National Assembly tried to include the Jews in the definition of non-Catholics, while others refused to do so. As a measure of compromise, the Assembly resolved, after having granted full rights to Protestants, not to decide anything about the Jews, whose status would be examined and acted upon at a later date.[20]

The Portuguese Jews were bitterly disappointed by this decision, and decided to react. They dissociated themselves from the Jews from eastern France, and asked to have their specific status taken into consideration. After all they had received many favourable Letters Patent from the kings of France and enjoyed many rights which a strict interpretation of the decision of 24 December seemed to take away from them. After a somewhat tumultuous debate, the National Assembly voted on 28 January 1790 to grant full rights to the Portuguese, Spanish and Avignon Jews. This satisfied the former, who returned home, dissolved the Portuguese *nation*, and set up a voluntary organisation which took care of their religious and charitable activities.[21] This change was accepted by them without undue difficulty: the long tradition of secrecy which had enabled the New Christians to survive as Jews had prepared them for a greater measure of independence and a greater flexibility than the Jews of Alsace and Lorraine were ready to accept. From that time on, they did not show much interest in the future of their brethren of the German *nations*.

The delegation of the Jews of eastern France joined by Cerf Berr himself had understood the danger in the decision the National Assembly was about to take: on the same day, 28 January, they addressed a petition to the speaker of the National Assembly, asking that 'our fate be decided at the same time as that of our brethren of Bordeaux.'[22] Whatever the reason – the petition may have reached the speaker too late, or the Assembly may have feared to antagonise the delegates of Alsace who were bitterly opposed to the Jews – no action was taken on their demand, no decision followed concerning the Jews of the German *nations*, who would therefore have to fight their war alone.

The district assemblies of Paris had voted to support the Jewish demands, but the National Assembly listened to their demands without being able to bring itself to the point of decision. The opponents of Jewish emancipation who were afraid of the precedent of the Portuguese Jews' emancipation did their best to prevent its use in favour of the Jews of the German *nations*. Hostility against them was rekindled, and many Alsatian municipalities, including that from Strasbourg, wrote to the National Assembly to inform it of their opposition to any favourable change in the status of the Jews.[23] The Assembly, which had enough difficulties on the eastern borders, chose not to act. It would have seemed that the Jews had lost their case, but for the internal dynamics of the revolutionary ideal.

On 27 September 1791, as the mandate of the Assembly was nearing its end, one of the deputies from Paris reminded his colleagues that on 24 December 1789 the Assembly had decided that a decision would be taken on the Jews' status, and that this had not yet been done. Despite the opposition of the leaders of the Alsatian deputies, it was resolved not to delay any longer. The principle of the emancipation of the Jews was then adopted unanimously. The next day the final version of its resolution was accepted:[24]

> The National Assembly, considering that the conditions necessary to be a French citizen and to become an active citizen are determined by the Constitution, and that every man who meets the said conditions, takes the civic oath, and undertakes to fill all the duties which the Constitution imposes has a right to all the advantages it confers, cancels all adjournments, reservations and exceptions inserted in the most important decrees concerning individuals of the Jewish persuasion who shall take the civic oath, which oath will be regarded as a renunciation of all privileges and exceptions previously granted in their favour.

Not wishing to antagonise the Jews' opponents any more, the Assembly decided to ask the Jews to prepare and hand over a list of their debtors and of the amounts which were due to them. The district directories were instructed to study the condition whereby the debtors could free themselves. The Alsatian directories were also asked to suggest ways and means to liquidate these debts, and to bring them to the attention of the Jewish leaders and of the Assembly. It does not seem that any action was ever taken upon these demands.[25]

Whatever happened, the Christian masses of Alsace did not react. The emancipation of the Jews was accepted there as the logical outcome of the revolutionary movement which could not be stopped or avoided. Did the Jews rejoice in their new freedom? Their reactions were probably very individual. It does not appear that the Jewish masses had shown great interest in becoming electors or gaining the franchise. They were more concerned for their security and welfare, to live in peace and to support their families. The fight for emancipation had been fought by the well-to-do, and mostly by the urban section of the Jewish population in Strasbourg, Metz and Nancy. Their considerable success would have destroyed the very existence of their communities, as the latter were in no way prepared to introduce a new form of administration. This would have had to be distinct from the autonomous tradition of communal organisation, which had just been destroyed by the Assembly's vote and which had made their new status conditional on their renunciation of all former privileges, but had not asked them to assimilate completely into the nation. They had become Frenchmen like all other Frenchmen, without being prepared for it, and more as a consequence of revolutionary logic than as a result of their own political activities.

Nevertheless, emancipation had become the law of the land, although its enforcement would still take some time. The 'law concerning the Jews' was published only on 13 November 1791, as the king had not been over-hasty in signing it. Some municipalities tried to prevent, or delay, the Jews from taking the civic oath, but very soon all opposition came to an end, and emancipation also became a fact.

In all the debates on the Jews' status, the problem of Jewish usury, essentially in Alsace, had assumed great, if not paramount, importance. Although the extent of Jewish loans had not yet been definitely assessed, there is no doubt that it was very large. Most loans, it would seem, had been made to the impoverished peasant class. The severe economic crisis which would eventually help to bring about the Revolution had not left the peasants untouched. They had had to borrow considerable sums to buy horses or agricultural supplies and were therefore very often indebted to Jews, as no other form of agricultural credit existed. In 1778 a considerable scandal broke out – the forged receipts case. In the Sundgau region, in Upper Alsace, many peasants began refusing to repay their loans to the Jewish leaders, as they produced receipts written in Hebrew characters, which, they maintained, gave proof that the loans had already been repaid. The lenders accused the peasants of using forged receipts and denied vehemently that they had received any payment. The scandal soon assumed such proportions that it became impossible for the authorities to ignore it any longer. An enquiry was ordered, which brought proof that the receipts had indeed been forged. The major culprits were severely punished: three were hanged, five were condemned to the galleys for life and four for short periods, and four others were sent to gaol and banishment. The real instigator of the fraud, Judge Hell, could not be convicted, as there were no clear-cut proofs against him. He was nevertheless exiled to Valence in southern France. He was later elected to the National Assembly and participated there in all the manoeuvres aimed at preventing recognition of the Jews' rights.[26]

Although it is impossible to determine the extent of Jewish usury, the fact remains that public opinion blamed the Jews for all the ills and difficulties of the peasants of Alsace. In later years, this problem would remain dominant, the central government having done practically nothing to remedy the peasants' situation.

The emancipation of the Jews of France had brought them complete freedom of movement. Whereas they would previously have had to secure a permit before coming to Paris or settling in other regions of France, they were now free to travel and to settle wherever they wanted, and they did not hesitate to use this new-found freedom. They began settling in important cities such as Strasbourg, Marseilles or Paris, and started the trend to urbanisation of the Jewish population of France. This process of migration was particularly evident in the former papal possessions of Avignon and Comtat Venaissin, which had been finally reunited with France on 4 September 1791. The Jews, who were living in terribly overcrowded quarters, fled the carrières: in less than twenty years about three-quarters of their population had left to settle all over France, but mostly in the south, where new communities came into being. In other parts of France, people moved more slowly, and the old centres retained most of their population.

This dispersal immediately created very important problems: the different Jewish *nations* had been dissolved as a consequence of emancipation, but their debts remained, and these were quite substantial. The former Jewish communities had indeed run into very heavy debt under the Ancien Régime while at the same time some of their members had become very rich. The very constitution of these communities was responsible for this paradox: in general, tax-payers had been divided, according to their wealth, into three classes, and the members of each class paid almost the same amount in taxes. The result was that usually the very rich paid as much as the rich, the difference being fairly small, and that the community was unable to share out its obligations in proportion to the personal wealth of each of its members. When an emergency occurred, such as the need to pay off some official or to give financial recognition to a renewal of privileges, the community was usually unable to face this expenditure with its own limited means, and had to take a loan. The community of Metz still had to pay the Brancas tax, which, despite all its efforts, continued to be reimposed. The other communities had also had to borrow large sums. On the eve of the Revolution, the Metz community owed about 500,000 livres to its creditors. The four communities of the papal province owed a sum of 800,000 livres. The Jewish *nation* of Alsace had debts comparable to those of Metz. The Portuguese Jews were about the only ones who did not carry such a heavy burden. With the general emancipation of the Jews and the end of communal autonomy, the different communities went practically bankrupt: they could not raise the necessary funds, as contributions which had up to then been received by force of law had suddenly become voluntary. The proud community of Metz, which had promised to repay all its debts, even though it had received its civic rights, found itself in a quandary: it wanted to keep the promise which had been given in good faith at a time when it did not even dream that it would have to give up its autonomous communal organisation – it was at the same time unable to do so as emancipation had deprived it of any legal possibility of collecting dues and taxes, except on a voluntary basis. It had requested that the Metz Jews be prevented from leaving the Jewish quarter until they had paid their part of the communal debt, but the sweep of emancipation had put an end to this hope.[27]

It was in these circumstances that the demand for nationalisation of Jewish debts first arose: the state, which had been the primary cause of the weakening of the Jewish community and which had deprived it of its resources, should therefore accept responsibility for its debts. The Jewish communities were ready to turn over to the state all their properties, which could then be sold, the proceeds being applied to the full or partial repayment of Jewish debts. In the Jews' view, such a step would be quite normal, as the National Assembly had already assumed the debts of the corporations and religious communities it had dissolved in October 1790: the state should therefore deal with Jewish debts just as it was dealing with the debts of these other groups. Whatever the merits of their demand, it was not accepted. The authorities decided that the Jewish debts would not be nationalised, and that they would have to be repaid.[28] The problem was complicated, as very often the loans taken by the Jewish communities had been underwritten by their elected or appointed officials, who were regarded by the Christian creditors as personally responsible for the debts. Therefore, any possibility of these debts being even temporarily suspended had to be abandoned. The result was that the Jewish communities or *nations* which had been dissolved with the proclamation of emancipation had to be revived under the guise and name of Commissions in Charge of Liquidation of the Debts.

They could therefore levy taxes and prosecute tax delinquents. In this way the old organisation of the *nation* was revived, as lists of former members of the dissolved *nations* – and of their children – were compiled. Names were checked so that nobody could escape the burden of the debt, even if he had moved to another residence. It is not surprising that these commissions took over some of the functions of the former communities, although their power was exclusively financial and their authority extended only to the reimbursement of the Jewish debts.[29]

But very soon Jewish worship was also attacked. At the height of Jacobin influence the Jewish religion was spared no more than was the Christian. The cult of Reason became more and more successful, as the old established religions had to fight the new ideal of a universal religion which would make other denominations unnecessary. The Jacobins thus brought the Voltairean ideal to its logical conclusion, in attacking Judaism as well as Christianity. Although the official policy was anti-Jewish and not anti-semitic, it may be wondered whether some remaining residual hostility to Jews did not exert its influence unconsciously on this new attitude. Whatever may have been the case, it would be difficult to call the Jacobins anti-semites, although their anti-Judaism cannot be doubted.

During the Terror, churches, temples and synagogues were closed, and often turned into Temples of Reason. The synagogue of Metz was less fortunate and was used as a stable. The district of Strasbourg forbade the Jews to pray in their synagogues, but prohibited at the same time all other gatherings, with the exception of those of the new revolutionary clubs and religion. Occasionally cantors or teachers were arrested with Catholic priests. Synagogues had to deliver up their silver and gold religious ornaments in order to support the war effort. Sometimes these were confiscated. Public prayer meetings were often organised with great difficulty and in secret places. This was the case in Paris, where services took place in a cellar, or in Haguenau, where a secret synagogue had to replace the former one which had been closed down by the local authorities.

The introduction of the revolutionary calendar, which now

replaced the week by the decade, made observance of the Sabbath very difficult inasmuch as what had hitherto been the seventh day of the week became a movable holiday. Religious education, at least in its public form, was practically discontinued, and the Metz and Alsatian *yeshivot* were closed down. In Strasbourg ritual slaughtering was forbidden, and at least one Jewish butcher who had sold kosher meat was prosecuted for having done so. In general, but with great difficulty, most communities managed to find a supply of it. Circumcision was attacked as a superstitious and useless custom: one rabbi who continued to perform this rite is described as having risked his life to do so. In the best of cases Jewish ministers had to perform their duties in secrecy, and to avoid any publicity.[30]

In their newly found freedom, a substantial number of Jews, intoxicated with the new ideas, took over the revolutionary ideals and participated in the fight against what they called the ancient superstitions which they themselves had renounced. There were many instances of Jews who renounced publicly the faith of their fathers, in favour of the new religion which was deemed superior to it. It is of course very difficult to assess how much was due to fear, and to the success of the revolutionary propaganda and atmosphere, and how much was due to an influence which would prove more permanent. In Saint-Esprit the revolutionary enthusiasm was extreme, as most members of the local Comité de Surveillance, the Jean-Jacques Rousseau committee, were Jewish: one of these even became the first Jewish mayor of the town; i.e. the first Jewish mayor in France.[31]

It is during this period that the first mixed weddings appear. Up to the French Revolution this had been impossible, as everything which was concerned with family life could exist only within a religious framework. Mixed weddings were impossible, as nobody would have performed them, the very idea of a civil ceremony being alien to the whole milieu of the Ancien Régime. With the introduction, and the triumph, of revolutionary ideas it became possible for a Jew to marry a non-Jewish person without either having to renounce his or her religion, and without having to go to any length to receive permission to do so.

There is no doubt that such occurrences were contemplated with great alarm by the Jewish community, which could do nothing about them.

It becomes quite obvious that for most Jews, the Terror, despite its egalitarian ideals, was looked upon as an obstacle, if not as a danger to Jewish life. Little love was lost on it, and its eventual defeat was not looked upon as a regrettable occurrence. David Sintzheim, Cerf Berr's brother-in-law – the latter had died at the beginning of the Terror – described in no uncertain terms the events he had experienced during this period:[32]

> It was in the year 1794, when the days of remembrance, the days of anger, arrived. The Lord opened His treasure and produced the instruments of His anger, and we said: we have been condemned. Were it not for the Lord's mercy on us, we would nearly all of us have disappeared and been lost, as they had proclaimed that they would destroy all the books written in Hebrew. Our numerous faults caused some Scrolls of the Law and precious books to be burnt, and precious treasures were then pilfered. I had to hide away my books. In this period of trouble and anger, those who know the ways of the Talmud stopped travelling and the ways of Zion were desolate. The doors of the Temple were closed to study and to prayer. I could not even study one chapter of a well-known Mishnah. I was in exile and moved from city to city, from border to border. Finally the Lord took pity on mankind, and freed the land from the evil beast. The anger disappeared and everyone returned to his home in peace.

There is no reason to believe that Sintzheim expressed only his own personal opinion. Most probably all the Jews of France had felt the weight of the Terror, and could not have brought themselves, only three years after having received their civil rights (for which they had not even strongly fought), to abandon without difficulty all the institutions and symbols of their religion. Nevertheless, it would be difficult to find a reaction or a condemnation of the Revolution *per se*. The Terror was looked upon as a deviation from the revolutionary ideal. Apart from some circles in the south-west and in Paris, there is practically no trace or sign of free thought among the Jews. All the rather weak attempts to bring about changes in certain aspects of Jewish religion or life remained unsuccessful. Zalkind Hourwitz, who had advocated putting an end to the rabbis' influence, could not make himself heard, and had to retreat into anonymity in this period.[33]

Meanwhile the younger generation began to find its way into the army. The number of volunteers increased steadily, although the great majority still could not contemplate any kind of life remote from their home. On the other hand, there was far greater understanding and readiness to serve in the National Guard, which did not entail service far from home: it is interesting to note that Jews very often asked not to serve on the Sabbath, which shows clearly that they had gladly accepted the new régime inasmuch as it did not interfere with their religious observance.[34] There was no love lost or regret for the Ancien Régime. Still the communities, left to their own devices and deprived of any authority over their former membership, were in not very good shape, and the general state of French Jewry was far from brilliant.

The problem of the debts of the Jewish communities had not yet found its solution, and the creditors regularly claimed their due, as nationalisation of the Jewish communities' debts had been definitely refused by the authorities. In Alsace the situation had somewhat changed as Cerf Berr, a short time before his death, had himself paid the debts of the Jewish community and had thus become the principal creditor of the German *nation*. His sons and heirs looked upon their father's act not as a gift, but as a service rendered, and therefore wanted to be paid back. The communities did not show any great enthusiasm for this proposal, and the heirs were therefore compelled to sue them. The situation became only more complicated as the internal migration of the Jews of France contributed to the dispersion of many old communities and to the relaxation of their influence and control over their former membership.[35]

Still there had been attempts to create some kind of Jewish organisation. In Bordeaux, the *nation* had dissolved itself and reappeared immediately as a welfare organisation. In Lower Alsace a number of Jews led by David Sintzheim, who seems to have taken over some of the responsibilities of his late brother-in-law, protested late in 1794 to the National Convention at the attitude of the local revolutionary bodies: they accused them of treating them very unfavourably, and of trying to take from them their rights as men and citizens. The city of Strasbourg had usurped the right to forbid them to enter it on certain days and at certain hours or even to remain there. It had also presumed to tell their womenfolk how to dress. They had been deprived of their part of the *biens nationaux*, and the title of French citizen had been taken away from them. The people's representative had indeed supported them, but they still would have liked to see stronger action taken against their enemies.[36]

There was probably some progress, but the reorganised voluntary communities do not seem to have been able to cope with all their problems. David Sintzheim, who had been appointed chief rabbi to La Communauté mosaïque de Strasbourg, could not receive his salary, which had been guaranteed to him by the richer members of the community and had to turn to the Ministry of Justice to try to obtain it. This step was forced upon him although he was a member of the foremost family of Alsatian Jewry, and its recognised leader, as his further career would amply show.[37]

None the less, a feeling of having become part of the French people had begun to show itself. In the Year VII of the French Republic (in 1798–9) an unknown author published a prospectus for a new prayer-book in Hebrew with a French translation. Called *Zemirot Israel* and very probably never published, it was supposed to follow the usage of the *Israelim Tsarfatim*, the French Jews. Without any doubt, there was more than a purely geographic indication in the juxtaposition of these two terms.[38]

On the other hand, although the state was not supposed to discriminate among the different religions followed by French citizens, it had not shown great enthusiasm in finding for the Jewish communities the same kind of organisation which had reorganised the Catholic church in France through the concordat of 1801. Even the Protestants had received a new organisation. Only the Jews were left out, although it had been recognised that their problem was outstanding. At the time of the discussion of the laws concerning the organisation of the different cults in 1801, Bonaparte had said in the Conseil d'État: 'As for the Jews, they are a nation apart, the sect of which does not mix with any other: we shall have the time to deal with it later on.'[39] The rapporteur of the law did his best to justify this delay, as this people 'so far as its priesthood and its cult are concerned, sees as one of its greatest privileges to have no ruler but those under which it has always lived, and sees as one of its great privileges to have only God as its lawgiver.'[40] The time was slowly ripening for a serious attempt at the organisation of the Jewish communities of France.

CHAPTER II

Napoleon's First Encounter with the Jewish Problem

It fell to Napoleon as Emperor to tackle the problem of Jewish organisation and survival in a free society seriously. Inasmuch as the Emperor ruled supreme, it is indispensable to examine his personal attitude towards Jews and Judaism in his formative years and in the first years of the Empire, although it is quite clear that the problem would have existed without him, and would have had to be solved anyway.

Napoleon Bonaparte had not met any Jews in his youth, and perhaps not even during his school years in France. His first contact with an organised Jewish community probably took place in Italy during the 1797 campaign. According to an anonymous Hebrew chronicle[1] which was certainly written very soon after the events it describes, the Jewish community of Ancona, still living in its small ghetto, was in danger of extermination, as the advance of the French revolutionary troops in Italy had exacerbated the reactionary and anti-Jewish sentiments of a large segment of the population: 'Each time it was heard that the Frenchmen overpowered their enemies like lions, it added to the hatred of these people against the Jews.' The chronicler added: 'One must know that the Frenchmen dearly love the Jews. The proof of this is that in all the cities and countries they have conquered, if there are any Jews there, they elevate them, lift them up, and debase the seed of Edom (Christianity).' It is in this connection that he mentions the commanding officer of the French army, 'who is called *Chelek Tov* [in Hebrew, 'a good part'], that is Bona Parte: he is good, will be good to the Jews and loves them.' He had not yet intended to come to Ancona, but when he heard of the dangers which threatened the Jews, he gathered his army and rushed to the city saying: 'For God's sake, don't delay, don't wait. Run, rush, don't stop, run to Ancona to save the Jews who are in great danger there. I know they are in great danger because the Christians want to kill them.' The French army saved the Jews of Ancona, who were overjoyed when they discovered that the first French soldiers who entered the ghetto were Jewish! The Frenchmen pulled off the yellow badge that the Jews had had to wear on their hats, and the Jews replaced it with the cockade. The 'liberator of Italy' abolished the laws of the Inquisition, and the Jews felt free at last. Three of them were appointed members of the new municipality, even as the ghetto memories were disappearing with staggering speed. In view of the danger that Ancona might be returned to the pope by the terms of the peace treaty which had been reached with him, the Jews, who greatly feared such a situation, went to Bonaparte, who advised them how to avoid this danger. Later on, when Napoleon returned to Milan, the Jews of Ancona sent a delegation to him to thank him for all he had done for them. He received them favourably, wined and dined them and told them: 'You are free men, you are free men . . . I shall maintain your freedom. Be strong, don't fear and don't worry.' For the Jews of Italy it is obvious that Bonaparte was the son of the revolution, bringing its ideal of freedom to their communities. They felt nothing but gratitude to him.

It is difficult to describe the feelings that the Jews of Egypt – the second great community he met and had to deal with – entertained toward Napoleon. He did reorganise their community, but very little has remained from this period which might illustrate his attitude to the local Jewish population. In an order dated 21 Fructidor of the Year VI (7 September 1798), he appointed two High Priests of the Jewish Nation: the title he had chosen to give to the spiritual leaders of the Cairo community gives new evidence of his natural inclination to relate the Jewish organisation to a somewhat imaginary and faraway past rather than to its most immediate present. He also appointed seven counsellors to assist them 'in the important affairs which concern the community'. In the third and last paragraph, he ordered that 'the two High Priests and the counsellors shall be responsible for any bad conduct and disturbances the Jews may commit.' The rudeness of the tone is no less evident than the desire to preserve the Jewish communal autonomy as a way to facilitate French control.[2] Still, the evidence is too fragmentary to be conclusive.

Another event is connected with Bonaparte's sojourn in the East, and his attempt to advance toward Syria and conquer Palestine. In the Paris *Moniteur Universel*, on 3 Prairial of the Year VII (22 May 1799), it was announced: 'Bonaparte has published a proclamation in which he invites all the Jews of Asia and Africa to gather under his flag in order to re-establish the ancient Jerusalem. He has already given arms to a great number, and their battalions threaten Aleppo.' This communiqué, dated from Constantinople, which did not exactly entertain peaceful relations with France at the time, alluded to events which have always remained baffling. The exact text of the proclamation has not been discovered. Some scholars were of the opinion that the announcement was planted in the press as a propaganda manoeuvre and tended to dismiss it completely. Others tried to explain the matter as a forerunner of political Zionism, Bonaparte having tried to implement a programme which would bring a solution to the contemporary plight of the Jews. This opinion was strengthened by the discovery of a letter sent to Barras, a member of the Directory, by an Irish patriot named Thomas Corbet who seems to have served in the French army, in which he suggested 'that a member of the Directory should dispatch an invitation to two or three Jews of the highest consequence and most respected among the members of their nation, and thus address them: "You are scattered over all the surface of the earth, nowhere as a nation, vilified, degraded by bigoted governments and insulted by the populaces..." ' As the Jews hoped to be once again a nation, they should show interest in the proposals made to them, and wish to see their land freed from the Turks, just as Egypt had been liberated from the Turks. Corbet also expounded different possibilities which could be suggested to the Jews, and which would allow them to subsist and prosper. He even wanted the Directory to tell them that they would be enabled 'in the armies of Bonaparte to learn that art in which you were formerly so distinguished, but from which you are at the moment excluded by all powers on earth.' This was of course an invitation to Jews to join the French army.[3]

It is by no means certain that this letter ever reached Bonaparte or that Barras paid any attention to it. It was written and probably sent on 29 Pluviose of the Year VII, which corresponds to 17 February 1799; had it been transmitted to Bonaparte, it could perhaps have reached him before he started the final phase of his Palestinian-Syrian campaign.

Some years ago it was announced that a document had been discovered[4] which contained the German translation of 'a letter to the Jewish Nation (1) from the French commander-in-chief Buonaparte [and another] (2) from Rabbi Aaron in Jerusalem', which were said to have been translated in 1799; that is, in the year they were sent. It has been argued that Bonaparte's letter was the long-sought proclamation, preserved by a Prague Jewish family who had eventually settled in Vienna, and who could have received a copy of it from a censor of Jewish publications in Prague with whom the family was on friendly terms. Dated 1 Floréal of the Year VII, which corresponds to 20 April 1799, the proclamation did not ask the Jews to join the French army but only 'to take over that which has been conquered, and with that nation's [France's] help to remain master of it, to maintain it against all comers.' Aaron son of Levi, Rabbi of Jerusalem, addressed himself very oddly to 'the children of Captivity in the Lands of sunrise and of sunset, of noon and of midnight'. His letter was dated the month of Nissan 5559. He described himself as 'after the passing of numberless generations, again first Rabbi and Priest in this Holy City', and called on all the 'men of Israel capable of bearing arms [to] gather and come up to us': the aim being to rebuild Jerusalem and the Temple. There is no allusion whatsoever to participation in the campaign against Syria or an attack on Aleppo.

Although it is rather difficult to pass judgment on a document which is known to us only through the English translation that the editor gave of the German translation of the French and Hebrew originals, and since there is no other mention of Napoleon's letter, and since Aaron son of Levi, who was certainly no rabbi of Jerusalem, cannot be identified with any measure of certainty,[5] the documents do not appear to be genuine. The use of the name Buonaparte, which the commander-in-chief of the French army had long given up for Bonaparte, the allusion to Jerusalem as his headquarters (although it is well known that he never went there), the use of some very curious expressions such as the land of noon and of midnight, the clumsy style of the translation, and the general appearance of the letters – all this makes it more than doubtful that these documents can stand the test of criticism. It is also curious to note that Bonaparte's letter is dated from 1 Floréal of the Year VII, which corresponds to 20 April 1799, i.e. to 15 Nissan 5559, which is the first day of Passover, the Jewish celebration of freedom from oppression, and that it does even make an allusion to it. Even Aaron son of Levi who is supposed to have written his letter in the same month does not mention this holiday! Obviously, if Bonaparte had wanted to impress the Jews with his proclamation, he would have issued it before Passover so that it could be read and distributed during the feast. It would therefore seem that if these forged documents were indeed written in 1799, they were intended to serve the same purpose as the famous communiqué published in the *Moniteur*, i.e. propaganda. It is therefore not very surprising that it should have finally landed in an enemy country, such as Austria then was.

There were echoes of this rumour in Palestine. In a circular letter sent by Rabbi Raphael Abraham Lev Aryeh, the 'lion-hearted', to the Italian communities – whose financial help he wanted to enlist for the impoverished and troubled communities of Palestine which had sent him to Europe – their plight is thus described: 'Since Egypt and its adjoining districts have been conquered, many troubles have been brought on us by the wickedness of the people who reside in this country who have slandered us saying that with the [French] army there are 12,000 good soldiers, who are our kin, children of Israel.'[6] This accusation had endangered the whole community of Jerusalem, which had to spend enormous sums of money to prevent a massacre, and was therefore in great need of help. In another letter the number of the Jewish soldiers was reduced to 10,000.[7] Thus the legend was created, and accepted in Europe, that many North African Jewish soldiers had joined Bonaparte's army. This is of course untrue, as they are not mentioned in any of the numerous records of the French forces in Egypt, which had indeed set up Moslem and Coptic contingents, but no Jewish battalions. But whatever the source or the explanation of these stories, one fact remains: nowhere does Bonaparte appear as hostile to the Jews. He is accused of, and thanked for, having brought them freedom, and supported their supposed national aspirations. This reputation followed him to Italy, after his return from Egypt: in 1800, after the battle of Marengo, he was still looked upon as the saviour, and all the Jews rejoiced when they heard about his victories in the Italian war.[8]

It is therefore rather surprising that a few years later he should have shown such violent hostility to the Jews. In a letter to his brother Jerome Napoleon, King of Westphalia, he was to call them 'the most despicable of men', and remind him that his intention was to correct them, but not to increase their number (6 March 1808).[9] The influence of traditional Christian anti-semitism cannot be dismissed, and there is no reason to believe that Napoleon had not been exposed to it. Perhaps the revolutionary period must be looked upon as an interlude during which he contained his reactionary tendencies, only allowing them full expression after he had assumed undisputed power.

It is interesting to note that in the view of contemporary witnesses this change of attitude was ultimately connected with the complaints lodged against the Jews in Alsace. At a discussion in the Conseil d'État which took place on 30 April 1806, Napoleon accused the Jews of being 'a nation within a nation'. He had heard many complaints against them from the Christians in Alsace and the prefect of Strasbourg when he had passed through the city on 23 and 24 January 1806. The Jews had replaced the feudal landlords and had to be protected against their own greed, otherwise they would be in danger of being massacred. He maintained that they were not citizens, and that civil law did not apply to them. They would have to be judged according to political law. Certainly at the demand of the Alsatian delegation he had met, he suggested limiting the number of Jews in Alsace to 50,000 and allowing the others to settle freely in other parts of France. In any case there would have to be control over their trade and loans.[10]

It is therefore of the utmost importance to know what the situation was in Alsace, or rather how the authorities presented it to the Emperor, who, it must be emphasised, never asked for the Jews' opinion on the matter, and did not care to have an enquiry made into it. As far as the authorities were concerned, those Jewish populations of eastern Europe who had been emancipated by the Revolution had not lost their economic identity. It is a fact that in Alsace, for example, beginning towards the end of 1801, the Jews as a group were being blamed for the considerable progress of usury. Whatever the precise extent of their activities and the justification of the claims lodged against them, it cannot be doubted that they were held responsible for it, and that they were most active in this particular field of economic life.

During the years 1803–5, one local Alsatian authority after the other complained about Jewish usury. Before, in the Year X, the general council of the Lower Rhine department had concluded that the Jews who had hitherto been busy supplying the armies during the war period had turned en masse to the credit business and were also busy buying real estate in order to break up large properties and sell them at great profit. The very dispersion of the Jews among the Alsatian villages enabled them to find out which peasant was in need of credit, and to ask for enormous interest. According to one report, the Jewish pedlars could then inform the lenders of the possibilities offered them and of the needs for loans. Thus Jewish usury was becoming a real plague in the country.

There can be no doubt that the opposition to the Jews' dealings had been largely inspired by the legacy of Alsatian anti-semitism, but, nevertheless, the extent of their dealings cannot be ignored. During the period September 1800 to December 1802, no less than 12,296,000 francs were officially lent to Alsatian peasants in the Strasbourg, Saverne and Selestat districts. It has been estimated that probably two-thirds of this sum would probably represent the real amount of the monies lent, as many deeds were registered twice. Even if this were so, the loans would amount to a sum far greater than the yearly income from all Alsatian farms and farming! It would of course be mistaken to attribute all these loans to Jewish usurers: there is no doubt that many Christians joined in the fray, and competed with the Jewish lenders, whose relative importance in this field does not relate in any way to their numerical importance among the Christian population. Their participation in the money business was therefore of paramount importance.

If the decisions of the local courts are to be believed, it becomes obvious that the need for loans, and therefore the practice of usury, was constantly growing. The Strasbourg court of justice decided in favour of Jewish lenders who had complained against their derelict debtors: in 1800–1, 40,000 francs had remained unpaid, in 1801–2, 215,000 francs, in 1802–3, 200,000 francs, and in 1803–4, 250,000 francs. During the first half of the year XIII (September 1804–March 1805), 150,000 francs had remained unpaid. The problem was therefore worsening, as pressure on the debtors increased.

Most of the lenders who had complained to the court were Jewish. The fact that the court usually sided with them does not reduce or diminish the social impact of Jewish usury. The very recurrence of the lawsuits again and again disclosed the importance of the Jews' dealings and the inability of their debtors to reimburse their debts. The seizures and sales, as ordered by the courts, which usually followed, the public character of which proclaimed the plight of the Alsatian peasants, could only increase the suspicion which had so long opposed Jews and Christians in north-eastern France. It is obvious that the precise nature and extent of Jewish usury can perhaps be suspected, but certainly not stated with great precision: the fact remains nevertheless that their debtors as well as the public authorities were convinced that it was responsible for the general plight of the Alsatian countryside. The Jews, it was maintained, endangered its very existence.

On 23 July 1806, Marshal Kellerman maintained in a report to the Emperor that only a very small number of Jews of Alsace refrained from usury and peddling. They were accused of taking very high interest. It was reported that their loans surpassed the sum of 30,000,000 francs. To stop this abuse, the Jews should be compelled to adopt a trade, or, if they refused to do so, they should be expelled.[11] In another report presented to the Emperor by the Minister of the Interior of 9 April 1807, which followed a number of complaints lodged in Alsace, it was reported that from the beginning of the year VII (September 1798) until 1 January 1806 the mortgages recorded in the administration's books in favour of Jews by the peasants of the Upper Rhine department alone amounted to 21,199,826 francs. Apart from this enormous sum, about another 10,000,000 francs was owed to the Jews, who had already acquired through expropriation or purchase a sizeable number of properties or farms. Their mortgages applied mostly to the poorer part of the working population. The Minister noted that at that time the whole annual land tax for this department amounted to no more than 1,800,000 francs. He deemed it necessary to add that the Jews had imitators in the departments where they lived, and that the situation of the peasants was no better in the departments where there were no Jews. It must also be added that the report did not distinguish between licit mortgages and usurious ones.[12]

The Jews did not agree with these one-sided accusations. In April–May 1803 the representatives of 'the citizens professing the cult of Moses' wrote to the Minister of the Interior that it was 'very painful for French citizens to hear only indirectly that particular complaints have been lodged against them, which have been accepted with too much reliance by the Prefecture'. The Conseil Général of the Lower Rhine department had prepared a report about this matter without even bothering to get in touch with them. They had suggested some measures which were not only unconstitutional but also punished the whole community for the fault of a few individuals. They requested therefore[13]

that every opinion concerning them be suspended, and to
authorise the communication to them of alleged information
incriminating them while imposing an interval to give useful
information to the government ... He who is entitled to a hearing
shall be condemned only after he has been heard. The guilty
alone shall be subject to losing their right to the protection of the
law ...

It became obvious that there was no intention of listening to the representatives of the Jews: the Emperor had already decided that the Jews had not really become French citizens, and that an effort should be made to remedy this situation.

What was the attitude of the liberal element, when confronted with this new Jewish problem? How did they react to it, as they were torn between their devotion to the revolutionary ideals and their discontent with the slow progress of the Jewish integration into the French nation? A former representative from the Vaucluse department, Moureau, published in 1819 his thoughts on the Jewish problem, which he called 'De l'incompatibilité entre le Judaïsme et l'exercice des droits de cité et des moyens de rendre les Juifs citoyens.'[14] He described in it his reactions when confronted with the problem of the recently emancipated Jews. To him it was evident that the Jews themselves were to blame for any opposition they encountered when wanting to receive or to use their civic rights, because they were not ready to give a guarantee in advance of reciprocity. The price had to be paid, unless it was agreed that there existed an absolute opposition between Judaism and the exercise of civic rights. He asked why a Frenchman could become a German, or a German a Frenchman according to the laws regulating naturalisation, whereas a Jew remained a Jew. A Jew born in Germany would define himself as a German Jew, and it is clear that the word 'German' is here an adjective governing the word 'Jew'! The fact is that Judaism is not only a religion, but also a social state. In Judaism, religion and politics are mixed. The Jew refuses to intermarry with the daughters of another nation. Therefore, if this nation has its own political laws which isolate it necessarily from other nations, if everything in it is religion, if everything turns into dogma, how can it seek to enjoy the social prerogatives of other nations, as there will always be a possibility of opposition between its religion, Judaism, and the duties which derive from these prerogatives? It is quite obvious, maintained Moureau, that the Jew does not look upon a man who is not Jewish as his brother. To illustrate his point, he recalled that during the Revolution when he served in the Avignon region as a prosecutor in the city of his birth, two Jews had been appointed members of the municipality: he could never manage to have them sign on the Sabbath the decision which had been agreed upon in council in their presence the same day. When he enquired into the reason of their refusal, they answered that the law of the Lord must be obeyed before the law of the land. After lengthy discussions, the result was that the two Jews finally stopped attending the meetings of the municipality on the Sabbath. There could be no doubt therefore that some principles of the Jewish nation are in opposition to the needs of a sound administration. The Jews want to be Jews before being men, therefore they are Jews before being citizens. How can they claim rights, while at the same time rejecting some of their implications?

They refuse to give their children the same education that their fellow citizens give their children: this is why they do not send their children to public school and do not use the opportunities open to them since their emancipation. Moureau accused them of remaining first of all Jews, because their religion forbade them to work on the Sabbath, and therefore their children from attending school on that day, as they would have to do some writing in school. Their religion forbids them to mix with other people. There is an obvious need to separate in the Jewish religion that which is demanded by reason and that which is a general consequence of superstition. The former has to be kept; the latter, being odious, atrocious and unjust, has to be rejected. The Jews must change their ways, give up selfishness and accept other men as their brethren. Meanwhile, a differentiation must be made between tolerance, which is due to them, and the granting of civic rights, which can only be a consequence of their integration into French society. They must become Frenchmen practising the Jewish religion. Judaism must become a religion and cease to be a people.

It is clear that apart from the specific complaints lodged against certain Jewish usurers, the misunderstanding was total. The Jews were asked to join a French society which had rejected the Christian meaning of the very Christian institutions it had maintained, such as the Sunday, which had become a day of rest and had ceased to be a holy day: they were supposed to reject Jewish practices, to which they were still attached, in favour of so-called French national habits, which had retained their Christian appearance despite the general decline of Christianity. The majority felt it had the right to impose the remnants of a Christian way of life, which had become part of the French lay tradition, on those who had never accepted the Christian heritage. It is not surprising to note that in this view the defects which were recognised in Judaism were looked upon not only as a consequence of the persecutions and legal segregation to which the Jews had been subjected, but also as a consequence of the very teachings of Judaism.

If this was the opinion of a representative of the liberal party, it is not surprising that the representative of the conservative camp, which denied the very value of the reforms of the French Revolution, should have adopted a more extreme and more violent position. In 1806, probably at the instigation of the government or at least with the blessing of its representatives in Alsace, the press joined in the discussion of the Jewish problem in France. The philosopher De Bonald, who represented the anti-revolutionary camp, violently accused the Jews of having virtually replaced the old feudalism as the effective rulers of Alsace, which they controlled with the help of the enormous amount of mortgages they held. The success of the Jews, he maintained, was of course a normal consequence of the regrettable errors committed by the French Revolution. There was great danger in the tremendous natural growth of the Jewish population, which should be contained. Bonald was convinced of the opposition between Judaism and Christian society: 'The Jews cannot be, and – whatever may be done – will not be citizens under Christianity, without becoming Christians.' Any sympathy shown to the Jews was in fact a consequence of hatred for Christianity. The Jews must be excluded from citizenship and from public functions: how could anyone agree to see Jews exercising any authority over Christians? Here again, the Jewish religion appears as the major hindrance to the acceptance of the Jews by French society.[15]

Another publication, issued by the lawyer Poujol, was to exert a much greater influence on the shaping of the Emperor's and the administration's opinion on the Jews. In his observations on the Jews,[16] the author mentions the fact that in January 1806 he had handed a short memorandum to the State Councillor who was at that time in charge of police in the Lower Rhine department. This civil servant, who obviously knew that the central government had shown lately great interest in the Jewish problem, had asked him to enlarge and complete his work, to study the different legal systems which dealt with the Jews, to suggest ways to contain their abuses, and to give the government the possibility of deciding whether the Jews should keep or be temporarily deprived of their citizens' rights, which, if maintained, would make any control of their activities illusory.[17] This pamphlet is then a good illustration of the complaints lodged against the Jews, and of the opinions held on the matter by the higher civil servants who had inspired it. It deals essentially with the problem of the Jews of Alsace.

Poujol is quite convinced that the Jews of Alsace have abused their newly won freedom. They have accumulated at least 35,000,000 livres of mortgages and the same amount in notes since 1797, and have escaped, as a consequence of their emancipation, any possibility of control. The National Assembly when it granted them citizenship had hoped that this step would assimilate them with the other citizens, and help rid them of their bad habits and customs. Experience had shown that this was a false hope, and that emancipation had only induced them to persist, and to strive, in their evil ways. Despite the opportunities the

Revolution gave them, they had not accepted any civilian or military duties. They had not changed anything in the education of their children, who did not attend public schools. They had taken up neither arts nor crafts, nor agriculture. Their religious code, which recommends them to practise usury, had not been amended. They had avoided being drafted into the army, and done everything which could harm the general interest. The Jews themselves were to be held responsible for this situation: why did they not use the new situation, as had the Lutherans, who were no less hated than they? 'They have made no useful use of their citizens' rights.'[18] They pretend that time and their own efforts will transform their condition in the future, but it would be dangerous and costly to wait until then. The government must act right away and decide whether their citizenship should be suspended temporarily. If this were not done, any reform would prove to be impossible. Therefore, one should not hesitate to treat them just as one would treat minors, and deprive them of the general protection of the law. The Jews were minors in modern society. When they have grown up; that is, when they have improved their ways, they will enjoy the full protection of the law.

It is obvious, adds Poujol, that the Jews have not become useful members of society. They are even harmful. It would seem that this recourse to an obviously unconstitutional step such as taking away, even temporarily, the Jews' citizenship did not harmonise with the general atmosphere and had to be justified not only on practical but also on legal grounds. He therefore reminded the reader that after it had emancipated the Jews, the National Assembly had decided to look into the problem of the loans they had granted. As this had not been done because of the prevailing circumstances, it would be justifiable to say that the essential condition of the Jews' emancipation had not been fulfilled, and that one could, or even should, implement this forgotten decision, and make the Jews' freedom conditional on a satisfactory settlement of the grievous problem of their usury. Only when they had rectified that, would it become possible to return to them their citizens' rights.[19] He then propounded a number of exceptional measures, which were also obviously illegal (inasmuch as they would apply to only a part of the population) which were intended to restrain, and to suppress, the Jews' usury. He suggested that the legality of their loans be reviewed by a special jury composed of Alsatian dignitaries, and that they be reduced by three-quarters of their value. So much for the past. As far as the future was concerned, he advised a limitation on the categories of persons who would be allowed to borrow from them, without bothering in the least to find a solution for the hard-pressed peasants whose needs had turned them into the most assiduous clients of the Jews. He recommended that all their contracts be passed before a notary, and other measures to the same effect. Citizenship would become not the consequence of a law, but a reward for good conduct: any Jew who opened a new factory would be entitled to it. But none of these aims would be really reached unless the Jewish religion itself were to be reformed. It must first of all be agreed that 'the days of rest of the minority religion coincide with those of the majority religion'.[20] This would help to further better relations among citizens of different religions and allow everybody to serve the state without infringing his religious law.

In the same spirit, circumcision, 'which is not related to the essence of their dogmas',[21] and dietary laws should be given up. The same could be said of the teaching of the Hebrew language, and the study of the Talmud. Mixed weddings must be encouraged as 'a most efficacious means to partake of . . . civilisation'.[22] Many Jews, Poujol affirmed, are eager to have these reforms approved. The best way for the government to reach its goal would be to supervise very strictly the activities of the rabbis who are their real leaders: if the government can enlist their help, it will ensure the quick success of its policy. It is therefore extremely important 'to give them a motive consistent with the views of the government'.[23] The best way to achieve this would be to set up a hierarchy of the rabbinate, and to give them a 'patriarch' who would have authority to supervise them and to dismiss them if they did not conform to his instructions. Poujol concluded: 'Once completely assimilated to other men, they will differ from them only in the manner of their worship of the Supreme Being, which, even as it differs among all people, tends only to what is the sole and common aims of all religions."[24]

Poujol's publication was impounded, probably at the demand of the Alsatian Jewish communities which feared the success of its none too friendly suggestions. It was later released for publication. The author maintained that he had sent two copies to the Emperor and that he would release the remaining copies 'when His Majesty the Emperor has approved it'.[25] No such approbation has been found, but the fact remains that these copies were soon released. It is almost certain that the Emperor had read his pamphlet and been impressed by it, as will be seen later. For Poujol and those who inspired him, Judaism had to accept its rôle as a minority religion, and adapt to this situation: the future fate of the Jews would depend as much on a change of their way of life as on a reform of their religion, the latter being looked upon as very largely responsible for the former. The Jews would have to show that they deserved to be citizens, and the government would have to be ready to go to the extreme step of taking away their citizenship in order to compel them to assimilate completely into the French Nation.

Poujol was not the first to criticise the originality of Judaism. Portalis had already proclaimed that 'the Jews were less a religion than a people'.[26] The same Portalis had written in 1803 that the Jews 'are French citizens as are the Catholics and Protestants. As such they must be assured of all the protection of the government.'[27] The legacy of the Revolution was too strong to be given up without any qualms: the jurist, despite his opinion about the Jews, found it difficult to ignore the constitution, and to circumvent the law of the land.

Curiously enough, at the time when some Alsatian and government circles were considering what to do about the status and activities of the French Jews, the Jewish communities of eastern France, probably aware of the benefits that the Catholic and Protestant churches had drawn from their new organisation, wished to reorganise their own activities, a step long overdue since the dissolution of the former Jewish *nations*. At the beginning of 1804, the leaders of the Metz synagogue wrote to Portalis, who was then Counsellor of State in charge of the different religions, to remind him that before the Revolution, the syndics of the *nations* were in charge of everything connected with the rites and ceremonies of Judaism and were empowered to raise taxes from their fellow Jews. After their emancipation they had lost their synagogue, which was closed down, and every kind of religious instruction had to be discontinued. It was only in Year IV that they recovered their synagogue and resumed their religious activities. They needed 3,000 francs to cover their yearly expenses and 1,500 francs to cover the costs of their hospital. Up to now these sums had been collected as voluntary contributions. This practice could not become permanent, as the salary of the rabbi, for instance, would depend on the whims, likes or dislikes of potential contributors. The writers proposed therefore the adoption of some kind of system which would regulate the designation, the term of office and the powers of the leaders of the community. They requested also that private meetings of prayer be forbidden, as their establishment would weaken the community which should remain united around its synagogue and they wanted to avoid every possibility of division. The leaders of the community should also be empowered to fine those who disturbed the prayers or the performance of other religious commandments. These did not seem to have been very rare occurrences. The leaders of the community requested therefore that the government ratify the regulations suggested by them, and thus ensure their application. They asked Portalis to empower the prefect of the Moselle department to appoint the administrators of the synagogue and to determine their number, and the length of their term of office. He should also authorise two of the members of the commission which handled the problem of the Jewish debts to associate with them three other Jews from Metz and empower them, under his control, to deal with all the problems connected with the financing of the needs of religious activities and of the hospital: this would include the right to raise taxes from the community, the basis of their assessment being the existing tax roll which had been established for the purpose of the reimbursement of debts. The existing committee should be allowed to determine the rabbi's salary. The commissioners should also be empowered to keep peace in the synagogue, and levy fines on those who disturbed it, the amount collected to be equally divided between the city's hospitals and the Jewish hospice. Private prayer meetings could not be established except with their consent, and only in exceptional cases. Religious activities should be freed from land taxes. Furthermore, they should be able 'to forbid all the members of the *nation* living in the Moselle department to celebrate any wedding or to slaughter any livestock intended for their use, without the permission and the delegation of authority by the rabbi.' Offenders would have to pay a fine.[28] This project was an attempt to return to the situation which had prevailed before the Revolution: it would have resulted in the reconstitution of the former Metz Jewish *nation* with the restoration of the right to impose a fine to the heads of the community and its rabbi and the definition of the latter's constituency as the department of Moselle, which corresponded to the former domain of the *nation*.

It is therefore not very surprising that Portalis neglected to answer these far-reaching demands. The Metz commissioners renewed their demand on 14 Floréal of Year XII (4 May 1804). It would seem that the Ministry of Cults asked then for their prefect's opinion; he then wrote to the Minister on 16 Thermidor of Year XII. He first noted that the legislator had not yet organised the Jewish religion, although this had already been done two years previously for Catholic and Protestant forms of worship. This failure did not mean that the exercise of Judaism had been outlawed. On the contrary, since emancipation and the taking of the civic oath, all of their former privileges had been abolished: since then their syndics and rabbi had become 'without strength and without any power to maintain religious discipline, to assess the taxes needed for the religion's expenses'. Some Jews had left the community and set up private prayer-rooms in their homes, the expenses of which they covered with the help of their friends. As a result, the synagogue lived very precariously: it had fallen into the greatest confusion and poverty. 'This state of anarchy has extended to nearly all the communes of the department.' In order to put an end to this most deplorable state of affairs, the Jews suggested to him a number of measures: five heads of the community would be chosen from among its twenty-five heavily taxed members. These would choose the rabbi by agreement with the government. They would submit their budget and the tax rolls to the prefect who would make them mandatory. No synagogue – that is, no community – could be established without the permission of the authorities, which would make it conditional on its having at least 500 members. All private prayer-houses would be closed. No book dealing with the teachings of Judaism could be published in the future without the permission of the Ministry of Cults. Any regulation adopted for the 'interior policing and discipline' of their religion would have to be submitted to the Minister. The right to impose fines was omitted in these suggestions.[29]

On 11 August the Minister of Cults showed interest in the prefect's report and approved its general lines. He nevertheless asked for suggestions from the Jewish notables themselves. The prefect thereupon addressed himself to the present leaders of the community and their predecessors who had been turned out of office after they had first brought their ideas before Portalis. It would seem that the richest element of the community had seized power once it had understood the importance and the possible consequences of the negotiations which the former commissioners had undertaken. They somewhat modified their first suggestions by asking that a general assembly of all the members of the community elect eighteen candidates, out of whom the prefect would choose six heads of the community. The recourse to the general assembly and to elections was obviously intended to preserve democratic rule in the community. The commissioners would also be empowered to call a meeting of the general assembly to elect a new rabbi.

The new commissioners presented a much more detailed plan, which was already a revised version of a former plan which the prefect had rejected. It renounced the principle of taxation in favour of voluntary contributions. As for the choice of the heads of the community, the suggestion was to leave it to the most heavily taxed members of the community: this would certainly help the finances of the community! In case of any difficulty or breach of peace in the synagogue, the incident would be reported to the authorities, who would then take the necessary steps to stop the offenders. These suggestions, inasmuch as they greatly restrained the recourse to democratic elections and avoided any possibility of taxation or fines, were much more acceptable to the authorities, who did not very much relish the application of all the rules of democracy. The prefect therefore recommended that the project of the new commissioners be taken into consideration, although he thought that voluntary contributions would be insufficient and that a form of taxation should be instituted, and that the authority of the heads of the community should not, in case of any disturbance, extend to more than the right to invite the police to put an end to it. He also thought it advisable to allow a synagogue to be set up (that is, a community) only where there was a population of 500–2,000 individuals, and then only through an imperial decree.[30]

On 14 February 1806 the government had not yet acted on any of these recommendations. The prefect of the Moselle department then wrote to the Minister of Cults to press the matter. He felt that the abuses concerning the celebration of marriages made it essential to act very expeditiously, as some Jews had blessed some marriages, although no civil marriage had first taken place. He felt that the only way to put an end to this abuse was to forbid anybody but the rabbi or his representatives to perform weddings. Therefore some form of regulation of the Jewish religion had become indispensable.[31]

Many other communities of the Empire had also turned to the Minister with their problems, and to ask for his advice and help. The fact remains nevertheless that he chose either not to answer their demands at all or to give only very fragmentary answers. Very probably, he had decided to prepare a more comprehensive legislation which would achieve for Jewish religion what had been done a few years before for the Christian denominations. In February 1805 he turned to a number of Jewish notables who either lived in Paris, or were frequent visitors there, and asked for their opinion. These then sent a circular letter to the different communities of the Empire in order to ask for their reactions. With the answers they had received, they prepared a 'Plan d'organisation du culte juif en France', which they now presented to him. Although the report is not dated, it can be safely assumed that it was handed in to the minister at either the end of 1805 or the beginning of 1806.[32]

This comprehensive plan, which was submitted among others by some of the traditional leaders of French Jewry – such as one of the sons of Cerf Berr – amounted to a detailed blueprint for the Jewish community of France. They first requested the same recognition as the other cults, as the law recognised the existence of Catholics, Protestants and Jews and did not differentiate between them. 'The Jews wish, like all Frenchmen, to be ruled by the same civil and political laws, and it is they who claim from the government the organisation of their cult'. They admitted that the rabbinate lacked some desirable things, but attributed this to their former separation from the body of the nation. This was, for instance, the reason why the rabbis did not speak one of the current languages of Europe. In order to remedy this situation, special seminaries should be established for the education of rabbis. Their duties should be very limited: to pray and lead prayers for the state and the health of the imperial family, and to perform weddings and divorces, but only after civil weddings and divorces had taken place. If they failed to do so, they should be punished accordingly. The power of excommunication would have to be taken away from them. They would give instruction on points of doctrine and belief, but only when requested to do so, and their decision would never entail exclusion from the religious society. In their instruction, they would never attack communicants of other state-recognised religions, or these religions themselves.

The rabbis should receive their salary from the state. This would of course be a very small expense, as their number would remain small (fifteen to twenty). Obviously the committee remained faithful to the general organisation of the rabbinate of the eighteenth century, which recognised essentially the provincial

– or *land* – rabbi as the head of the Jews of the province, and did not feel that every local community should employ its own spiritual leader. They wanted one rabbi in every department where the number of Jewish families reached at least 200. Only in the Seine department, which included the city of Paris, was there justification for two rabbis. These would be elected by a council of notables and would have to be French citizens, and be approved by the Minister of Cults. The prefect would administer their oath of office, just as he administered the oath to Protestant clergy and Catholic priests. From the year 1818 on, nobody could be elected rabbi who had not studied at one of the approved seminaries. The rabbi would reside in the town of his department which had the largest Jewish population, where there would also be established the council of notables. These – there would be six of them – would be elected in each department by the twenty heads of family most heavily taxed. These notables would communicate with the prefect and decide whether to build or remove a synagogue. The regulations they would draw up for the synagogues would have to be approved by the prefect and the Minister.

The establishment of two seminaries, one in the north and one in the south; i.e. one for the German Jews and one for the Portuguese Jews, was a very important part of this programme. Instruction would be given there not only in sacred studies but also in French or other modern languages. The different communities would have to cover the expenses of the seminaries and of the synagogues in general.

The committee members were afraid that their proposals would not receive due consideration, and hoped that the Minister would overcome all the difficulties which endangered the enactment of their project. Little did they know that while they were working on their plan, other bodies were also considering different projects for the organisation of the Jewish religion in France. In more than one way, it was rather symbolic that this unanimity in considering the need for some kind of regulation or law organising Jewish worship in France did not in the least correspond to a community of aims. Whereas the representatives of the Jewish interests, who had never completely lost their nostalgia for the Jewish *nations* of the past, their organisation and their discipline, wanted essentially to re-create a form of Jewish organisation, and to re-introduce some logic into their religious and financial affairs, the government was mostly moved by its desire to solve social problems, to redefine the place of the Jews in French society. The Jewish community was convinced that the legitimacy of the teachings of Judaism as a religion would not be questioned, whereas some government circles and their associates felt that the evils they thought they detected in the Jewish community were no less a consequence of the laws and teachings of Judaism than a result of their age-long oppression. The Jews felt very secure in their newly-won citizenship, whereas some officials did not hesitate to contemplate the possibility of suspending or abolishing it. From this radical misunderstanding of each side's motives or intentions would result much greater misunderstandings, and, as far as the Jews were concerned, the feeling that they had been tricked. It is true that they were definitely in a weaker position in these negotiations, for the government and the higher civil servants knew what the Jews wanted, but they themselves did not know precisely what the government's policies would be.

CHAPTER III

The Calling of the Assembly of Notables

All contemporary witnesses agree that it was during Napoleon's short stay in Strasbourg on 23 and 24 January 1806 that he finally decided to take action on the Jewish problem, as explained to him on his return from his German campaign.[1] There had been complaints already, but it is clearly on Napoleon's insistence that action was now taken. It must be noted that there existed at the time no legal definition of what constituted usury, and the Council of State did not feel that the economic conditions prevailing in a country at war made it possible to adopt a definition and to determine what was an acceptable rate of interest.[2] Only on 3 September 1807 was a law enacted which fixed the rate of private loans at 5 per cent and commercial loans at 6 per cent. By that time, the Jewish assemblies had long ago dispersed! This fact made the whole matter more difficult, for there was no legal precedent which might have helped in the search for a solution.

The *Grand Juge* (the Minister of Justice) decided not to wait until a general measure was enacted. He did not accept the Council of State's position which had reminded him that in the absence of a law, it had been agreed 'that conventional interest may exceed the legal rate, as long as the law does not forbid it', on condition, however, that it be put down in writing. According to the Council, this system had worked out very satisfactorily.[3]

45

Nevertheless, the Minister wrote to the Emperor on 3 March 1806 to bring before him the claims which had been lodged against the Jews; these, he maintained, were the result of the freedom now enjoyed by the Jews, whose numbers had greatly increased since the Revolution. All proposed remedies were useless; he therefore suggested taking specific action against the Jewish lenders to control their activities, and to take measures against the multitude of foreign Jews who had settled in France and who 'enjoy all the rights attached to the quality of Frenchmen, without fulfilling any of the citizens' duties.' In view of the importance and delicate nature of this matter he suggested that it be handled by the Council of State.[4] Thus the Minister of Justice thought it advisable to bring before the highest judicial body of France an obviously illegal and unconstitutional suggestion: for he suggested discriminating between Jewish and non-Jewish citizens of France, and reintroducing a state of affairs which had been done away with by the National Assembly in 1791.

It is quite possible, and even probable, that he was not acting on his own, but only putting forward the opinion of the Emperor who had by then already made up his mind on the problem. On 6 March Napoleon answered the Minister, requesting the legislative section of the Council of State to study whether it was possible to cancel all mortgages received by the Jews, to forbid them to receive new ones for ten years, and to ask those who had no property holdings to pay a licence fee, all these measures applying particularly to Jews newly emancipated. The answer of the Council of State would obviously decide what the new régime's attitude to the Jews would be. Would it attempt to bring a change in the economic habits of the Jews by means of persuasion and within the framework of existing general laws, or would it, in one way or another, agree to a renewal of discrimination? The problem was brought before the section of the interior, whose chairman was Regnault de Saint-Angély, who during the Revolution had supported the Jews' fight for emancipation. He asked a young and recently appointed *maître des requêtes*, Molé, to look into the matter. Molé therefore prepared a very long report, where he reviewed the whole question and suggested ways and means to correct the present situation and prevent its recurrence. He requested a meeting of the section to which he might present his report and suggestions. The chairman, shocked by this unusual demand, decided to study the report first.[5] As one of the witnesses wrote in his recollections: 'To politicians and lawyers, there seemed to be no difficulty or matter for doubt. No legal disposition gave authorisation to establish the least difference between citizens, whatever religion they professed. To inquire into a lender's belief to decide whether he is entitled to be paid is a strange idea, opposed to principles as it is to present customs.'[6] Nevertheless Molé surprised his colleagues when he proposed to enact laws of exception against the Jews, at least so far as their private transactions were concerned. The councillors just smiled, and there was no discussion of the report. Every member, except the *rapporteur*, held a different opinion. Oddly enough, Molé, who himself attributed his appointment as *rapporteur* to a 'distraction' of Regnault,[7] had adopted a point of view which was not expected from a newcomer at the Conseil d'État. If Chancellor Pasquier's memoirs are to be believed,[8] Napoleon had shown great sympathy for the young jurist: is it impossible that he influenced him?

According to the rules of the Conseil d'État and despite the hostile attitude of the members of the section, the problem was now brought before the full Council. A *rapporteur*, Councillor Beugnot, was appointed, and presented his report to his colleagues. He admitted without any difficulty that the Jews in Alsace, whose conduct he described as detestable, constituted a serious problem. The reason was obvious: 'France alone has opened its doors to the Jewish Nation and incorporated them without any conditions into all the rights and benefits of its social order.' This 'unwise generosity' had attracted many Jews to France. There were only two possible solutions: either to reform the Jews, or to expel them, 'as there is no compromise between these two solutions for a wise government'. Laws of exception would be dangerous to the economy of France, as the Jews would emigrate with their capital. On the other hand, it would be dangerous to give the courts the right to function as a commission of review of the Jewish loans. The sections of the Council had therefore rejected nearly unanimously (i.e. except for Molé) the enactment of an exceptional law against the Jews. But as the prevailing situation required that action be taken, he recommended that the courts use the weapons they already had against illegal rates of interest, which they had not done – and expel the 'fugitive and vagabond' Jews from France. He also suggested the possibility of suspending for one year, but no longer, the payment of the Jewish debts, but on condition that every case be reviewed by the public prosecutor before action was taken. It was suggested that a census be taken – 'with prudence and discretion' – of the Jews of France, their profession and capital. This would make it possible to expel those who had no right to live in France. The Minister should also instruct the courts not to prosecute or condemn delinquent debtors with too great rigour. Beugnot also pointed to the need to provide other sources of credit for the French peasants such as local banks or loan-banks.[9]

The Council then agreed that the problem of usury was neither purely Jewish nor purely Alsatian. If an inquiry were to be made in the Seine department, where there were obviously very few Jews, it would probably show that the problem of usury was worse there. Measures against the Jews would be very difficult to apply, as there was no possibility of suppressing mortgages without bringing proof of their illegality. How could Jewishness be proved? The Constitution did not oblige anyone to own property. To ask that every Jew pay for a licence for his trade would be a return to the pre-revolutionary situation with its special taxes on Jews. Therefore the two sections concluded:[10]

That it is not possible to enact a particular law for the Jews in order to curb usury;
That this evil, which is too widespread in France, requires general cures, and that the law which will deter them must be common to the whole Empire;
That time has not yet come to deal with this matter;
That for the time being, the usury blamed on the Jews of the kingdom and foreigners cannot be repressed except through administration and police measures.

This opinion contradicted everything that Cambacérès, the Chief Chancellor, knew of the Emperor's intentions. He therefore put an end to the discussions and asked that they be renewed in the Emperor's presence. This new meeting took place at Saint Cloud on 30 April 1806. Beugnot, who probably knew by then what Napoleon really wanted, presented his report. It would seem that in the Emperor's presence he was not at his most eloquent. While listening to him, Napoleon grew more and more furious. When Beugnot had concluded, Napoleon made some sarcastic comments about those who make Christian prejudice responsible for the Jews' plight, and forget the curse which follows them.[11] According to Pelet de la Lozère's report, Napoleon was very violent: the government cannot stand still while the Jews strip Alsace. 'The Jews must be considered as a nation, and not as a sect. They are a nation within a nation.' Legal measures must be taken against them. He went so far as to deny their citizenship, and decided that they must be judged according to political and not civil law. 'They do not belong to the same category as the Protestants and the Catholics.' He also reminded the councillors of the need to protect Alsace, a border province, from the Jews who are potential spies, 'without any ties to the country'. Perhaps their number there should be limited to 50,000, and the others allowed to settle anywhere in France. They could also be forbidden to trade, and all their transactions annulled.[12]

Beugnot was astounded and did not answer. Only Regnault gathered enough strength to defend the Council's views, and mentioned that a serious study of the problem had been prepared by a junior member of the Council. This was of course Molé. When the Emperor asked for his report, Molé answered that he had handed it to the chairman of the commission of the interior, whereupon the Emperor asked that it be published. It was obvious that he had seen Molé's report beforehand.[13]

The meeting ended without any decision being taken. Molé used his newly won popularity and was received by Napoleon the following Sunday. The Emperor again told him that he did not acknowledge the Jews as fully-fledged Frenchmen. Despite the legal difficulties of which he was aware, he was of the opinion that the situation required action. The Talmud was again accused of fostering hatred of Christianity and of unworthy teachings. In the Emperor's opinion, this warranted and required supervision of the Jewish schools and rabbis. These should be organised and given some kind of hierarchy. He did not care about this cursed race, which would be the only one left unredeemed, but only about saving Alsace from their hands. Molé told Napoleon that such views meant that he had no hope of their regeneration, and that he, Molé, must disagree with this opinion. Napoleon did not answer.[14]

On 7 May Napoleon again discussed the Jewish problem in a meeting of the Council of State. He rejected as insufficient the suggestion that vagabond Jews be expelled and the courts instructed to use their discretionary powers against usury. Only laws of exception would help solve the problem. To expel the Jews would be a show of weakness; to reform them would be a sign of strength. Trade should be forbidden to the Jews, as they made ill use of it. This law must mature. He then called for a meeting of the Estates General of the Jews; that is, to gather fifty or sixty of them in Paris, and to hear their reactions. The evil done by the Jews 'does not come from individuals but from the very temperament of this people'. It was now clear that the Emperor had definitely made up his mind, and that he would order the Council of State to act accordingly. There would be exceptional laws against the Jews.[15]

Regnault de Saint-Angély prepared a draft of the preamble which was intended to justify the law and indicate the aim it pursued. He was extremely embarrassed, and produced a very long and diffuse project which tried to hide the fact that this was to be a discriminatory law. He called it: 'Project of a decree on the convocation of an assembly professing the Jewish religion', as if hoping to blur the economic aspect of this project. It was the duty of the Emperor, he wrote, to try to stop the present evil and to prevent its future reappearance. Payment of Jewish debts would be suspended for a year, but he explained this away as a warning against usury. This suspension would not prejudice payment of these debts, nor eliminate the payment of interest. He added that there could be no difference between the citizens of the Empire on account of their religious practices or beliefs. The best way to know the wishes and demands of the Jews would be of course to call a meeting of their representatives, and these could then make the Emperor's intentions known to their brethren: he did not want anybody to be judged by his beliefs, but by his actions. The meeting would aim only to make the Jews worthy of their rights. There was no intention of isolating them within the Nation, but only of consulting them. Let the Jews, he concluded, entertain no fear but only hope for a better and more stable fate.[16]

Whatever the merits of this long dissertation, which tried to deny the obvious, the Emperor rejected it and decided to produce a new draft himself.[17] He told the Council of State on 21 May that he did not think that he had to justify himself, as though he could be accused of evil intentions. On 30 May, the imperial decree was published: its language was very different from that of Regnault's project. He accused the Jews in the northern departments of the Empire of enormous usury, and declared that he had thought it his duty to help their victims. It had also become urgent to revive among the Jews the sentiments of civil morality which had been weakened during their long debasement. The Emperor had therefore decided to call an assembly of the principal Jews, with whom he would communicate through his commissioners. The aim was twofold: to inform the Jews of the Emperor's intention, and, on the other hand, to receive their opinions on the best ways 'to replace the shameful resources to which many of them have resorted from generation to generation for many centuries'. It is clear that the Jews received no inkling whatsoever of what was in store for them. It would also seem that the legalistic approach of the Council of State had made an impression on him, as he now wanted the Jews to bring him suggestions. It would thereby be a permanent instruction to the government's representatives to try to secure the Jews' agreement to the government's measures, or at least to have them ask for governmental action. This of course would take away the stain of illegality from any discriminatory action against the Jews: after all, they had either agreed to or asked for it.

The decree also suspended for a year the execution of judgments and contracts – except where there was need to prevent limitations – which had been obtained against farmers who did not engage in trade in the eight departments of Sarre, Roer, Mont Tonnerre, Lower and Upper Rhine, Rhine and Moselle, Moselle and Vosges; that is, the former province of Alsace, the region of Metz and the parts of annexed Germany west of the Rhine. The Assembly of the Jewish representatives was summoned for 15 July in Paris. The prefects of those departments mentioned in the list annexed to the decree were to choose the delegates from among the rabbis, landholders and other distinguished Jews according to the numbers mentioned therein. As for the other departments, the prefect was empowered to appoint one delegate for a Jewish population of between 100 and 500 persons, two delegates for a population between 500 and 1,000, and so on. The delegates were requested to be in Paris by 10 July.[18] It was significant that the minister in charge was the Minister of the Interior, not the Minister of Cults: Napoleon had definitely chosen the political, not the civil, path to deal with the Jews!

The most visible part of the Emperor's decision was of course that connected with the loans given by the Jews. Nobody knew exactly how to apply it, and the Minister of Justice could suggest only recourse to the courts, should any problem of interpretation arise. The prohibition on usury could be, and was in some cases, easily circumvented.[19] On the other hand, the Jews of France, who knew nothing of the dealings which had preceded the publication of the decree (they were not yet, despite citizenship, represented in all sections of French society), had great confidence in Napoleon's justice. Nevertheless, if we are to believe a petition presented to the Minister of Justice on 1 September 1806, a substantial number of Jews were almost ruined by this decree, for it was in fact very difficult to distinguish between legitimate contracts and practices that were forbidden or frowned upon. The courts of justice had completely altered the meaning of the decree by over-extending it. The deputies of the departments concerned asked that an end be put to this abuse.[20] In the atmosphere of this period, when the Emperor ruled supreme, the fact that they dared complain at all is sufficient proof of the disorder created in Jewish life by Napoleon's measures. It must also be added that when the end of the year of suspension approached, it became obvious that no permanent measure had yet been taken concerning the Jews' affairs. It was therefore extended in May 1807 until the Emperor might decide otherwise.

The prefects had meanwhile begun to implement the provisions of the decree and were busy choosing the Jewish delegates. It soon became evident that there existed no reliable statistics of the Jews of France. The prefects collected information on the numbers of Jews in their departments. Many errors were corrected. In the Vosges department, for instance, their number had to be reduced to 250 from 6,513, while in Gironde it had to be increased from 600 to 2,131. This required an increase in the number of deputies.[21]

When it came to choosing the delegates, opinions differed, and pressure was often exerted on the prefects. Naturally they turned to the former leaders of the Jewish *nation*, or to its leading families. It is not surprising that Cerf Berr's brother-in-law, David Sintzheim, who had by that time become the rabbi of Strasbourg, should have been joined by three of Cerf Berr's sons, one of them, Theodore, representing the Seine department, the second, Lippman, representing Upper Rhine, and the last one, Baruch, representing Lower Rhine. One of their relations, Auguste Ratisbonne, was also appointed. Finally eighty-two notables were designated, not counting thirteen supplementary delegates from the Italian departments. On 10 July a new decree had decided that the Jews of the Kingdom of Italy would also be invited: a further sixteen delegates were therefore added, who could not attend the first meetings of the Assembly as their appointment had come too late. The Assembly, which by then had become the Assembly of the Israelites of France and of the Kingdom of Italy, and which was later called the Assembly of Notables,[22] totalled 111 members, who would rarely, if ever, be present at the same time in Paris.

CN

As a matter of fact, they did not expect that they would have to stay in Paris for a prolonged period. Very soon it became apparent that the merchants among them could not afford to remain for long away from their business. The poorer members pretty quickly had great difficulties in supporting themselves. The dossiers of the Assembly are full of demands for leave of absence, which was very often granted. The government had not even thought of the expenses – travelling and maintenance – which the deputies would have to meet. It was only very late during their stay that the problem was solved – not through a governmental allocation, but through a forced contribution of the Jewish communities, which were made to pay for delegates chosen for them by the prefects at the central government's command.[23]

When the deputies arrived in Paris and registered with the Ministry of the Interior, it became evident that nothing was yet ready for their meetings, which had to be delayed. Only about 14 July was a place chosen for their meetings; this ironically proved to be a secularised chapel behind the Paris Town Hall. Napoleon finally decided to delay no more. The first meeting was to take place on 26 July. Molé himself pointed out to the Minister of the Interior that 26 July fell on the Sabbath and that it would perhaps be advisable not to call a meeting on the Jews' day of rest, as there was great danger that the more observant deputies would not attend the meeting for this reason. The Minister of the Interior nevertheless stuck to the date previously fixed, perhaps to show that the French state did business on the Sabbath, and that all citizens were to take cognisance of this fact.[24] A few days before, on 17 July, the Minister had tried unsuccessfully to have the whole matter handed over to the Minister of Cults, maintaining that it is 'from the religious beliefs of the Jews that originate all the difficulties which prevent them from being citizens, like the other subjects of Your Majesty.' He had asked in the same letter that commissioners be appointed to represent the government at the Assembly.[25]

On 22 July, Napoleon appointed three commissioners, all of them *maîtres des requêtes* at the Council of State. Not surprisingly,

Molé was one of them: Napoleon had not forgotten his newly won expertise in Jewish matters and the opinions he had defended before the Council of State. He was joined by the future Chancellor Pasquier, and by Portalis junior, who was none other than the son of the Minister of Cults who had been left out of this consultation. Molé became the chairman of this small group, and was its main representative in its dealings with the Jewish Assembly. In the same letter Napoleon communicated the text of the questions which were to be submitted to the Jewish Assembly, with the aim of 'reconciling the belief of the Jews with the duties of Frenchmen, and to turn them into useful citizens, being determined to remedy the evil to which many of them apply themselves to the great detriment of our subjects.'[26]

There is no indication as to who had drafted the questionnaire which was to be handed over to the deputies. It is probable, but not certain, that Molé had some responsibility for it. Quite possibly a final report sent to the Emperor on 8 July 1806, i.e. only a week before the supposed meeting of the Jewish assembly, had served as a final inspiration to those who had drafted the questionnaire. It reaffirmed that the Jews constituted a people, not a sect, and had survived as such despite their dispersion, due to their religious institutions. 'The code of the Jews included at the same time the religion, the political and the civil laws, the habits, the manners and all of the customs of life. These diverse things, which everywhere else are separated, are here mixed in the same code . . .' The modern Jews are not different from the ancient ones. They do not mix with their neighbours, and marry only among themselves, according to their own rules. 'They have their particular manner of existing among us.' They recognise as their brethren only those who profess their religion. They appear in court only when they litigate against Christians. As for the lawsuits which they have among themselves, they bring them before their rabbis. Even their dietary habits differentiate them from the Christians. In general, religion deals only with problems of conscience: among the Jews it includes everything which establishes and rules society. Therefore the Jews are a nation within the nation. It then becomes clear 'that it was not advisable

55

to proclaim them citizens, without investigating if they could or even wanted sincerely to become so. It follows also that it would not be unreasonable or unjust to submit a type of corporation, which, on account of its institutions, principles and customs, remains constantly separated from general society to particular laws.' The Emperor had imposed a suspension of one year for Jewish loans, but this was not a conclusive solution, which could be found only through a regulation of Jewish loans. A commission should be appointed to review all loans granted by Jews. Did this mean that only specific usurers should be punished? This would and should generally be so, but in view of the fact that Jewish usury was a consequence of Jewish religious teachings, which, if they did not ordain it, did still allow it, a general measure would be justified. The best way would be to make all loans public, as usury hates the light of day. Mortgages should also be regulated. If it was desired to limit usury, the number of potential usurers should also be limited and Jewish immigration into France forbidden or restricted. Today they were not persecuted any more, so there was no reason to offer them a refuge. 'One should not give the Jews a fatherland, before making sure that the fatherland that promises to accept them will find in them real citizens.' Naturalisation of a Jew should be conditional on his having a useful profession. All Jews should be compelled to send their children to public schools: this would bring them near to the body of the Nation. As for foreign Jews, they should report to the police, to ensure they settle in towns rather than in villages. The Jews in general should not fear or suspect the intentions of the Emperor: the proposed measures would only re-establish equality between all Frenchmen and themselves.[27]

It was in this climate that the questions brought to the Assembly were elaborated. There were precisely twelve:

(1) Is it lawful for Jews to marry several women?

(2) Is divorce allowed by the Jewish religion? Is divorce valid, even when not pronounced by courts of justice and by virtue of laws that contradict the French code?

(3) Can a Jewess marry a Christian, or a Christian woman a

Jew? Or does the law order the Jews to marry only among themselves?

(4) In the Jews' eyes, are Frenchmen considered as brethren or as strangers?

(5) In either case, what relations does their law prescribe for them towards Frenchmen who are not of their religion?

(6) Do the Jews born in France, and treated by the law as French citizens, acknowledge France as their country? Are they bound to defend it? Are they bound to obey its laws and to follow all the provisions of the civil code?

(7) Who appoints the rabbis?

(8) What police jurisdiction do rabbis exert among Jews? What judicial power do they exert among them?

(9) Are these forms of election, this police jurisdiction, requested by their law or only sanctioned by custom?

(10) Are there professions which are forbidden to Jews by their law?

(11) Does the law of the Jews forbid them to take usury from their brethren?

(12) Does it forbid them, or does it allow them, to take usury from strangers?[28]

It is clear that these were all leading questions which had only one common aim: to compel the Jews to choose between their religious law and the duties of patriotism. The first question looks particularly odd in this connection: who could have imagined at that time that Jews still engaged in polygamy? It may be wondered whether the questionnaire's aim was not to put the Jewish deputies in a position of inferiority from the outset and to take away from them any possibility of adopting an aggressive stance. The second question on the validity of Jewish divorce was intended to compel them to choose between Jewish and civil divorce: would the Jewish delegates be ready to proclaim that a religious divorce pronounced according to all the rules of the Jewish code becomes invalid if not confirmed by French laws and courts of justice? The third question asked practically the same question: whereas French law allows mixed marriages, does

Jewish law oppose it? Does Jewish law, in opposing mixed weddings, forbid what French law allows? In the mind of the questioner it was of the utmost importance to show that Jewish law negated French law and, if so, to compel the Jews to renounce established Jewish usage.

The fourth and fifth questions were intended to extract from the Jews a definition of their attitude towards their fellow French citizens: did a common nationality create a bond among Frenchmen of Christian and Jewish religion, which would be as strong as that which linked the Jews of different countries? Would the Jews be ready to transform themselves from a nation into a sect? After all why should the bond between Jews be stronger than the bond between Christians? The latter cared little for their common religion once their leaders had decided to fight each other on the battlefield! Even in these extreme circumstances they did not feel that their Christian conscience or belief was endangered by the hostilities which opposed them.

The next three questions which dealt with the organisation and the powers of the rabbinate were clearly designed to compel the Jews to decide what would be the power of the rabbinate, and whether it could be reduced to the same status as that of the Catholic hierarchy; that is, be incorporated in one way or another into the structure of the state. Would the Jews be ready to renounce this form of judicial autonomy, and to say so? Would they be ready to admit publicly that the whole conception of the rabbinate was based on custom, and could therefore be looked upon as an addition to Judaism, and not as one of its central elements? Any refusal to do so would of course have to be construed, and condemned, as an affirmation that Jews were ready and willing to recognise a judicial system which was not common to all the citizens of the state.

The last three questions dealt with the Jews' economic occupations, and essentially with the problem of usury. Was there a legal difference between usury towards Jews and usury towards non-Jews? If there was, would this not be definite proof that Jews had a double standard of morality which would allow them to seek from Gentiles a profit which they were forbidden to make from Jews? If they denied the legality of usury to Jews and non-Jews, this would then be an admission that the Jews looked upon their fellow-citizens as brethren, and that the practice of usury, the existence of which it was of course impossible to deny, was an evil consequence of a long period of submission and persecution, and must be done away with. This would justify the intervention of an external power which would cleanse the Jewish body of this sickness through appropriate means; i.e. with the help of exceptional laws which would apply to Jews as such. Therefore it was not at all fortuitous that the question concerning money-lending to Gentiles was the last one: it was the only one which could produce the kind of answer Napoleon wanted to receive.

When the Assembly first met, it knew nothing of the Emperor's real intentions. The deputies were told only that they would have to organise their meeting, and that when this had been done the government commissioners would come to tell them what was expected of them. They were therefore unable to prepare themselves for the forthcoming meeting and to agree on any line of conduct. They met for services on the Sabbath morning of 26 July in the small synagogues of Paris which were only a few hundred yards away from the hall where the meetings of the Assembly were to take place. It has been reported that, despite the proximity, a number of delegates chose not to walk there, but to use a coach. This echoed a clash which occurred during the meetings of the Malesherbe commission in 1788, when the leaders of the German *nation*, including the well-known leader of the Alsatian Jewry, Cerf Berr, and the leaders of the Portuguese *nation*, headed among others by their former syndic, Abraham Furtado, clashed on religious grounds, the former reproaching the latter for the laxity of their religious practice. Anyway, the majority of the delegates, if not all of them, did not hesitate and, despite the Sabbath, went on to attend the meeting which had been called for 11 o'clock in the morning.

Although a preparatory meeting had been called at the house of one of the Paris deputies on Friday 25 July, to try to adopt a common attitude, at least as far as the religious aspects of a

Sabbath meeting were concerned, there was no agreement between the delegates on this point.[29] The agenda called for the election of a chairman, two secretaries and three scrutineers. The vote took place under the presidency of the oldest member, Solomon Lipmann from Colmar. Immediately, the differing religious attitudes became apparent: a few of the rabbis had put down their choice in writing the day before; other delegates were willingly helped by Jacob Lazard, a Paris delegate; others wrote down their choice themselves without further ado.[30] Abraham Furtado, a delegate from Bordeaux, was elected chairman with 62 votes, while his rival, Berr Isaac Berr, received only 32. Whatever their other differences they had one thing in common: both of them had definitely received a good French education and were completely at ease in the French language. It is therefore not surprising that they were considered two good candidates.[31]

As a matter of fact, the problem of language greatly complicated the work of the Assembly as many delegates knew only German or Italian, and a sizeable number of the French-speakers knew no other language. It became therefore soon necessary to translate all documents into German and Italian, which was not particularly easy when legal documents were concerned. Isaac Samuel Avigdor and Rodrigues junior were elected secretaries, Olry Hayem Worms, Theodore Cerf Berr and Emilio Vitta, scrutineers.

The commissioners, who had not attended the meeting, were not dissatisfied with the choice which had been made: the chairman was a Portuguese Jew 'who knew the writers of the 18th century better than the Talmud, and sought for truth in Voltaire much more than in any other Jewish or Christian author.' Nevertheless they were later to discover that it was this very characteristic which made Furtado unacceptable to most of the other deputies, whose religious convictions were much deeper.[32] The measure of influence he managed to secure was mostly used in his functioning as chairman and the part he took in drafting the minutes of the meetings, which he was also accused of having somewhat altered or toned down.[33]

When the election had been carried out, Furtado addressed the Assembly and thanked it for its confidence. He warned it against tumultuous meetings, which any lack of discipline would make unavoidable, as the number of the assembled deputies was so large. He was applauded and the name of the Emperor and his family duly acclaimed. One of the delegates suggested sending a deputation to the Emperor to assure him of the loyalty, respect and love of the Assembly, which would consider the suggestions brought before it with all sympathy. Another delegate suggested that the Minister of the Interior be asked to transmit the deputies' wishes to the Emperor.

Lippman Cerf Berr, who represented the Upper Rhine department, asked his fellow deputies to be worthy of the trust which had been put in them and to forget their differences: 'let there be no longer Alsatian, Portuguese or German Jews'. The step taken by Napoleon was unprecedented. 'No sovereign has ever done what Napoleon has now performed for the people of God.' All the Jews of Europe knew it and had their eyes fixed on the Assembly. He therefore suggested that the text of the Imperial decree of 30 May 1806 be engraved on a marble tablet and hung in the hall of their meetings and later in the major synagogues of the Empire: it is significant that he did not include among its provisions the first one, which dealt with the suspension of Jewish debts! A bust of the Emperor should be placed in the hall, and an address of thanks sent to him. The Saturday following 26 July should thereon become a permanent festival for all the Jews of France, who should also institute a prayer for the Emperor and his family. This suggestion was not acted upon in view of its comprehensiveness, but it was agreed that the whole Assembly would ask to be received by the Emperor in order to express its gratitude. The meeting was then adjourned, and Furtado went to see the Minister of the Interior to report on the whole proceedings.[34]

Did the deputies realise that a diatribe against the Jews, published in the *Moniteur* the day before (25 July), was the result of research done at the suggestion of Regnault de Saint-Angély before the Jewish problem was examined in the Council of State and that it had been written by Molé, who had just become the senior representative of the Emperor to the Jewish Assembly? Molé's first contacts with them should have left little room for doubt. When the second meeting was called on 29 July, it was announced that Messieurs Molé, Portalis and Pasquier would appear before the Assembly in order 'to make known to it the intentions of his Majesty the Emperor and King'. According to the report of Pasquier 'the speech which he (Molé) pronounced at the opening of the Assembly, on 29 July, was very hostile to the Jews, and was not designed to give them confidence in the government's dispositions'.[35]

Molé first declared that the Jewish deputies were aware of the Emperor's intentions and knew that some of them had given cause for complaints which had reached the throne. The Emperor had stopped the progress of this evil, and had decided to hear and consult the Jewish delegates before taking any final decision how to cure it. The purpose of the meeting was therefore to enlighten them and to co-operate with them. For the first time the Jews would be judged with justice: a Christian prince would determine their fate. 'His Majesty wants you to be Frenchmen: it remains with you to accept such a title and to bear in mind that not to prove worthy of it would be to renounce it.' For good measure, he added a threat: not to answer truly the questions which would now be put to them would give evidence of guilt and blindness to their true interests. The answers, as soon as they were drafted, should be transmitted to the commissioners. The wish of the commissioners was to report to the Emperor that all the Jews of the Empire were determined to conform to the laws and morality which were incumbent on all Frenchmen. After this haughty and somewhat threatening speech, the twelve questions were read to the deputies. It is known that when the sixth question was read, which asked whether the Jews looked upon France as their fatherland, and were bound to protect it, the deputies shouted: 'to the death!' Whereupon Furtado turned to the commissioners and made his speech.

He thanked them for the communication they had just made, and expressed his joy at the opportunity 'to dissipate more than one error, and to put an end to many prejudices.' This would help to demolish the wall which had so long separated the Jews from the other nations. He asked the commissioners to assure the Emperor of their loyalty.

After having refused to answer questions put to them by the deputies, the commissioners departed. The president then appointed a Committee of Twelve which was intended to prepare a draft of the answers to be put before the Assembly, which would have to accept or modify them, before sending them to the commissioners. This committee included, among others, David Sintzheim (also called Zinsheimer), rabbi of Strasbourg, Segre, rabbi of Vercelli in Italy, Abraham Andrade, rabbi of Bayonne, Berr Isaac Berr from Nancy, his son Michel Berr, Baruch Cerf Berr, nephew of David Sintzheim and son of Cerf Berr, and Jacob Lazard, the well-to-do jeweller from Paris.[36]

The discussion could now begin.

CHAPTER IV

The Meetings of the Assembly of Notables

It has been maintained that 'the only deep difference between the members of the Assembly was a consequence of their financial status . . . some were rich, the others were poor.' The rich, who had to look after their interests, and ensure the reimbursement of the loans they had extended to Christian borrowers, were therefore ready to compromise and reconcile 'their beliefs with the duties of Frenchmen'. The poor, who had nothing to lose, could afford to be more uncompromising and more obdurate as far as their religion was concerned.[1] This view is totally unacceptable: despite the uniform style of the official reports of the Assembly of the Jewish Notables, it is quite obvious that there were few, if any, meetings during the Napoleonic dictatorship which witnessed such freedom, and even temerity, of expression in the defence of religious belief and resistance to external pressure. There are enough witnesses to demonstrate this without leaving room for any doubt.

Chancellor Pasquier, in his memoirs, described the course of events after Furtado's election:[2]

It soon became clear that the Portuguese Jews were suspect to all their coreligionists who considered them as apostates. President Furtado was more suspect than anyone else. They seemed to believe that he was connected with his religion only by the feeling of human respect which allows one to leave the religion in which one was born only when moved by the strongest of convictions. Now this was not Furtado's outlook: philosophical indifference was the foundation of his opinions. The rabbis of Alsace, and those of the former Comtat of Avignon, whose knowledge brought them to the forefront, said of their president that visibly he had learned the Bible only in Voltaire. His influence was nil on an assembly of men moved by the strongest religious conviction.

It would seem that these rabbis soon enough won the grudging respect of the commissioners. Pasquier told of his own surprise:[3]

They had been generally suspected to be occupied only with their pecuniary interest and to hold to their religion only from habit, and primarily as a result of the conveniences it provided their conscience with, in enabling them to live at the expense of all the countries which had received or tolerated them. One found oneself in the presence of men who were very superior to the rabble they had been identified with. Very carefully taught in their religion and in its principles, they were strengthened in their attachment to it by the reproof it attracted to them: their very cultured minds were estranged from no human knowledge.

Even Molé admitted to the fact that there was quite a number of very distinguished men in the Assembly, 'even some Jews of good faith'. He was particularly impressed by a number of rabbis to whom his door was always open.[4]

Apart from the differences of origins which separated the Portuguese, Italian and German Jews from each other, there existed also another disparity: the commissioners had themselves very soon realised that there was a philosophical camp and a rabbinic camp, the first ready for change and reform, and the latter completely and unalterably opposed to anything which would seem to create a danger to the integrity of their religion. Again and again the commissioners allude to this opposition and to the need for a compromise between the two camps.[5] It is obvious that the rabbinic party systematically increased its influence, and that the philosophic camp very soon found itself needing to strengthen itself, although the election of Furtado as chairman against Berr Isaac Berr, who was considered one of the leaders of the other group, would have seemed to indicate an absolute victory for the philosophers.[6] That this was not so was due in great part to the action of David Sintzheim who, wrote the commissioners, was looked upon as 'the main supporter of Jewish orthodoxy'.[7] If a contemporary report from a pro-rabbinic source is to be believed, 'there were great quarrels between them, because there were present – on account of our faults – a great number of bad and so called modern Jews, who were ready – God forbid – to abrogate a part [of the law], but the honourable Chief Rabbi Sintzheim intervened and vowed: no dot over an i will be taken away from our religion . . .'[8] Sintzheim himself in a letter to the rabbi of Prague told of his difficulties and his hope of preventing the success of those who were ready to give up practically everything. He maintained to his correspondent that the Emperor himself did not want anything so extreme.[9]

Each camp tried to enlist help or understanding for its cause. Sintzheim seems to have written to many well-known European rabbis,[10] and to have imposed himself as the real leader not only of the rabbinic camp, but of the rabbinate itself. He dismissed Andrade, the so-called rabbi of Bayonne, as a cantor who had more than heretical tendencies, and Segré as a plain schoolteacher from the little Italian town of Vercelli: he was a man of culture, but no great Hebrew scholar, and was not to be confused with the rabbi of Turin, who did not attend the meetings.[11] On the other hand the Paris delegates Worms and Lazard did not hesitate to write to an Italian friend in order to call him to Paris because the presence of enlightened men was required there, as the opposition to their views was steadily growing.[12]

A man like Lazard was quite convinced that the Jews of France were in danger of having to choose now between conversion and expulsion and this would also be the problem of the other Jews of the Empire, and that the only solution would be to become a different kind of Jew: he wrote to his Italian friend asking him for his opinion on the reform of the Talmud and legal Codes which could prove necessary to the salvation and the happiness of the Jews.[13]

There can be no doubt that the differences of opinion cannot be attributed to a difference of economic status: the fight over the answer to the twelve questions was an argument over principle, and on the integrity of the Jewish inheritance in a modern world.

Curiously enough, both camps were convinced, at least at the beginning, of the Emperor's support, or lack of interest, as far as purely religious problems were concerned. Both erred, but for different reasons.

If the differences of opinion were as sharp as the witnesses thought, it may be asked: who was responsible for the answers given to the twelve questions – the philosophers or the rabbinic party? There can be no doubt that Sintzheim himself did most of the writing. The public rumour as expressed in a private letter,[14] the testimony of one of the members of the Committee of Twelve[15] and, more important, a letter of Sintzheim himself attest to this: In order to stop, or limit the enterprise of the philosophers, he wrote that he had taken upon himself the task of drafting the answers.[16] As these are known to us in their French translation, a language which Sintzheim did not speak (although it is quite probable that he understood it), it becomes obvious that the French text of the answers, which was to be transmitted to the commissioners, was more polished than the Hebrew original from which it could not have greatly diverged. In general it must be considered as a text prepared in full agreement with the rabbinic camp and under its influence and control. It is clear that Sintzheim's influence and prestige were great enough to help reach a consensus during the discussions.

When the notables met again on 4 August 1806, they were informed that the Emperor was to receive them in an official reception, once the first results of their discussion had been reached. The report of the Committee of Twelve on the first three questions was then presented with the draft of a declaration, which was intended to serve as an introduction to the answers. The full discussion was then started.[17]

In the preamble the deputies defined themselves as 'the French deputies professing the religion of Moses', assured the Emperor of their love and respect, and proclaimed their adherence to the Talmudic principle that the law of the land is the law – 'Dina d'Malkhuta Dina'.[18] 'Their religion', they said, 'orders them to consider the laws of the prince as the supreme law in civil and political matters.' The acceptance of this principle meant that any civil or political disposition[19] of their code, or the religious interpretation given to it, which might be at variance with the French code, would automatically become obsolete, as the Jews had first of all to recognise and obey the law of the land. It is quite obvious that it was the rabbinic party which had decided to quote well-established rabbinic law as a basis for their deliberations, and to justify their answers on purely religious grounds, and to avoid political and sociological justification: Jewish law should influence and shape all their decisions. However sound this point of view might have been, it did not spare them many difficulties which were soon to appear during the discussion of the problems of marriage and divorce. These acts had always had a religious meaning in Judaism: the Revolution had decided to turn them into civil ceremonies, and Napoleon had not seen fit to change this new definition and to restore to them their religious connotation. What would then be the relationship to, or opposition between, Jewish wedding or divorce, and French civil wedding and divorce? The commissioners who had received the minutes of the meetings from the chairman and examined them before reporting to the Emperor or the Minister of the Interior showed considerable interest in the distinction between the religious and the political or civil laws: they wondered whether this differentiation was legitimate, as the laws of Moses appeared to constitute an indivisible code. They also expressed some surprise at the affirmation of the preamble according to which the Jews had always obeyed French law since the Revolution: could this be true so far as their marriages and divorces were concerned? The commissioners were primarily interested in uncovering all the possibilities of differentiating between different aspects of Jewish law: if it could be proved that all laws had not the same relevance and that the Jewish code was less than monolithic, the door would be opened to a reform of Jewish usage.[20]

In this respect, the answer to the first question, which dealt with the problem of polygamy, appeared to them as a superb illustration of the possibilities of action open to the rabbis. The Assembly had answered that the law of Moses neither ordered nor forbade the Jew to take more than one wife. In the Orient, polygamy still existed, but in the West it had been suppressed by a synod of a hundred rabbis which had met at Worms during the eleventh century under the chairmanship of Rabenu Gershom. Although this prohibition was not intended at the time to be permanent, it had become accepted usage. The commissioners then asked what was the real nature of the rabbis' power: when were they empowered to restrict the application of Mosaic law and when could Mosaic law be invoked in order to condemn their initiatives?[21]

The second question, concerning divorce, gave cause for misunderstanding: the notables had been asked whether the Jewish religion permitted divorce, and they had answered that it allowed repudiation; that is that the husband could issue a writ of divorce to his wife, but that the opposite was not possible. The commissioners agreed that the error had been committed in good faith, and recognised the situation as it was. The delegates declared that the Jewish divorce could be pronounced only after the civil divorce had been pronounced. They made a point of justifying this on *halakhic* grounds, declaring that according to Jewish law, a repudiation becomes final only inasmuch as each and every bond between husband and wife has been broken. This would obviously not be the case where the law of the land made civil divorce compulsory. Therefore the civil repudiation would have to precede the religious one. To repudiate his wife, a Jew must therefore obtain two divorces: a civil and a religious one. Therefore Jewish religion did not contradict French law in this matter. It must be noted nevertheless that the notables managed to avoid any mention of the validity of a civil divorce, which had not been followed by a religious one. It would have been difficult for them to recognise its validity in the absence of a religious ceremony. The same problem also of course existed for Catholics.[22]

These two answers were accepted by the Assembly without any difficulties. The answer to the third question, which dealt with the problem of mixed marriages, was far less easy to give. It is well known that the rabbis were a small minority in the Assembly – about 15 among nearly 100 lay delegates – but this did not cause them to abandon even a minute part of their authority. It may be gathered from the discussion that there was no agreement over this question in the Committee of Twelve, which reported two opinions.[23] When these were brought before the plenum, a violent argument broke out. One of the rabbis declared from the start that when purely theological – by which term he referred to religious practice – questions were examined, the rabbis should be more particularly consulted. The chairman maintained that the majority rule applied to all the discussions of the Assembly. A secretary then read the opinion of the rabbis, which was probably a minority opinion, and which, it would seem, expounded the absolute opposition of Judaism to mixed marriages. The discussion was then resumed; it would seem that all agreed that the rabbi's opinion was essentially correct, but that it did not take into consideration the problems of the hour. Rabbis and laymen agreed on the essential brotherhood of all Frenchmen, but not on the means of expressing it in their answers. Should all the dangers of mixed marriages be explained to the government? A representative of the lay members declared that no law demands that marriage partners should belong to the same religion, but that one should not hide the problems mixed weddings were liable to create. For another delegate, the political advantages of mixed weddings considerably surpassed the religious drawbacks. It became obvious that the Assembly was deadlocked and that the rabbis would not give in. It was therefore suggested that an attempt be made to reconcile the two texts and to reach a common answer. A small committee was set up which soon agreed on a lengthy reply. It declared that the law neither prohibits, nor recommends, marriages of Jews with Christians. It forbids only marriages with idolaters, which the Christians are not. Nevertheless, the rabbis are opposed to such unions, as they cannot be sanctified when the two partners do not belong to the same religion. In such a case they can be married civilly, but not religiously. Therefore, they would not need a religious divorce if they were to separate. The reply concluded:[24]

> This is the opinion of the rabbis who are members of the
> Assembly. In general, they would be no more inclined to bless the
> wedding of a Christian woman with a Jew, or of a Jewess with a

Christian, than Catholic priests would agree to bless such unions. The rabbis recognise, however, that the Jew who marries a Christian woman does not therefore cease to be a Jew in the eyes of his co-religionists, any more than he who marries a Jewess civilly and not religiously.

When the commissioners received their opinion, which had been accepted unanimously, they had no difficulty in detecting that it contained not one, but two, answers. They agreed among themselves that the rabbis' opinion was the correct one 'and that all the amendments which accompanied it were dictated by the fear that a great number of deputies have of endangering their civil status through too great a candour about their religious discipline.'[25]

It is clear that the discussion of the problem of mixed marriages constituted a turning-point in the history of the Assembly: the rabbinic camp had not only won its fight against the philosophers; it had also managed to impress the commissioners, who were now convinced that their opinion had greater importance than they had earlier thought. From now on, they were recognised as the persons to deal with, and the measure of their influence on the Assembly's debates was fully felt. This development was to have important consequences later on.

When the Assembly resumed its discussions on 7 August, it tackled the next four questions. Moïse Levy from Nancy, who was one of Furtado's supporters, brought the draft of the Committee of Twelve before the delegates. The fourth question had asked for a definition of the Jewish attitude towards the French people: would the Jews be ready to recognise Frenchmen as brethren? It is evident that the Twelve could not, and would not, give a negative answer to this question, as it would have been tantamount to a rejection of the whole revolutionary inheritance, and a declaration of intention as to the real importance of emancipation for the Jews. The delegates were in no mood for this. The draft answer was divided into two parts: the first declared that, in the eyes of the Jews, the Frenchmen were their brothers, and not foreigners. The law prescribes love and aid for those who observe the Noachide laws and this applies to Christian

Frenchmen. Here again the answer meant that Christianity would no more be considered as a form of idolatry. It was rhetorically asked: could it be otherwise 'when they inhabit the same land, when they are ruled and protected by the same government and the same laws, when they enjoy the same rights and fulfil the same duties?' Moreover, the Jews owe a debt of gratitude to their fellow French citizens for the rights they have received. Nevertheless, the Assembly maintained that fraternity had to be mutual: equal rights and equal duties. This was a rejection of any exceptional measures against the Jewish community.[26]

The second part of the draft contained a distinction between the Jews of the north and the south: the latter had made greater progress towards civilisation because they had been less unhappy than their co-religionists from the North. This statement was construed as a form of discrimination among the delegates, and some deputies protested against it. It was therefore deleted from the proposed text, which was then accepted unanimously, the deputies again emphasising that 'France is our country, all Frenchmen are our brethren, and this glorious title, while honouring us in our own eyes, becomes a pledge that we shall never cease to be worthy of it.'[27]

When the commissioners received this answer, they could not hide their displeasure: they accused the Assembly of quoting many texts which recommended hospitality and love towards all men, and of having failed to show that biblical and rabbinic law did indeed authorise the Jews to consider to be their brethren men who were not descended from the chosen people and professed another religion. They declared that the purpose of the question was to determine whether the Jews looked upon themselves as a family, a tribe or a specific people. The deputies had avoided answering the question. The commissioners felt that Jewish law had aimed to separate the Jews from the other peoples: any indication of tolerance on their part was not to be understood as a desire for universal fraternity, but rather as an attempt to give some protection to foreigners, and to prevent the Jews from becoming completely unsociable. The commissioners reported their dissatisfaction with this answer to the Minister of the Interior.[28]

The answer to the fifth question, which concerned those relations which should exist between Jewish and non-Jewish Frenchmen, raised no special problem and was unanimously accepted. Relations with Gentiles could not be different from relations with Jews, as Christians and Jews differed only in the way they adored the Supreme Being. This answer repeated that Christianity was not an idolatrous religion. This was justified by biblical and talmudic law as well as by modern usage. The Jews considered the end of the Jewish nation, and their integration into the great French nation as an improvement which made any discrimination on their part between Jews and Gentiles impossible.[29] The commissioners were not completely satisfied with this answer, and suspected the Jewish delegates of having preferred to describe the present situation of the Jews in France rather than actually discuss the matter on its legal merits.[30]

The sixth question dealt with the attitude of French-born French-Jewish citizens to their fatherland: did they consider France as their fatherland, and did they feel bound to defend it? Did they feel that they had to comply with its laws and all the dispositions of the civil code? The answer was obviously positive. The delegates declared that love of the fatherland had made French Jews feel foreign even among English Jews. This feeling was strong enough to make French Jews fight Jews of other countries with which France was at war, and this had not made them conscious of any special problem. Curiously enough, the commissioners accepted this answer without even remarking that the deputies had not answered the last part of the question which concerned automatic compliance with the civil law. Anyway, the deputies accepted its formulation by a unanimous vote.[31]

The Assembly then turned to the seventh question: who appoints the rabbis? The deputies sought to differentiate between the pre-revolutionary appointments and the present situation. One of them asked whether it would be advisable to describe the usage of both periods or be satisfied with the latter? Another wished to explain the difference between the officiating rabbis as such and those rabbis who did not engage in the practical rabbinate (although they had received the rabbinic title). It would seem that the deputies felt that a comparison of the respective status of rabbis and priests would in any case compel them to explain this purely Jewish feature. In the final draft, which was accepted by a majority vote, it was decided to refer exclusively to the post-revolutionary situation and to declare that wherever the number of the Jews warranted it, a rabbi was appointed by a majority vote of the local heads of families. Nevertheless, there were innumerable exceptions to this rule, and it had to be admitted that the whole matter was not very clear. During their examination of this answer the commissioners received further clarification: a rabbi had to receive a certificate of ability from another rabbi in order to be allowed to exercise rabbinic functions.[32]

The Assembly then adjourned until 12 August when it tackled the last five questions. The delegates from the Kingdom of Italy had meanwhile arrived in Paris and now took part in the discussion of the notables. They asked that the Kingdom of Italy be mentioned as well as the Empire in the resolutions to be adopted. The delegates then examined the draft of the answer which dealt with the powers of the rabbis. They described the origins of the rabbinate and explained that when the Jews lived in small communities during their dispersion a rabbi joined by two assessors presided over a Jewish court of justice in order to render judgment. This could be done only with the authorisation of the local authorities. Since the Revolution such Jewish courts had completely disappeared from the Empire and from Italy. The Jews, having become citizens, had everywhere conformed to the laws of the state. As for the rabbis, they were now satisfied with preaching, performing weddings and pronouncing divorces. At the request of a Portuguese or Italian delegate, it was stated that in the south a marriage could be, and often was, performed by a lay person, or a member of the family, even in cities where there was a rabbi. This made it imperative that this kind of marriage, and not only those weddings where a rabbi officiated, be regulated by law, in order to avoid confusion or possible abuses. In their report the commissioners concurred with this wish, and agreed generally with the virtually unanimous answer given to this question by the deputies.[33]

The ninth question, which concerned the method for electing rabbis and their police power, had lost its meaning with the answer to the eighth question. The deputies said so, and added that any rabbinic jurisdiction or any rule for the election of rabbis could not be a consequence of the law, but only of usage. The commissioners did not even find it necessary to react to this answer.[34]

The tenth question enquired whether there were any professions forbidden to the Jews by their law. The deputies quoted the Talmud and said that according to Jewish law it was a foremost duty of the father to teach his son a trade. The commissioners, although not convinced by the answer – they were perhaps thinking of such laws as the Sabbath, holidays and dietary laws which made some trades rather difficult for practising Jews – decided not to pursue the matter further.[35]

The last two questions dealt with the problem of usury: the first, which was the eleventh, asked whether Jews were forbidden to take usury from their fellow-Jews. The deputies first gave the Hebrew definition of usury: it meant the prohibition not of an exaggerated interest but of *any* interest. This was forbidden to the Jews, as one of the aims of their law was to strengthen the bonds of brotherhood between them. When they borrowed money, it was only because of a pressing need: to lend money to the needy was a most commendable gesture, but to take interest from them would have been a misuse of power at a time of need. Therefore, usury was forbidden, because it would have negated the duty of charity. On the other hand, a commercial loan, even to a Jew, could include some very moderate form of interest, as this would then be a gain proportionate to the risk involved. Thus it became clear that any loan, in the nature of assistance, given to a Jew or a non-Jew, must be free of any interest. The problem would be different if the loan were given for a business reason. The dispersion of the Jews had relaxed the bonds of brotherhood which would normally have bound together the nationals of the same country. Thus it had also brought about a measure of disregard for the principle involved: without any undue scruples, as was well known, Jews had made interest-bearing loans to Jewish businessmen as well as to persons belonging to another religion!

The answer, which very skilfully linked loans made to Jews with loans made to Gentiles, was intended to prove that even when Jews granted such loans, they did not differentiate, as a consequence of any principle, between Jewish and Christian borrowers. It also established a distinction between loans made for consumption and those made for business reasons. This could hardly have pleased the commissioners, who maintained that the possibility of granting interest-bearing loans to foreigners was to be understood as a means to enable the Jews to get rich quick, rather than as a consequence of any subtle legal distinction. They most certainly did not agree with the spirit of the answer. It must be noted that the Assembly itself, although it eventually adopted the proposed text with barely a dissentient voice, had discussed it in great detail before agreeing to it.[36]

The answer given to the twelfth question, which dealt with the legitimacy, or lack of it, of usury to Gentiles, did not raise any problems. Without any discussion, the Assembly accepted unanimously the draft prepared by the Committee of Twelve. This declared that the law allowed for commercial loans to foreigners, but not to Gentiles living among the Jews. As Moses had legislated only for the Jews, he could obviously not have forbidden them to extend commercial interest-bearing loans to members of foreign nations, as he did not know whether these nations would reciprocate or not. In any case commercial loans were not to be confused with loans to the poor: as long as the interest remained moderate, the first were permissible while the latter were forbidden. Maimonides' opinion, which would recommend taking usury from a Gentile, was not shared by the other rabbis and remained therefore a private opinion which was not binding.[37] The fact that there existed a number of Jewish usurers did not, and could not, reflect on the whole Jewish community. Therefore, one individual who deviated from the existing laws could not bring blame on a hundred thousand others. The problems of usury, the deputies implied, was the problem of a few Jews individually and not of the whole community.[38]

The commissioners, in their report to the Minister, refused to accept this answer, and accused the Jews of maintaining a double standard: one for loans to Jews and one for loans to Gentiles. They noted that if the answer were to be accepted, the absolute prohibition of all but commercial loans would be recommended. The Jews' doctrine on loans would then be more severe than that of the Catholic theologians. In reality this was not so, as it had never prevented the most religious of Jews from practising usury.[39]

Concluding their report, the commissioners remarked that the Assembly had been more interested in presenting a vindication of the Jews than in providing a scrupulous description of their beliefs and practices. To achieve this aim they had quoted alternately Moses and the rabbis, without determining their relative authority, using or rejecting them according to need. They also felt it necessary to give the Minister an analysis of the membership of the Assembly, which did not exactly prove their understanding of its workings. According to them, it was divided into three different parts: a small group more attached to the letter of the law, and rejecting any concession; a second, formed of the majority of the Assembly, and wishing to reconcile the interests of religion with the enjoyment of civil rights. A third group, the smallest one, took control of everything and included the richest, most polished and ablest delegates: they had little regard for their religion and kept its name and appearances only as a matter of self-respect. These remarks showed that the commissioners had by no means fully understood the importance of the role of Sintzheim.[40] Other observers were to be more careful in appreciating his role during the proceedings.[41]

Having handed in its answers, the Assembly now awaited developments. Champagny, the Minister of the Interior, having received the reports, proceeded to prepare his own more general report to the Emperor. This he did in two communications, on 30 July and 20 August.[42] He sent the Emperor the minutes of the Assembly's meetings, and analysed its composition. Although the

Portuguese Jews on the one hand, and the German and Italian Jews on the other, had agreed on all the essential tenets of their faith, they still differed from each other and did not hesitate to set up different synagogues even when they lived in the same city. Among the German Jews themselves there were other differences: the Jews of Metz were more liberal than the Alsatians, and the long-established residents of France more so than the newcomers. Nevertheless, Champagny wrote, the debates had been pursued in good spirit, as the deputies had sincerely wished to meet the views of the Emperor: 'they have done, I believe, everything they could to comply with Your Majesty's intentions.'[43] They had shown themselves to be Frenchmen in their enthusiasm for him, although it had occasionally been difficult for them to find a middle way between their wish to comply with the laws of France, and the precepts of their religious code. Champagny was more receptive than the commissioners to the Assembly's declaration that religious law required the Jews to accept and respect the political and civil law of the country they lived in: this had always been the case as experience amply showed. Anyway, it would be always possible to request – and to obtain – that every Jew give a written promise to comply with the law of the country. He then examined the answers given by the deputies to the twelve questions.

He found no major difficulty in the first two answers, as the Jews were willing to comply with the laws of the land, rejected polygamy, and were ready to make the granting of a religious divorce conditional upon the previous granting of a civil divorce. The Minister agreed that any marriage between members of different religions would be bound to raise difficulties.

He expressed particular admiration for the strength of the Assembly's declaration on brotherhood. As a country, France, he declared, had behaved in a most favourable way towards the Jews. The Jewish nation should not be recognised as a nation anymore, but the Jewish religion was entitled to the protection of the state, as long as it did not contradict its laws. Nevertheless, Champagny wrote, it must be admitted that the Jews could not recognise the Christians as their brethren in a religious, but only in a political and civil sense. Moses, when he legislated for his people, could not have done so for the present situation, that is for the Jewish dispersion. Therefore, when dealing with the general problems of brotherhood, the deputies had been absolutely justified in turning to the rabbi's opinion and not to that of the Bible: this was of course a severe criticism of the commissioners' opinion on this matter. Champagny also dissociated himself from their remarks on the nature of the Jewish religion, and wrote that in his opinion the Jews did not look upon the Christians as idolaters.[44]

When it came to the problem of the Jews' military duty to their fatherland, Champagny recognised in the Assembly's positive answer a direct consequence of its acceptance of the civil laws of the country the Jews lived in. So far as rabbinic jurisdiction was concerned, he would have preferred an answer declaring that in civil matters the rabbis exercise only those functions which the state had turned over to them, and not others which must come as a result of the title they bore. When Champagny discussed the answer to the tenth question which dealt with the professions of the Jews, he expressed his surprise at the commissioners' reaction, as he could not understand why they doubted the accuracy of the answer of the Assembly. If some religious practices such as a rigorous observance of the Sabbath might eventually complicate the practice of some profession, other qualities such as the sobriety of the Jews, their thrift, their dedication to work and aversion to entertainment more than compensated for that. Their law showed indeed that, during their national existence in their country, they had practised all trades and professions.

The problem of usury was not forgotten. According to Champagny, Jewish law permitted the lending of money at interest to Gentiles, but did not order it. Civil law could therefore forbid it without any difficulty, as there would be no danger of conflict between the two systems. The usurers would be punished by civil law in such a case.

On the basis of these remarks, and in a direct rebuff to the commissioners, Champagny concluded that the answers of the Assembly were sincere. The deputies could not have given more positive answers without infringing the principles which the orthodox considered sacred. Moreover, even if the strictest views of the Jews were adopted, it still proved impossible to find one rule which commended what French law forbade, or which forbade what French law enjoined. There would therefore be no difficulty in turning the Jews into faithful and obedient citizens.[45] He then suggested a number of practical measures to make this possible.[46]

Three days later, on 23 August, Napoleon answered Champagny and sent him his instructions 'on the directions which I intend to give the Assembly of the Jews and what the commissioners to this Assembly will now have to do'. Napoleon's intentions were to transform the Assembly of Notables into a Great Sanhedrin, which would review the answers of the deputies, and convert them into a second body of legislation for the Jews, following the law of Moses.[47] This new plan does not seem to have been in existence at the time the Assembly began to meet. Everything points to the fact that when Napoleon began dealing with the Jewish problem, he thought that the Notables alone could do the job. In fact the number of rabbis who took part in the Assembly's meetings was rather small. What then had happened to cause the Emperor to change his mind and request the establishment of a new body, the name of which showed clearly enough that he intended to give it powers far greater than those the Assembly had been granted? Napoleon never explained why he chose to act in this way, but the commissioners, especially Pasquier, seem to have felt that the idea of the Sanhedrin arose as a direct consequence of the way the discussions had proceeded in the Assembly, and how decisions had been reached. In Pasquier's words:[48]

after a few weeks we had not moved further than on the first day; besides the difficulties of the subject-matter and even while recognising on nearly every point the fairness of the propositions which had been made to them, the more enlightened, the more influential members of the Assembly told the commissioners that the statements which were requested from them were not only embarrassing for them and delicate for their conscience, but that they would obviously be completely useless; that they had no authority to order their co-religionists to comply with them; that the very fact that they had been chosen by the government made it impossible for them to be considered as the representatives of the Jewish people, with authority to legislate in its name. Several times they had quoted the name of the ancient gathering of doctors which was known under the name of the Great Sanhedrin; this gathering alone, they said, had been empowered to render decisions on such matters when the Jewish people was constituted as a separate nation, and it alone would be empowered to pass judgment upon them. When the commissioners reported these observations to the Emperor, he did not hesitate to seize hold of the idea, and soon it became known that he was very much inclined to authorise the summoning in Paris of a Great Sanhedrin, which would be composed as far as possible following the rules and according to the ways imposed by the law of Moses.

Molé attributed this turn of events to the influence of the rabbis, which had grown tremendously during the meetings of the Assembly, and the discussions which had occurred between the Committee of Twelve and the Emperor's representatives. There is evidence that Sintzheim himself had greatly contributed to this change: in a private letter he expressed his pleasure at the meeting of the Sanhedrin, as it would re-establish the authority of the rabbis, who would certainly constitute a majority of its membership, and at the same time reduce the pressure of the lay delegates.[49]

Napoleon explained his intentions in a note which he sent with his letter to Champagny: since the fall of the Temple to Titus, no Assembly of Jews comparable to the present one had been able to meet. The present circumstances were quite different as the Jews were not expected to give up their religion, or to adopt any modifications which would be repugnant to its letter and its spirit. At the time of their persecution, new teachings or practices had been accepted, and the rabbis had arrogated to themselves the right to explain the principles of their religion when the need appeared. As the right of legislation could not belong to an individual, it would be advisable to turn the Assembly which was at present meeting in Paris into a Great Sanhedrin, 'the decisions of which shall be placed next to the Talmud as articles of faith and principles of religious legislation'. Therefore, the Jews of all nations should be invited to send their deputies to Paris in order to take part in the proceedings of the Great Sanhedrin. A notification would be sent to all the synagogues of Europe, and an official invitation to those of France. The answers which would then be given to the questions posed 'will be turned into compelling theological decisions or teachings, so that they will have the strength of ecclesiastical or religious law and will become a second legislation of the Jews, which, while keeping the essential character of that of Moses, will adapt itself to the present situation of the Jews, to our ways and our usages.'

The Emperor then repeated the twelve questions which had been put to the Assembly and added the answers he expected to receive. As far as polygamy was concerned, the Assembly or the Sanhedrin must forbid it in Europe. It must also prohibit divorce except in those cases which French law allowed, and decree that they cannot be pronounced unless already pronounced by the civil authority. When the problem of mixed marriages came up, Napoleon was positive: the Sanhedrin must decide that the religious ceremony could take place only after the civil ceremony had been performed. Moreover it must declare that mixed marriages are permissible: it should recommend the conclusion of such marriages for the protection and propriety of the Jewish people. The Sanhedrin must recognise, as had the Assembly, the brotherhood of Jews and Frenchmen, and establish as a principle that the Jews are the brethren of the inhabitants of these countries which had granted them not only toleration but also protection and in which they enjoyed political and civil rights. It would also reveal the differences which existed in this matter between French and Italian legislation and that of the other countries.

The Sanhedrin would proclaim that the Jews must defend France as they would defend Jerusalem, 'for they are treated in France as they would be in the holy city'. As far as the rabbinate was concerned, the Sanhedrin would determine who should appoint the rabbis, how they should be organised and paid. It would establish in Paris a rabbinic council, the members of which would be the superiors and the supervisors of the Jews. It would also determine their precise functions. Moreover, it would forbid taking usury from Frenchmen and from the inhabitants of those countries which had granted them civil rights. It would therefore interpret the law of Moses as ordering them to consider all the places where they were citizens as equal to Jerusalem. The Jews are foreigners only where they are persecuted on account of the law of the country: only there may they indulge in illicit profits. In his conclusion, the Emperor repeated the principle on which his Jewish policy had been all along founded: when problems of principle had been settled by the Sanhedrin, consideration would be given to research into methods which might end or contain their evil ways. Laws of exception should appear as a consequence of the Jews' wishes!

The commissioners, who were retained in office, were ordered to study these general instructions and to discuss them with the most influential members of the Assembly. When they had agreed on the steps to be taken, they were to report to the Assembly and tell it of the Emperor's satisfaction with their zeal. They were to inform it that in these extraordinary circumstances, the Emperor's intention was to prevent their newly-won rights becoming illusory and 'make them find Jerusalem in France'. The Assembly should then set up a Committee of Nine of its more enlightened members which would prepare, together with the commissioners, the formation of the Great Sanhedrin.[50]

The three commissioners, directed by Molé, immediately began to study this new task. On 2 September they reported on the results of their efforts and brought their suggestions before the Emperor and the Minister of the Interior.[51] On receipt of the Emperor's instructions, they decided to meet one by one, or collectively, the most important members of the Assembly, to ascertain their real intentions and to explain to them the Emperor's demand that the answers given to the twelve questions receive a religious sanction. These meetings yielded very varied reactions. Some delegates were interested exclusively in their political and civil advancement and cared very little about the religious aspect; they were convinced that the passage of time and the progress of religious indifference would reduce the number of believing Jews: this was one of the reasons which made it impossible for them to understand the Emperor's wishes. The 'real Jews of the Assembly who are in the opinion of His Majesty's commissioners the representatives of the majority of the Jews, or, rather, the only representatives of the Jews who are Jews' and who were the real objects of the Emperor, were overjoyed when they heard of his intentions, and were told that he wanted to maintain the integrity of their religion.[52] They were convinced of the advantages of a religious assembly and insisted on the authority which would thus be conferred to the answers given to the Emperor's questions: no Western Jew would be in a position to refuse to adhere to them. They also remarked that religious assemblies had their own traditions, and that every religious synod which had met since the destruction of the Temple had been composed exclusively of rabbis and that when the Sanhedrin admitted lay members, these had always been recommended by their knowledge and piety. A modern Sanhedrin should therefore be composed of two-thirds of rabbis if it were to have any authority in France or abroad. The commissioners thereupon remarked that this was a major reason for the reluctance of the philosophers: they were afraid of losing most of their influence. The consultations they had had with the deputies showed that the philosophers scarcely acknowledged the existence of the rabbinate, and sapped its authority in order to silence religious opinion. They neglected no opportunity to keep them away from the meetings where the resolutions brought to the Assembly were prepared. On the other hand, the philosophers had to admit that only the rabbis had any authority in religious matters, and that any instruction to the French, Italian and German synagogues could be sent only and exclusively by these rabbis who were at present members of the Assembly.[53]

The commissioners suggested therefore the following measures: they would pay the Assembly a visit and one of them would inform them of His Majesty's general satisfaction with the spirit of their answers. He would also confirm them in the use of their political rights and full freedom of religion, and explain to them the Emperor's plans in order to persuade them in favour of summoning a Great Sanhedrin. The Great Sanhedrin, not counting its president, would be composed of seventy members, two-thirds of whom would be rabbis. In order to fill this quota, thirty supplementary rabbis would be invited to Paris from the synagogues of France, Italy, Spain, Portugal and Germany to join the present rabbinic members of the Assembly. They should be in Paris before 15 October, which would be the day of its opening meeting. The other third, composed of lay members, would be chosen among the deputies to the Assembly in these proportions: nine Portuguese, eight Germans and eight Italians who would be designated by a secret ballot in the presence of the commissioners. The participation of former members of the Assembly would then assure the continuity of its work. A Committee of Nine should be elected from the forty members of the Assembly – rabbis and elected lay members – who would sit in the Sanhedrin, in the proportion of six rabbis to three lay members.

The next day Napoleon sent his instructions to the Minister of the Interior.[54] He did not agree that part of the membership of the Assembly should be sent home: they should remain 'the basis of the operation', as they had already answered the questions put to them. One should avoid leaving 'the certain for the uncertain'.[55] Thirty new rabbis should be invited to join the fifteen already present. With some of the most important members of the Assembly they would compose the Sanhedrin. But the Assembly should retain its full membership: it was only to be enlarged by thirty rabbis. This would enable the deputies to exert great influence on the reluctant or fanatical rabbis, as it would compel them to choose between compliance with the answers, and – the Emperor did not hesitate to use the word – the danger of a refusal, which would cause the expulsion of the Jewish people.[56] Nobody would be sent home, but the Assembly was to declare that a Great Sanhedrin would be chosen among its membership. The result would be that a large Assembly would take its decision according to the interests of the Jewish people and its own interests. It would try to avoid being made responsible for the miseries of the Jewish people. The Sanhedrin would be the committee of the General Assembly of the representatives and elders of the Jewish people. The Assembly for its part would deal with problems of discipline, organisation and finances. Before inviting other rabbis, it should be ascertained that the fifteen already present agreed with the answers previously given to the twelve questions, as it would be ridiculous to bring to Paris thirty new rabbis only to have them 'declare that the Jews are not the brethren of Frenchmen'.[57]

With these instructions in hand the Minister of the Interior prepared the meeting of the Sanhedrin. First of all, the rabbis who were members of the Assembly were asked to sign a declaration of agreement with the decisions of the Assembly; this was done on 10 September. Seventeen rabbis, not fifteen as had first been estimated, signed this declaration, which was formulated with great care. They declared that the Assembly's answers conformed to the laws and traditions of Judaism, and that, in view of the fact that they would have to be rewritten by the Sanhedrin, they would contribute to this 'in limiting ourselves to the positive meaning they express'. This was of course a way of preventing undesirable surprises, but the commissioners nevertheless admitted their statement without any difficulty.[58] Everything was now ready for the communication to be read to the Assembly, a meeting of which was called for 18 September. Molé appeared before it with his colleagues and made a resounding speech.

He first informed the Assembly officially of the Emperor's general satisfaction with its answers. He proclaimed the Emperor's intentions 'to assure you the freedom of your religion and the full benefit of your civil rights, but in return for the august protection he grants you, he requests a religious guarantee of the complete observance of the principles proclaimed in your answers.' The Assembly, as it stands today, cannot give such a guarantee, Molé continued, and therefore a Great Sanhedrin will be called composed of seventy-one members, two-thirds of whom will be rabbis, among whom will sit the rabbis who are members of the Assembly of Notables and had accepted its decisions, and one-third lay members chosen from the deputies. The Assembly itself would not be dissolved with the establishment of the Sanhedrin and would continue its work. The Sanhedrin would ratify the decisions of the Assembly and give a greater weight to its answers. A Committee of Nine would be chosen among the membership of the Assembly giving equal representation to the Portuguese, Italian and German delegates. This was of course an attempt to turn the more orthodox element into a permanent minority. The Assembly would send an appeal to all the synagogues of Europe to invite them to send deputies who would be able to enlighten the government, and be deserving of communicating with the Assembly.

In his answer Furtado, the chairman of the Assembly, thanked the Emperor for the interest he took in the organisation and advancement of the Jewish religion. Now that it had been demonstrated that the code of Moses contained nothing which would justify the exclusion of its followers from the possession of the civil and political rights all Frenchmen enjoyed, the time had come to give the Assembly's decisions full religious sanction.

The Assembly thereupon voted in favour of the recommendations the commissioners had brought before it and began to prepare the meeting of the Great Sanhedrin, and the continuation of the Assembly's work.[59]

CHAPTER V

The Great Sanhedrin

As a first step toward the meeting of the Great Sanhedrin, the Assembly elected the Committee of Nine. Although Molé had hoped to have six rabbis designated as members, only four were elected: three Italians and one Portuguese. As the commissioners reported, the Alsatian rabbi Sintzheim, the foremost representative of Jewish orthodoxy, and the German rabbis, were eliminated with the victory of the philosophic party.[1] The mediocrity of this rabbinic representation was soon demonstrated as the Assembly had to decide to ask David Sintzheim to help the new committee prepare the proclamation which was to be sent to the Jewish communities of Europe![2] Later on the Assembly designated by a secret vote the twenty-five lay members who were to sit on the Sanhedrin. The commissioners reported that a number of the deputies elected had aroused the deep disapproval of the rabbinic camp on account of their very lax religious practice. Some were accused of being atheists or of not having their children circumcised. This criticism does not seem to have impressed the commissioners, who decided to ignore it. In any case, they did not intend to weaken the philosophers' camp, and so strengthen the rabbinic party.[3]

The Committee of Nine seems to have been dominated by the president of the Assembly, Furtado, and by Jacob Lazard, deputy of Paris, who engaged in constant feuding with Berr Isaac Berr, deputy of Nancy, who belonged to the orthodox camp and who was soon reduced to silence. The commissioners met regularly with the Committee of Nine to prepare the meeting of the Sanhedrin.[4] On 24 September the Assembly accepted unanimously the draft of the appeal to be sent to all the Jewish communities of Europe which the Nine had prepared with Sintzheim's help. Dated Paris, 24 Tishri 5567 – 6 October 1806 – the letter of the Assembly of the deputies of the Israelites of France and the Kingdom of Italy was addressed to their co-religionists, informing them that the Great Sanhedrin would begin its meetings in Paris on 20 October, under the protection of Napoleon, who intended to abolish every humiliating distinction which separated the Jews from his other subjects. Let the leaders of other communities support this enterprise with their help and advice, and choose representatives to send to Paris to participate in this great enterprise, initiated by Napoleon the Great.[5]

It had already become obvious that the meetings of the Assembly would be protracted and that many deputies and, later, rabbis would find themselves in reduced and difficult circumstances should nothing be done for their support. It was decided to approach the Minister of the Interior to secure his support in raising within the various Jewish communities the funds necessary for the support of the needy delegates. In order to make it possible for the rabbis to come to Paris, it was finally decided that the Jewish communities would have to pay for the upkeep of their envoys to Paris.[6]

The choice of the rabbis proved more difficult than expected. The government had not taken into account the fact that according to ancient usage there were very few rabbinic seats in France, the religious organisation being regional rather than local. Previously the *nation* had a rabbi, but not the local community. This had been the case in Metz or in Lorraine. Even in Alsace before the Revolution there were officially only five or six rabbis, with a few substitutes. The number of persons who possessed the rabbinic title was of course much greater, although they did not hold – nor had they ever held – any rabbinic position or responsibilities. The choice of the future members of the Sanhedrin became rather difficult, and was very often criticised. Furtado frequently complained of their general mediocrity. Lazard himself expressed his displeasure at the choice of the rabbis from Paris: one of them was a hawker of handkerchiefs and muslin; another looked to him more of a simpleton than a rabbi. They had of course the great disadvantage of belonging to the orthodox camp, which did not particularly endear them to the Paris deputy.[7] The search for rabbis willing to come to Paris – many refused because of reasons of age or fear – was to take much longer than expected, and caused deferment after deferment of the Sanhedrin's first meeting, which finally took place on 4 February 1807, i.e. two and a half months after the day set aside for its opening session! The rabbis themselves added to the delay when they refused to admit such unlikely members of the Sanhedrin as the Parisian Jews Zalkind Hourwitz and Moses Ensheim who were known as extreme reformers: a few rabbis had warned that they would rather leave than sit with them. The idea was therefore given up.[8]

On 31 January 1807, Molé reported to the Minister of the Interior about the progress of his and his colleagues' work. He proposed the appointment of a chairman of the Assembly and of assessors. The commissioners had agreed that the best choice would be the Chief Rabbi of Strasbourg, David Sintzheim. He justified this choice of a northern chairman by the need to bring about a change of opinion among the very Jews against whom there had been complaints; these were none other than the northerners, that is, the former members of the German *nations*. He added that these Jews did not recognise the orthodoxy of their brethren of the south, concluding that 'Rabbi Sintzheim fits the position intended for him on account of his great age. He enjoys the respect of all his co-religionists, belonged to the first Assembly and had taken part in the drafting of its answers.' As assessors, they suggested two Italian rabbis: Segré and Cologna, whose help they greatly appreciated. Their suggestions were accepted by the Minister, who informed the Assembly accordingly.[9]

Meanwhile the Committee of Nine and the commissioners had agreed upon by-laws regulating the seating and deliberations of the Sanhedrin. It would not meet until all its members had arrived in Paris and until its head, his two assessors, and its two scribes, i.e. its secretaries, had been appointed. The Committee of Nine was empowered to verify the powers of the members, in the presence of the commissioners: the rabbis would be required to show the prefect's order appointing them, and give proof of their rabbinic title and of their knowledge of Hebrew. For the other delegates, the prefect's letter of appointment would be sufficient. The Minister of the Interior was to appoint the chairman and his collaborators from a list presented to him by the commissioners. Four days before the opening of the Sanhedrin the Assembly of Notables would meet to hear the report prepared for the Sanhedrin by the Committee of Nine.

The by-laws also provided for the seating arrangements: in an obvious attempt to draw inspiration from antiquity, it was decided that the members would be seated in a semicircle, according to age, the oldest member sitting immediately to the left of the chairman, and so on. There could be no deliberation if those present numbered less than sixty. The meetings would take place on Mondays and Thursdays. In order to avoid discussions, it was decided that every report presented to the Great Sanhedrin would be brought to it by two *rapporteurs* who were members of the Committee of Nine. Once the report was submitted, deliberation would be suspended for eight days, each member who so desired being allowed to send his written remarks to the Committee of Nine which would then bring them to the attention of the commissioners, and, at the expiration of the interval of eight days, before the Sanhedrin. There would be no discussions in the Sanhedrin. Votes would be by roll-call, the only answers permitted being yes or no. The by-laws also stipulated which prayers should be said and in what manner and even indicated when members of the Sanhedrin would have to cover their head. It was clear there was no room for surprises, and there were none.[10] After a first meeting on 4 February, which dealt with the composition of the Sanhedrin, a second meeting was called for 9 February, when a special service took place in the most important Paris synagogue, and prayers for the Lord's blessing and inspiration were offered. The members of the Sanhedrin then proceeded to the meeting-hall where David Sintzheim, now called *Nasi* according to ancient usage, took the chair, with his two assessors, the *Ab Beth Din* and the *Hacham*, at his side. Sintzheim's speech, translated into French, was read: he promised to ensure that the purity of divine law and the respect of human law would both be kept in mind, and that the Sanhedrin would merit the protection of the Emperor and the confidence of all the Jews. It was thereupon decided to send the minutes of the Sanhedrin's meeting to the Minister of the Interior and the commissioners. Then Furtado, and Cracovia, the rabbi of Venice, both members of the Committee of Nine, were appointed *rapporteurs*, and the debate began.[11]

Furtado brought before the Sanhedrin the first doctrinal decisions which it was asked to act upon. He had himself taken a major part in the preparation of at least the first six proposals brought before the Sanhedrin.[12] By contrast with the Assembly, the Sanhedrin was to discuss nine proposals only, as the three questions dealing with the rabbinate and its powers were not included in the list of problems submitted to it, but were left to the Assembly's discretion.

During the meetings, much attention was given to decorum, and the members, lay people or rabbis, wore uniform during the sessions. These sessions seem to have been very short: at the beginning the commissioners had thought the Sanhedrin should deal with one problem at a time, but as they recognised the smoothness of its proceedings, they agreed to have two or three questions brought up at the same meeting.[13] Furtado was the principal orator in the name of the Committee of Nine, and took a major part in the proceedings, where he and Sintzheim were the foremost speakers. The proposals of the Nine did not differ greatly in their content from the Assembly's answers, but revealed an important change in tone: whereas the Assembly had given advice, the Sanhedrin gave orders. It forbade polygamy where the Assembly had shown that it was no longer practised among western Jews.[14] The Assembly had admitted that a religious divorce would be invalid if not preceded by a civil divorce: the Sanhedrin ordered the rabbis not to issue any writ of divorce unless they were sure that a civil divorce had already been pronounced.[15] The only point where it took a decision which did not appear in the Assembly's decisions concerned the difficulties of Jewish soldiers who were to be excused those religious obligations which were incompatible with a soldier's duties.[16] In general, the importance of the observation of the Noachide laws was emphasised: in those countries which gave protection and hospitality to the Jews, those who observed these laws should be regarded as brethren of the Jews and all the laws of brotherhood applied.[17]

An important preamble preceded the Sanhedrin's decision: it first thanked Napoleon for having decided to summon the Sanhedrin in Paris, and confirmed that it was empowered to take decisions which would serve as an example to all Jews. It distinguished in Jewish law between religious and political decrees. The first were independent of circumstances and therefore permanent. The second applied only when Israel constituted a nation in its own land. This distinction had always been known to the rabbis, but only the Sanhedrin was at liberty to draw from it the necessary consequences. This had not yet been done, because no Sanhedrin had been able to meet since the dispersion of Israel, but now the time for this had come. Drawing its authority from the laws, decrees and customs of Israel – the name of Napoleon was not mentioned – which empower the Sages of every generation to take those measures which circumstances make necessary in order to preserve the written and oral law, it proclaimed the duty of obedience to the law of the country in civil and political matters. Any Jew from France or Italy who disregarded those laws or rebelled against them would have sinned against the Lord. The Sanhedrin then turned the Assembly's answers into religious commandments and made them a part of Jewish religious legislation.[18]

The only high points of the meetings were the speeches presenting or defending the proposals, which were unanimously accepted. In Furtado's view, there would be no difficulty in achieving the Sanhedrin's aims, as this would be a natural application of Jewish law. He maintained that the evils which could be found among some Jews were a consequence of the persecution they had suffered, and not of the teachings of their religion. This was of course a refusal to accept Molé's theories to the contrary. The Sanhedrin would avoid the dangers of fanaticism and superstition, and show that there existed a perfect harmony between Jewish and French law. Sintzheim felt it necessary to speak himself on the problem of usury: he could do so without qualms as he himself and Cerf Berr's sons had not been accused of practising it.[19] He warned against the consequences of such a practice, as it begins inconspicuously but finally brings about the destruction of whole families. The only excuse he could find for the Jewish usurers was that a long tradition of persecutions had made them turn to usury, because all other trades were closed to them. This was no longer true, as the Jews now enjoyed the rights of full citizenship. Therefore they should take it upon themselves to put an end to usury and to combat it. What is forbidden towards Jews cannot be tolerated towards Gentiles. Let the Jews now enter new professions to which they had had no access before. The Great Sanhedrin must nevertheless establish a difference between usury and a commercial loan which would justify a moderate rate of interest. Sintzheim concluded that Jews should conform to the government-imposed interest rate. In this way he rejected any special measures which would regulate Jewish money-lending, and declared that French law would be quite sufficient to deal with the problem.[20]

Furtado, acting as a *rapporteur*, made a speech on the same subject. He felt it particularly appropriate that a Jewish religious court should condemn in no uncertain terms the evil practice of usury. This would *inter alia* result in putting an end to the collective guilt which had up to now applied to all Jews, whether they practised usury or not. If the Jews had been accused of being a nation within a nation, this too was a consequence of the persecutions they had been subjected to, and which had compelled them to close their ranks in order to facilitate protection against their enemies. The fact that Jews were to be found in different countries had brought them the reputation of being cosmopolitans with no strong ties with the country they lived in. Furtado strongly denied this last accusation: the Jews' law had made it imperative upon them to accept the laws of the countries they lived in. It was evident that in their dispersion, the Jews had not known a form of central authority. Thus the Great Sanhedrin had fallen into oblivion. Therefore the proclamation of the Jews' attachment to the country they lived in was of great importance, as it would finally dispel the error which was so prevalent among Gentiles in this connection. Jewish history would at last stop being a history of bloodshed, expulsions, massacres, and would know a period of peace and happiness.[21]

On 9 March the meeting of the Sanhedrin came to an end: Furtado read a letter from the commissioners which authorised its president to conclude its proceedings.[22] Sintzheim then made a speech in Hebrew, later translated into French, in which he analysed the results and the efforts of the Sanhedrin. He made it very clear that in proclaiming the duty of the Jews to conform to the civil and political laws of their country, the Jews had only drawn the consequences of their own law. This had been done, he maintained, without impairing in the least any commandments of their religious laws. They had proclaimed at the same time a clear line must be drawn between religious and political duties. Any attempt to cross this line would only bring confusion and scandal. He then reviewed the decisions of the Sanhedrin, and applauded its declaration about human brotherhood. The Sanhedrin had acted wisely in accepting the principle of the ruler's authority and the duty to comply with his laws. He was quite outspoken when it came to the problem of mixed marriages: 'you have recognised the validity of certain civil acts, but you have admitted their religious incoherence.'[23] Alluding to polygamy and divorce, he said that the Sanhedrin had condemned some customs which were tolerated in Palestine, but had become unacceptable in Europe. For the sake of peace, the Sanhedrin had accepted that in certain ceremonies the public sanction should precede the religious sanction! It had also agreed that in certain conditions, there could be an exemption from some religious duties: but this could occur only when the sovereign and the state were in danger.[24] He considered that the decisions of the Sanhedrin constituted a 'social pact'[25] signed between the people of God and the nations which had accepted it, and refused to see them except as equals. For him there was no need for excuses and apologies. On the contrary, he called upon all mankind to recognise that the law of Israel was perfect, and rejected thereby any implication that the problems of the Jews were a result of Jewish law, and that there was any need for religious reform. He then thanked the commissioners for their great help, and the Emperor for having made the Sanhedrin possible. He finally rendered homage to his colleagues and reminded them that 'whoever betrays the divine laws will soon trample underfoot the human laws.'[26] At the suggestion of Furtado, the Sanhedrin thanked its chairman for the way he had fulfilled his duties.[27] The Sanhedrin now dispersed. The Assembly of Notables which had been interrupted for the duration of the Sanhedrin's meetings thereupon resumed its meetings.

At this point in the proceedings, the general agreement which had been reached during the debates between the Jewish deputies and the Sanhedrin seemed to indicate that the general problem of the Jews' assimilation was nearing a quiet solution. As a result of the conformity that was said to exist between Jewish and French law, a general spirit of confident optimism prevailed, as though the whole matter had only been the result of a misunderstanding which could easily be solved by a restatement of Jewish doctrine. The hostility of Alsace and the Emperor's personal position on the matter – inasmuch as it could have been known to the Jewish leaders – were completely forgotten in the mutual applause. It was precisely at that time that the Emperor's instructions arrived and events began to take a significantly different turn, although the Jewish deputies did not yet suspect this.[28]

Furtado himself seems to have believed that it would be possible to solve the problem through negotiation. In a private, and probably secret, letter to de Gerando, the secretary-general of the Ministry of the Interior, he put down in writing his suggestions concerning the problem of Jewish usury in Alsace. He first tried to explain the persistence of usury in this region and blamed it on the generally unfavourable attitude of the Christian population towards the Jews, and on local conditions. Contrary to accepted opinion, Furtado maintained that in the eight departments where the suspension of the debts due to Jews had been enacted since 30 May 1806, there were no more than 600 persons living exclusively from the loans they had granted, and not all of these were usurious. The usury attributed to the Jews was very exaggerated, and out of proportion with what had taken place in reality. Therefore the accusation of usury which had been lodged against all Jews could apply to only a small number of individuals. Moreover what was described as usury was really a form of swindling, which police measures could easily prevent. The evil ways of fifteen or twenty individuals – he would not hesitate to give their names – were endangering the reputation and interests of 45,000 Jews. This, of course, did not justify a general measure against all the Jews, as most of these were completely innocent. What then could be done to alleviate the condition of the Alsatian peasants who were in debt to the Jews? Furtado's suggestion was to give these debtors, who would not be asked to repay their debts immediately, an interval of five years to free themselves from this burden: they would pay a fifth every year, the interest being limited to 5 or 6 per cent. Thus it would be possible to solve the problem in a comparatively short period, without any need for special legislation.[29]

The naïveté of Furtado and his fellow deputies becomes obvious when they are confronted with the instructions finally sent by Napoleon to the Minister of the Interior and the commissioners in February 1807; that is, after the meetings of the Sanhedrin had already begun. In a four-part instruction, Napoleon first gave his directives for the meeting of the Sanhedrin. He asked that this body proclaim that Jewish law contains religious and political dispositions. Only the political instructions could be modified. The Great Sanhedrin was empowered to establish a distinction between religious and political laws. This had not been necessary as long as the Jews had lived in their land. Since their exile there had been no Sanhedrin. This introduction was followed by the questions which were to be brought before the Sanhedrin and the answers which were expected. It may be said that the Sanhedrin accepted all the Emperor's views with the exception of the recommendation on mixed marriages, which it had firmly rejected. The influence of the Emperor's views on the Sanhedrin's decision is obvious: Molé himself informed the Minister of the Interior that there would be no problem in getting general agreement to these modifications. The Emperor, except for the problem of mixed marriages, had not asked for any extraordinary change, and his instructions had not greatly changed since August 1806.

The three other parts of the Emperor's instructions were quite different and showed what the Emperor's intentions really were. It is therefore necessary to give them in their entirety:[30]

(II) Measures of organisation and discipline should also be taken, and they seem to pertain to the General Assembly. Therefore the General Assembly shall determine:

(1) the organisation of Sanhedrins or administrative consistories on an *arrondissement* or departmental basis, and of a consistory or central Sanhedrin, and the prerogatives of these institutions, which shall exercise a strict supervision over the rabbis;

(2) the number of rabbis, how they shall be paid, their obligations and their prerogatives;

(3) the necessary conditions governing authorisation to trade, and how this authorisation shall be granted with the agreement of the local authority;

(4) the prohibition of every kind of commerce, the right to draw bills of exchange, to deal in second-hand goods, to keep shop, to any individual who has not obtained the above mentioned authorisation;

(5) the prohibition for ten years to all Israelites who are unable to show that they own property in France, to grant loans on mortgages, and the authorisation to be given to property-owners to grant such loans, while confining their right to accept mortgages to the value of the property they possess;

(6) the duty, in each department or *arrondissement* where there is a Sanhedrin or a consistory, to authorise in every three marriages only two between Jew and Jewess and one mixed marriage between Jew and Christian. If the application of this disposition should prove to be too difficult, measures must be taken to engage to instruct, to encourage, to command in order to reach this aim;

(7)   the duty to provide a number of recruits proportionate to the size of the Israelite population, no Israelite to be replaced except by another Israelite.

Other provisions may be prescribed but they will come later.

(III) Among those mentioned above, some are not only disciplinary measures, but belong also to the province of legislation and require the help of the Council of State. Thus the Great Sanhedrin will explain the political provisions of the law of Moses, and prescribe as dogma the objects which belong to its province. The General Assembly of the Israelites, concluding a kind of agreement with the administration and in consideration of the advantages which the Revolution has granted the Jews, will prescribe the organisational disciplinary provisions. The Council of State will finally enact the necessary rules for the fulfilment of the above-mentioned provisions and prohibitions.

There is in all of this a mixture of dogmas, discipline, legislation, from which follows the necessity of a Great Sanhedrin, of a General Assembly of the Israelites, and reciprocal aid from the public authorities.

It will require much reflection and discernment to distinguish with precision what must appertain in this plan to the Great Sanhedrin, to the General Assembly and to the Council of State.

If a senate decree were necessary, there would be no difficulty in this, but it would not be possible to proceed by means of the law, as it is a question of achieving political results through civil provisions.

(IV) The principal aim in view was to protect the Jewish people, to come to the help of the countryside and to free some departments from the disgrace of having become vassals to the Jews, as the mortgaging of a great part of the lands of a department to a people, which in its ways and its laws constituted a particular nation within the French nation, is a real vassalage. It thus happened that in a period very near to us mortmain threatened to take hold of the territory and it became necessary to set obstacles to its progress. Likewise with the Jews' suzerainty spreading unceasingly through usury and mortgages, it becomes indispensable to set bounds to it. The second aim is to weaken, if not to destroy, the Jewish people's inclination to such a great number of practices which are contrary to civilisation, and to the good order of society in all the countries of the world.

The evil must be stopped through obstruction; it must be obstructed by the transformation of the Jews.

This set of proposed measures should have two results. When,

99

out of every three marriages, one is between Jew and Frenchman, the Jews' blood will lose its particular character.

When they are prevented from dealing exclusively in usury and peddling, they will accustom themselves to crafts: the inclination to usury will disappear.

When some of their youth are required to join the army, they will stop having Jewish interests and sentiments: they will acquire French interests and sentiments.

When they are submitted to civil laws, they will, as Jews only, uphold dogmas and they will have left that condition where religion is the only civil law, as prevails among the Moslems, and as the case has always been during the infancy of nations. It is frivolous to say that they are debased only because they are molested: in Poland – where they are necessary in order to replace the intermediary class of society, where they are respected and powerful – they are not any the less abject, dirty and prone to the practices of the lowest dishonesty.

Thinkers would doubtless suggest that we be satisfied with the introduction of improvements in their legislation; but this would be insufficient. Good is produced slowly and a mass of vitiated blood can be improved only through time. Meanwhile the peoples suffer and cry, and it lies in His Majesty's intention to come to their aid.

Two means must be used concurrently, one of which will stop the spreading of the fire and the other extinguish it.

From this springs the necessity to have recourse at the same time to the Great Sanhedrin, the General Assembly of the Jews, and to lawful provisions decided in the Council of State.

The Great Sanhedrin is supported by the wishes and the thinking of everything that is enlightened among the Jews of Europe. With this support, it is empowered to remove from the legislation of Moses those laws which are atrocious, and those which pertain solely to the situation of the Jews in Palestine.

The Emperor's instructions proved very clearly that he had not renounced his intention to enact the laws of exception against the Jews in order to 'regenerate' them. The hopes of the deputies and the members of the Sanhedrin would soon prove to be illusory, but they did not yet know what was in store for them, and did their best to conform to the Emperor's wishes. The Sanhedrin even agreed to include a dispensation from religious duties for Jewish soldiers in the army, although the Assembly had not even discussed the matter. Furtado's efforts to avert a general measure against the Jews on account of the usury of which they were accused proved futile, even before he had begun to plead the cause of the mass of the unjustly accused Jews of the north-eastern departments. For a long time, he did not know that the Emperor did not share his views on the matter.

Champagny, the Minister of the Interior, immediately understood the meaning of the Emperor's instructions. In his answer of 17 February, he wrote that he was expediting the completion of the Sanhedrin's meetings, in order to bring to an end the purely religious part of the operation. Nevertheless he would not reveal to it the full scope of the Emperor's views, 'which could frighten a few rabbis who are too slavishly attached to their ancient practices'.[31] In any case it would be very difficult to keep the Sanhedrin in session for an extended period, as it was practically impossible to maintain its seventy members for any duration in Paris. He would therefore soon have to release those among its members who did not have to participate in the Assembly's meetings. Champagny was nevertheless uneasy about the unconstitutional aspects of the proposed law against the Jews, and hoped to find a way to justify it. That is why he wrote to the Emperor that he 'would try to get it [the Assembly] to agree to invite the public authority to prescribe and to have carried out, what it could only, at most, recommend.' This request would allow him, he added, to send the Emperor the text of the measures which would be required. He nevertheless warned the Emperor that it would not be possible to secure the delegates' agreement to his instructions concerning the necessity of mixed marriages.[32]

On 26 February, Champagny sent Molé an explicit letter:[33]

I am very insistent that the General Assembly, while expressing its wishes for the regeneration of its co-religionists, and recognising the insufficiency of its means to perform it, should request the public authority to agree to intervene in order to complete the enterprise; it seems to me necessary that it should point out with the greatest precision possible, the different matters on which this authority should take action, such as the mixing of the Jewish race with the race of Frenchmen, conscription, the repression of usury, the exercise of crafts, and especially of agriculture . . .

It seemed impossible of course to ask for such a statement from a purely religious body such as the Sanhedrin. The commissioners would have to extract it from the Assembly of Notables, although this was hardly a representative assembly, as its members had not been elected, but chosen by the prefects. It is also a fact that they had been very careful in their handling of the rabbinate, as they were not fully convinced that they would be able to persuade it to agree to everything they wanted. They were rather satisfied at having been able to come to an agreement with it. In their report to Champagny on the conclusion of the Sanhedrin's meetings, they insisted on the care they had taken to conform with the Emperor's wishes, although it had been difficult to explain to the rabbis and make them understand that the preamble, with its distinction between religious and political laws, did not attack either the dogmas or the traditions of the Jewish religion. The only great problem they had met was that of mixed marriages, and they thought that they had made the best of the situation in persuading the Sanhedrin to agree that those Jews who entered such marriages should not be excommunicated. Even the head of the Sanhedrin, who was the most understanding of its members, would go no further! They were therefore rather pleased with the result of their endeavours.[34]

The Sanhedrin having been dispersed, the Assembly of Notables continued its work. As a matter of fact it had continued to meet during the time the preparations for the Sanhedrin's meetings were in full swing, although a very large part of the discussions had taken place within the framework of the Committee of Nine. On 9 December 1806 the deputies met to hear a member of the Committee who was to present a report on the organisation of the Jewish cult, which had been agreed upon in a meeting between the Nine and the commissioners. The *rapporteurs* declared that everything that could infringe on the religious teachings or usages of Judaism had been discarded. The Jewish religion would at last receive a legal status and a well-defined organisation; its ministers would be recognised by the public authorities and see their functions specified, their salary assured and their influence turned to its proper end. This recognition of the Jewish religion would not place the Jews in an isolated situation, but would only express their religious diversity. He then described the proposed organisation of the Jewish cult and its internal policing system.[35]

This system was based on the division of France into a number of synagogues and Jewish consistories, which would submit to the authority of a Central Consistory. Obviously, the term 'consistory' was borrowed from the Protestant neighbours of the Jews, who had used this term for a long time. This put Judaism and Protestantism clearly in a minority position in comparison with the Catholic church. The use of the term 'synagogue' was later to create extreme confusion as it sometimes applied to the whole Jewish population which lived in a given circumscription, sometimes to the circumscription itself, sometimes to the building, and sometimes to the administration of this circumscription. This confusion had its origin in the very impression which surrounded the term 'church', which could also apply to different objects.[36]

The basis of the system was the synagogue – that is, the circumscription which was to be headed by a consistory; such a synagogue would be established in each department which counted at least 2,000 members of the Jewish faith. If a department did not include 2,000 Jews, it would unite with one or more neighbouring departments until this minimum number was reached. The seat of the consistory would always be in the town with the largest Jewish population. In no case could there be more than one synagogue – that is, one consistorial circumscription – in one department. No particular synagogue – in this case a subdivision of the consistorial synagogue – could be established unless the consistorial synagogue had so suggested to the competent authority. It would be administered by a rabbi and two appointed notables. Each consistorial synagogue would have a chief rabbi, and would be administered by a board consisting of the chief rabbi, another rabbi if possible, and three notables, two of whom had to be chosen from among the residents of the city of the seat of the consistory. The eldest of these four or five members would become the presiding officer, and would be called the *Ancien* or Elder of the consistory.

The competent authorities would appoint in each consistorial circumscription twenty-five notables, chosen out of those Jews who paid the highest taxes or were the most respected members of their faith. These notables would elect the members of the consistory, who would still have to secure the agreement of the competent authorities. Persons who were under thirty years of age, or had been adjudged bankrupt and had not redeemed themselves in an honourable way, or were known to have practised usury, could not be elected to the consistory. Every Jew who wished to settle in France or in the Kingdom of Italy would be requested to inform the nearest consistory within three months of his decision.

The duties of the consistory were to ensure that the rabbis conformed in public and in private to the Sanhedrin's decisions, to maintain order in the synagogues, to supervise the administration of the particular synagogues, to receive and spend the funds necessary in the exercise of the Jewish cult, and to see to it that no assembly of prayer was established without its express authorisation. It would also encourage by all possible means the Jews of its circumscription to enter useful trades, and inform the authorities of those who had no acknowledged means of existence. It would also annually inform the authorities of the number of prospective Jewish conscripts.

These regional consistories would be headed by a Central Consistory with its seat in Paris, and composed of three rabbis and two lay people. These rabbis would be chosen from among the existing chief rabbis, and the lay members would be subject to the same conditions as the members of the regional consistories. Each year one member would leave office, but would always be eligible for re-election. The remaining members of the Central Consistory would vote in this election, but their choice would have to be ratified by the competent authorities. The Central Consistory's duties would be to correspond with the consistories, to see to it that the new regulations were applied, to inform the authorities of all the infractions, or non-observances of these rules, to confirm the appointment of the rabbis and to bring before the authorities any motion to have rabbis or members of the consistories removed from office.

The chief rabbis would be elected by the committee of twenty-five notables, and their choice would have to be ratified by the Central Consistory. Nobody could be elected rabbi unless he was a native-born or naturalised French citizen, or an Italian citizen in the Kingdom of Italy, and unless he had produced a letter of authorisation signed by three Italian chief rabbis if he was Italian, or three French chief rabbis if he was a Frenchman. From the year 1820, candidates who did not know French in France, or Italian in Italy, would no longer qualify for the rabbinate. Those with some knowledge of Greek or Latin would be preferred to candidates who had a comparable level of Hebrew knowledge. Their functions were: to teach the Jewish religion and the doctrine of the Sanhedrin, to proclaim the duty of compliance with the laws, and especially with those which dealt with the defence of the country, even more so at the time of enlistment, to teach the Jews that military service was a sacred duty during which the religious laws which proved to be incompatible with it would be suspended, to preach in the synagogues and to lead the prayers for the Emperor and his family, to celebrate weddings and to perform divorces, but only after having examined the certificate of the civil wedding or divorce.

The salaries of rabbis of the Central Consistory and of the consistorial synagogues was determined. As for the salaries of the rabbis of the particular synagogues, these would depend mostly on the decision of the Jews who had asked for their establishment. The different consistories would be empowered to raise among the Jews of their circumscription, with the consent and help of the authorities, the sum necessary for the payment of their rabbis, while funds necessary for other expenses would be raised by the authorities at the request of the consistories. Part of the sums raised in the different consistories would be set aside for the payment of the rabbis of the Central Consistory. Each consistory would appoint a treasurer, who could not be one of its members, to collect the sums which would have to be raised in this way. This treasurer, who could not be a rabbi, would be responsible for paying the rabbi, and other expenses, and would account annually for those expenses.

Any unemployed rabbi who wished to remain in France and Italy would be required to declare his adhesion to, and sign, the decisions of the Sanhedrin, and this declaration was to be transmitted to the Central Consistory by the consistory which had received it. The former members of the Sanhedrin were to be preferred as far as possible in the choice of the chief rabbis. The draft ended with a motion on the duty of all French and Italian Jews to serve in the army and fight for their country, and with the wish expressed by the Committee of Nine: that is, without the concurrence of the commissioners, to have the salaries of the rabbis paid by the state, as was already the case with the clergy of the other recognised religions. The Assembly thus showed that it was not fully convinced that this matter had been settled in a favourable way. Whatever their merits, the proposed regulations fitted completely into the Napoleonic political scheme: the Jewish religion was not so much organised as controlled. Its centralised organisation, the need to obtain official recognition for any appointment and any taxation, the *de facto* suppression of democratic procedures with all the powers handed over to appointed bodies, all this very well expressed the Emperor's political philosophy. Judaism had to be centralised in order to be kept under supervision.

This proposed constitution was not accepted without great discussion. The deputies did not easily agree to allow the consistories to receive such exorbitant powers, and asked for local representation at the local level when the budget of an individual synagogue was to be discussed, and also the departmental level when the financial affairs of a multi-departmental consistory came up for review. The salary of the chief rabbi should be the only common expense, and the city where he officiated should pay a proportionately larger part of his salary, as it received greater services from him than the others, and would therefore be able to do without a local rabbi.

A member of the Committee of Nine then told the full Assembly of his reservations concerning the proposed text. He felt that it was unreasonable and even vexatious to have stipulated that no one could become a member of the consistory if he had been accused of usury. He could not accept the implications of such a condition, which amounted to a suspicion of all Jews. The usurers were a very small minority, and their mention was therefore out of order. He also felt that the police, and not the consistories, should keep under surveillance those Jews without any known means of subsistence: this would be anyway very difficult in practice, as the consistories would not be able to keep check on what was going on in their whole circumscription. Moreover, their responsibilities were religious, and had nothing to do with the police. He also thought that the instruction given to the consistory to inform the authorities every year of the number of conscripts, was unacceptable: did this mean that the consistory would have to keep a register of births of all the Jews in its district? The law of conscription applied to all Frenchmen: to present such an extraordinary demand to the Jews would seem that they were less enthusiastic than their fellow-Frenchmen in the defence of the fatherland. This was of course false, he maintained. Anyway the consistories would be less able than the public authorities to deal with this problem. The proposed law would introduce a civil difference between Frenchmen on account of a religious difference, and this was unacceptable. He complained also that two-fifths of the membership of the proposed consistories which were to supervise the rabbis' activities were to be composed of rabbis: how would these be able to fulfil their duties? He also rejected the proposals defining the financial workings of the consistories, perhaps because he felt that to accept them would mean that it had been established that the Jewish religion would not be entitled to the same help that other religions were already receiving from the state.[37]

Another member of the Committee of Nine rejected these restrictions, and thought that the intended measures would have great pedagogic value: anyway, how could anyone who was persuaded of the good-will of the authorities, and of their great wisdom, dare to think that they needed the deputies' advice on the best ways to achieve the Jews' regeneration? There was nothing insulting either in the condition on usury, the aim of which was to ensure that the proposed members of the consistory were fit to serve, or in the check on destitute Jews, as the government was perfectly entitled to the necessary statistical information. Was there any harm in controlling the immigration of foreign Jews to France? Other deputies added their remarks in favour of, or against, the text of the Committee of Nine, and the proceedings became difficult. In order to find a solution, one of the deputies proposed the adoption of the draft, and to mention in the minutes the criticism and reservations it had raised. This proposition was accepted by the majority. The chairman then summed up the remarks concerning the provision against usurious consistory members. He added that there existed no legal definition of usury, which made its enactment arduous. On the other hand, they should have enough confidence in the twenty-five notables who were to elect the members of the consistory not to choose anybody unsuited for this function. This condition should therefore be removed: if it were to remain, it could only have as result the debasement of the men the Emperor wished to honour.[38]

The following meeting which took place on 11 December 1806 discussed that part of the committee's draft which dealt with the Jews' military duties. Several of the deputies thought that the whole matter was not only superfluous, but also insulting: the Jews served in the army no less than their fellow-Frenchmen. Some of them did not want to be known as Jews in the units in which they served and therefore took an assumed name. This was a rather surprising admission of the problems met by some Jewish conscripts during their military service. The majority nevertheless decided to accept the proposed text.[39]

The Assembly was to meet again on 15 December to discuss the problems of the rabbis' salaries as it had been raised in the motion reported by the Committee of Nine. A number of delegates who probably felt that the Assembly was nearing the end of its existence thought that the motion, which was to be sent to the Emperor, should also include an appeal for the modification of the decree of 30 May 1806, which had suspended payments due to the Jews. There were problems of application, as those authorities responsible for it had deemed fit to give it a greater extension than had been originally planned.[40] After discussion, it was decided to separate the two problems, and the motion was thereupon accepted by a majority vote. The discussion of the appeal on the suspension of the repayment of debts started immediately after. The decision was taken to request that the Committee of Nine be entrusted with the investigation of this matter, and that one deputy from each of the eight departments concerned be added to it for this purpose. The eight new members were at once appointed.[41]

On 25 December the Assembly resumed its meetings. It first heard a letter from the envoy of the Prince of Lucca and Piombino to the Emperor which informed it of the permission now given to any Jew to settle in that principality and enjoy the same rights as all its other inhabitants. He asked permission to inform accordingly the deputies to the Assembly and to the Sanhedrin, and all other Jews those bodies might require to communicate with. It would seem that the Assembly had by that time been recognised as the representative body of all the believers in Judaism, and could therefore be asked to act as such.[42]

The Assembly was also requested to deal with a complicated problem of inheritance about which the Emperor had been petitioned and which the Council of State had turned over to the Assembly, which had set up a committee to look into the merits of the affair. This committee had now reported on the decision reached, and asked that 'in the name of religion and honour' certain payments be made.

A number of deputies asked whether the Assembly was entitled to turn itself into a court of justice. The proposal made was accepted with virtual unanimity only after it had been specified that the Assembly had only lent its good services and that its intervention had been officious. It thus refused the role which even the Council of State had tried to attribute to it.[43]

The same day, the Assembly was told of the difficulties encountered in certain departments where the Jewish population refused to take part in the payment of the expenses of its deputies in Paris. The Minister of the Interior wanted to know which departments had refused to do so, as he intended to take a general measure in this matter. The Assembly rejected unanimously any general measure which would apply to all the Jews of France, and agreed that all problems be brought to the chairman, who would then inform the Minister.[44]

On 5 February 1807, the Assembly heard the text of the decisions which were to be brought before the Sanhedrin. One of the members, Avigdor, then made a rather lengthy speech where he differentiated between the persecutions the Jews had suffered in their history and the generally understanding attitude of the Church. He expressed the hope that the present leaders of the Church would use their influence with all Christians to foster the sentiment of fraternity 'which nature has put in the heart of all men', and which the moral teachings of every religion should support. All this led to a motion which expressed gratitude for all the good deeds of the Christian clergy towards the Jews during the ages, and the shelter that some popes and other ecclesiastics had granted to Jews who had been expelled from other countries. The Assembly was therefore asked to express its gratitude for the kindnesses of the Christian clergy. This motion, which was accepted by a unanimous vote, was sent to the Ministry of Cults.[45] The timing of this motion (which was presented on the eve of the Sanhedrin's meeting), and the fact that it was not sent to the Minister of the Interior, seem to show that the Assembly was now intent on having Judaism recognised as a religion equal to all others, and based its request on the public proclamation of its reconciliation with Christianity. It is impossible to decide whether this step was a result of pressure on the part of the commissioners, or of the philosophers, or was the result of a private initiative. The proclamation of human fraternity which it included could not have displeased the Emperor.

The Assembly did not meet during the Sanhedrin's session. Its next meeting took place on 25 March 1807, when it heard a report on the Sanhedrin's resolutions, which was presented by Furtado on behalf of the Committee of Nine. He expressed his pleasure at the agreement given by 'a body of doctors equally enlightened and pious' to the draft of the resolutions which had been presented to them. They had decided they were in harmony with the letter and spirit of scripture, and had therefore endorsed them unanimously. The Sanhedrin had agreed to the assembly's deliberations: 'the content is the same, the form only differs'. The principle of 'Dina d'Malkhuta Dina' – described in Furtado's words as the fundamental principle which establishes that in civil and political matters the law of the prince is religiously binding – had been reaffirmed, as is well shown by the preamble to the Sanhedrin's decisions. The Jewish nation having disappeared and been incorporated into the great French nation, there would be no longer any reason to differentiate between citizens of the Jewish faith and the others. He reminded the Assembly that one of the reasons for its meeting was the problem of usury: he repeated the same arguments he had already used in his private communication to the secretary general of the Ministry of the Interior, and maintained that there was no justification in punishing all the Jews for the crimes of a few isolated usurers. He regretted deeply that the absence of the Emperor, who had left for the wars, had prevented him from officially receiving the deputies, as he had previously intended to do.

Furtado then read the address he suggested be sent to the Emperor. It was in the main an expression of gratitude for the Emperor's interest in the Jewish faith. From now on all faults would be personal, and public opinion, which was now sufficiently informed, would no longer blame the misdeeds of the few on the whole Jewish community. The integration of the Jews into French society was now assured. The decisions of the Sanhedrin would make it possible to put a stop to many abuses, and this would warrant action on the suspension of the payment of the debts due to the Jews which had been decreed on 30 May 1806. Let the guilty alone be punished: this would be the surest sign of the Emperor's protection!

Furtado then brought a final motion before the Assembly; this was obviously what the commissioners had been instructed to extract from the Assembly. It declared that the regeneration of the Jews implied not only the rectification of false opinions, but also the curing of vicious habits. Only the government was in a position to prepare and take those measures which would further the attainment of this aim. The Assembly had done its duty in showing the public authorities what had to be done. Therefore, Furtado suggested in the name of the Committee of Nine, that the notables should ask the commissioners to transmit to the Emperor their wish that measures be taken in order to prevent a few culprits pursuing their peddling or money-lending, which were so often detrimental to the good name of their co-religionists.[46]

A very rough debate at once broke out. Some deputies felt that in view of the Sanhedrin's decisions, the motion had become useless: the doctrine of Judaism on usury was already well known, and there was no point in discussing it again. One of the deputies asked whether this motion meant that the Assembly's and the Sanhedrin's decisions were completely meaningless: 'Should we still take or provoke measures in favour of the regeneration of our co-religionists? Should we implore His Majesty not to treat us like other citizens, ask for special laws for those among us who might in the future commit the same excesses which are blamed on some Israelites of the north?' Why, therefore, should the Assembly pay attention to the bad conduct of some Jews? If they have erred, it is up to the police and the government to settle this problem, not to the Jewish community. The law must apply to all Frenchmen, Jews and Gentiles. The motion was therefore useless and dangerous and should be rejected. The misunderstanding became apparent right away, as Furtado maintained that the proposed draft had not been properly understood, and was very far from the meaning some deputies had wanted to read into it. Nevertheless the Assembly refused to pass judgment on the merits of the motion, although it had been willing to approve the report on the Sanhedrin's meeting and an address to the Emperor. In a very close vote – twenty-six against twenty-three – it adjourned its decision until its next meeting which took place on 27 March.[47] Even then no decision could be reached, and it was decided to appoint a special Committee of Eight to meet the commissioners in order to clarify the implications of the proposed motion. The discussion was renewed on 30 March, as the Committee of Eight reported on its meeting with the commissioners. These had been told of the Assembly's doubts and fears: did the government intend to draw a line between Jews and Gentiles? Was French law to apply to all Frenchmen or not? The commissioners said in their answer that no general measure would be taken which would apply to all the Jews of France and Italy. How could anyone doubt the good-will of the government, which had so assiduously studied the problems of the Jewish religion and given it so many proofs of its understanding? They very cautiously added nevertheless that they did not know what the Emperor's intentions were. They recommended that the motion include a reference to the need for action to prevent the disorders which had brought about the decree of 30 March 1806. This would be a sign of loyalty and the negation of the growing fears of the Jews. They concluded that the Emperor did not in the least plan special legislation for the Jews. They accepted a few amendments which somehow toned down the proposed text. The Assembly was not yet fully convinced, and Furtado had to make an impassioned speech in which he reproached the deputies because they now refused what had been asked before; that is, the possibility of drawing a line between usurers and other Jews. The Assembly thereupon adopted the motion which had been brought before it by a majority vote. It had taken the commissioners at their word, although many of its members were aware of the dangers of the proposed motion. Thereupon a vote of thanks to the chairman was proposed and accepted.[48]

The Assembly met again on 6 April 1807. The chairman reported that he had received a letter from the commissioners the day before which informed him that the Assembly could now disperse, as it had completed its programme, and the Emperor had already received its address and its last motion. The chairman thanked the deputies for the confidence they had given him. All differences of opinion which had appeared during the discussions related to the choice of the means to achieve the proposed aim, but not to the aim itself. He himself had not felt any fears when he had been invited to join the Assembly, although the reason given was rather threatening and he felt that hitherto everything which had happened confirmed his impression. He admitted that in order to be fully integrated the Jews would still have to do much by themselves, but time would help. The Assembly agreed with his views and assured him of its gratitude. After a final exhortation, the meeting was closed. The Assembly, following the Sanhedrin, had now completed its proceedings.[49]

CHAPTER VI

The Duped

The deputies of the Jews dispersed with the feeling that they had done their best to answer the questions put to them without having in any way prejudiced the principles and the interests of their religion. Under the prodding of David Sintzheim, they had always been careful to give a sound *halakhic* basis for all their decisions, and not to yield to the Emperor when they felt that principles were endangered. They had not budged in the least on the problem of mixed marriages, the religious incoherence of which Sintzheim had not hesitated to proclaim during the last meeting of the Sanhedrin. It is now clear that during the meetings of the Assembly and of the Sanhedrin, he had made a point of corresponding with some of the most renowned rabbinic authorities of Central Europe. He had reported on the Assembly's work to the chief rabbi of Prague, Baruch Benedikt Jeiteles, and told him of his successful efforts to prevent any deviation from Scripture and the Talmud.[1] He had also corresponded with the recognised leader of Central European orthodoxy, Moses Schreiber, the rabbi of Pressburg, better known as the Chatam Sofer, who held him in very great esteem as a talmudic scholar and as a religious authority. On 10 December 1812, shortly after Sintzheim's death, Schreiber eulogised him publicly in Pressburg, and did not hesitate to compare him with Joseph who had known how to represent and protect his brethren before Pharaoh without compromising his faith:[2]

Such was this just man whom we are eulogising today: the Gaon, the late Rabbi David Sintzheimer, the author of the *Yad David*. During his lifetime he was honoured and was very close to the monarchy in Paris; he was asked a number of questions and knew how to answer his questioners. He was great and much honoured in the eyes of the Emperor and his ministers, and they honoured him greatly when he passed away, as is well known. Nevertheless he was greatly respected by the Jews and busied himself all his life with the study of the law, and went through the study of the whole Talmud a number of times. He knew perfectly the works of the ancient and modern rabbinic authorities, as is evidenced by perusal of his book. I knew him in my youth, and also lately in his exchange of letters with me; I have seen his uprightness and integrity. He achieved leadership through his knowledge of civil and political matters, but remained the ruler through his great courage: he did not allow others to rule over him, and was not seduced into following them, God forbid! After he had revealed one handbreadth, he concealed two handbreadths. His integrity stood by him, and his flavour did not vanish.

According to Moses Schreiber, Sintzheim had therefore managed to preserve the integrity of Judaism before Napoleon and his commissioners, and where he seemed to have given in, he had in fact taken back much more than that which a superficial judgment might have accused him of having sacrificed. In Moses Schreiber's opinion, Sintzheim had been able to resist pressure and to reply with dignity. It is remarkable that Schreiber expressed his admiration for Sintzheim's ability to hold his own in Paris without in the least changing his way of life: for the study of the law remained his principal occupation.

One of the foremost rabbis of Italy, Ishmael ben Abraham Isaac ha-Cohen, had also been invited to take part in the Assembly's meetings as a delegate of the Jewish community of Modena, of which he was rabbi. In view of his great age – he was eighty-three in 1806 – he had not come to Paris, but this did not prevent him from trying to answer the twelve questions put before the Assembly. It is quite possible that some Italian deputies were influenced by this. Whatever the case, his answers came from a reputed rabbinic authority, and had been written far away from Paris, without fear of any hostile reaction, and with no pressure exerted on their author either by the orthodox or by the more liberal delegates. It is interesting to note that his independent opinion based itself mostly on the principle of 'Dina d'Malkhuta Dina', which had been so often invoked by the Assembly and the Sanhedrin. His answers did not differ on essential points from the decisions of the Sanhedrin. The problem of idolatry was central in his thinking: if the Christians could not be accused of practising an idolatrous religion, it became obvious that they should be looked upon as brethren and the Jews would have to behave to them 'in love, brotherhood, peace and friendship'. He emphasised the good relationship which must exist between the followers of the different monotheistic religions. When it came to the problem of the rabbinate, he declared that the police powers it had once used were the results of privileges which had been granted for that purpose, and these no longer existed. He denied of course the religious validity of mixed marriages. As far as usury was concerned, he admitted the possibility of commercial loans among Jews, and the legitimacy of agreed usurious loans to Gentiles, but advised against them as a mark of religious zeal. The final conclusion might well have been written by the deputies who met in Paris. As a matter of fact, Ishmael ha-Cohen did not in the least criticise the competence of the Paris meeting, and declared that only reasons of health had prevented him from participating.[3]

The Jewish deputies were then at peace with their conscience, and convinced that their answers had met with the agreement of the Emperor, and that all misunderstandings had now been overcome: their declarations had finally opened the door to full integration in French society. They had thanked the commissioners and the Emperor for their good-will and desire to help them. They would have been satisfied with the passage of a law that fixed the legal rate of interest, and punished all those, Jews or Gentiles, who did not abide by it. When the law fixing the interest on loans at 5 or 6 per cent, depending on the kind of loan which had been granted, was finally published on 3 September 1807, the Jewish community felt that the whole matter had now been definitely solved. Since usury had become an easily recognisable crime through its very definition, the police and the courts would deal with individual usurers, and no longer look towards the Jewish leaders who had condemned this practice. Little did these know what was then being prepared in the government's councils.

As early as 20 August 1806, after receiving the text of the Assembly's resolutions and expressing his approval, Champagny, the Minister of the Interior, had broached in his report to the Emperor a number of measures which he felt were necessary in order to ensure that the national character of Jewish existence in France would disappear, and which would help to put an end to the bad habits of the few without punishing the mass.[4] Freedom of religion should be maintained. Those Jews who were deserving of it should be 'raised to the dignity of Frenchmen', as though this had not been the case since 1791. Those undeserving should be chastised or expelled.[5] He felt that a distinction should be made between the different sections of French and Italian Jewry: the Portuguese Jews and those of Tuscany and Metz had reached a social status very superior to that enjoyed by the Jews of Alsace. Champagny suggested that every Jew be invited to affirm or take an oath that he felt himself bound by the civil and political laws of the empire. The taking of this oath would be the condition for obtaining French citizenship.[6] The rabbis should be confirmed by the government after their election and provision should be made for the regular payment of their salaries. He also suggested an organisation of the Jewish religion, whereby rabbis would encourage the Jews to enter the different trades, and where the elders or lay leaders would inform the authorities of any cases of usury or disregard of civil laws. He was of the opinion that all Jewish children should be compelled to attend public schools with due regard to their religious obligations,[7] but feared that the sorry state of the public schools would make this rather difficult. Compulsory apprenticeship could also be very useful, but all these steps would take time, and significant results could not be expected before the next generation. On the problem of usury he noted that all measures to restrict or contain it would be powerless as long as no legal definition of this crime were forthcoming.

Should this exist, the Jews would have to obey it exactly as they would have to respect any other law. He cautioned against harsh measures until something was done to solve the problem of credit, perhaps by the establishment of *monts de piété*, or municipal pawnshops. As a last step he proposed that the term 'Jew' be replaced in public usage by the term 'Hebrew', which would designate the religion, without recalling the painful connotations associated with the first epithet. In general, he did not recommend special laws against the Jews, perhaps out of respect for legal tradition and for the constitution.

When, on 9 April 1807, he reported on the conclusions of the Assembly's and the Sanhedrin's meetings, the tone had changed. He emphasised that the Jews themselves had asked for the Emperor's intervention in order 'to bring more prompt and efficient remedies' to a situation which 'the more honest and enlightened Jews' deeply deplored. Any measures taken to this effect would escape the accusation of arbitrariness, 'as they had been asked for by those to whom they shall apply'. He then recommended control on Jewish immigration into France, admitting only those Jews who could justify their ability to live and deal in a useful way.[8] Every Jew wishing to enter commerce, with the sole exception of wholesale dealers, manufacturers or farmers, should obtain from the local authorities the necessary permission. This authorisation could be withdrawn. Any Jewish pedlar who plied his trade far from his home would have to register with the police. This was not construed as an obstacle to the freedom of trade but as a measure designed to prevent abuses. Any loan given to peasants, working-men, women or minors would become valid only if a notary testified that the whole sum had indeed been handed to the borrower in his and two witnesses' presence. Mortgages should be limited to the value of the lenders' possessions. Measures should be taken to prevent the harmful results which a sudden removal of the suspension granted on 30 May 1806 to the debtors of the Jews would be likely to bring about. Some loans should be repaid right away, but others should be paid back over a period of six years. The Jews' account-books should now be kept, not in Hebrew, but in the language of the land. To conclude, Champagny again emphasised the need to prepare alternative sources of credit for needy country people, and he recommended the general institution of public pawnshops. All through Champagny's report, his reluctance to suggest exceptional laws against the Jews is strongly felt, and he took great pains to justify his position. It is certain that the Emperor imposed his own will in this matter.

The Council of State was soon entrusted with the task of preparing the special laws which would deal with Jewish religious organisation and the limitation of their economic activities. What had hitherto been kept secret, now began to become known: laws of exception were in the making, which were justified by the wishes of the Jewish deputies themselves. The philosophers' party, which had led the fight in favour of the measures requested by the Emperor and which had justified the motion addressed to the Emperor in order to ask for his active intervention, felt duped. As some Portuguese deputies remarked, it was quite probable that the deputies would never have voted for these motions if they had been informed of the use it was intended to make of them.[9] Furtado, who seems to have been particularly shocked at this turn of events, and who probably felt that as a former chairman of the Assembly he bore a greater responsibility than other members, did not hesitate to leave Paris in the company of a Nancy deputy to meet the Emperor at Tilsit. There is no report of the meeting, or whether it took place.[10] Nevertheless it would seem that Furtado still had some hope of securing a favourable answer from the Emperor. He continued his campaign in France after his return, but was unsuccessful. In the meantime, the one-year delay for the repayment of the debts due to the Jews, which was to elapse on 30 May 1807, had to be extended, as nothing had yet been decided in this matter. It was probably then that Furtado, who signed as the ex-president, published, with considerable courage, and great dignity, his protest against the projects which were discussed by the Council of State.[11]

He first mentioned that the Assembly had asked that the salaries of the rabbis be paid by the state and that the suspension of the repayment of debts due to Jews be lifted. Alluding to the memorandum he had sent to the Ministry of the Interior, he wrote that after the Assembly had concluded its work in a satisfactory way, only two decisions remained to be taken: the enactment of the proposed organisation of the Jewish religion, and the measures which would lead to a peaceful removal of the suspension of debts. Instead three drafts were now being examined by the Council of State: the first dealt with the organisation of the Jewish religion and was incomplete, as it avoided the problem of the salaries; the second dealt with the conscription of Jewish soldiers, and was useless, as the law on military duty applied to all Frenchmen, Jews and Gentiles; and the third dealt with the debts due to the Jews, and was dangerous, as its results would encourage the practice of usury and not prevent it. The application of the Assembly's recommendations would certainly have achieved the desired result in an easier and more efficient way.

On the problem of the salaries of rabbis, Furtado noted that Jews paid taxes, including that part of them which was used to cover the expenses of the different religions. Thereby they helped to meet the expenditures of the Christian religion: why shouldn't these funds be employed in the same way for the needs of Judaism? When it came to conscription, he wanted to know where the Jews differed from the other religions: they were called to the army in the same way, and could buy replacements on the same conditions. They had no possibility of avoiding the law's implications. Therefore, any special measure enacted for the benefit of the Jews would cast aspersions on their love for their country. In view of this he rejected the proposed law, which would have compelled two-thirds of the Jewish draftees to serve in person, or to take only Jews as replacements. It was also mentioned in the draft that should this be disregarded, the different government ministers would no longer suggest to the Emperor that any public appointments be offered to Jews. Why should this category of Frenchmen be looked upon as collectively accountable for this crime, solely on account of its common religion?

He used much stronger terms for the proposed decree on the debts. The measures which it contained, Furtado argued, would result in the further estrangement of the Jews from handicrafts, the access to which would be made more difficult. Their adoption would be tantamount to an invitation to return to the practice of usury. He wanted to know why all these measures concerning the Jews were necessary. The answer generally given was that they were intended to put an end to the activities of a few crooks and help a few victims. In fact there were no more than twenty or twenty-five persons who justified these measures among a mass of 50,000 Jews! Civil rights were as sacred as property rights. One could not attack the latter without harming the former. This would indeed be the result of the laws of exception. Why should innocent persons be treated this way? Why should punishment precede the supposed crime, and not follow it, as had always been the case? Furtado concluded that there was no escape from the dilemma: either the presence of the Jews in France was looked upon as an evil, and they should be expelled, or it was not so considered and then they should be treated as Frenchmen, and not as Jews! They could not accept the discrimination intended and would rather be exiled than disgraced. The proposed laws should be looked upon as a return to the age of feudalism. To accept them would be to misunderstand the Emperor's intentions. Furtado asked that the Council of State inform the Emperor of the Jews' reaction, believing that this would result in a change of policy. It is difficult to say how much of this hope was sincere, and how much lip-service. It remains a fact nevertheless that Furtado's trip to the Polish frontier in order personally to inform Napoleon of the Jewish fears seems to show that he still entertained some hopes. It is remarkable that in a private letter of 15 March 1808, he still thought that his efforts had averted the danger of the proposed decrees.[12] He had not yet understood what the Emperor's intentions really were, and how he had been taken in by the deft manoeuvres of the commissioners. Two days later, on 17 March 1808, no room was left for doubt.

On that day three decrees were published which gave official expression to Napoleon's views on the Jews. The rather long interval which separated their publication from the end of the Assembly's meetings and the Council of State's study of the projected measures – its report had been completed by 13 June

1807 – is rather surprising. The councillors' propositions were sent to the Emperor only at the end of February 1808. This was a delay of eight and a half months, which looks strange, as Napoleon tended to impatience. It is quite possible that the delay was due to a certain uneasiness at measures which so clearly contradicted the constitution and judicial conscience of the council's members. They had perhaps hoped that the intervention of Furtado and his friends would bring about a change of attitude on the Emperor's part. Whatever the reasons, the delay had no effect, and the Emperor's intentions did not change, as revealed in the three decrees of 17 March 1808.[13]

The first decree dealt with the organisation of the Jewish religion of France. The deputies' demands notwithstanding, the responsibility for the rabbis' salaries was not assumed by the state and the mention of the practice of usury among the moral blemishes which would disqualify applicants from membership of the consistories was not removed. The demands of the Jews had been rejected outright, although the general recommendations of the Assembly on the organisation of the Jewish bodies had been accepted, as they had been worked out with the Emperor's commissioners. In order to allow it to function, a second decree, published the same day, was absolutely necessary. It instructed the Minister of Cults – not of the Interior – to prepare the list of the consistorial synagogues which were to be established. This would be done in consultation with the Central Consistory. The Council of State would have to give its authorisation for the opening of any 'particular synagogue', on the recommendation of the Minister of Cults. This would also require the agreement of the consistorial synagogue, that is, of the department or multi-departmental organisation, of the Central Consistory and of the prefect of the department concerned. A list of the Jewish population was also to be provided. The leaders of the particular synagogues would have to be appointed by the departmental consistory and approved by the Central Consistory. The size of the new circumscription would be determined by the decree which would establish it.

The notables were to be appointed by the Minister of the

123

Interior – not of Cults – at the suggestion of the Central Consistory and with the advice of the prefect concerned. The appointment of the members of the departmental consistories must be made at the demand of the Minister of Cults on the advice of the prefect, or prefects, of the departments of their consistorial circumscription.

The first Central Consistory would be appointed by the Emperor himself at the suggestion of the Minister of Cults: its members would be chosen among the former members of the Assembly or of the Sanhedrin. The new member who would be elected annually to replace the outgoing member would also have to be recommended by the Minister of Cults to the Emperor, who would appoint him.

The assessment of the Jewish contributors to the expenses of their cult would be prepared by the regional consistory which would apportion the assessment in accordance with the number of departments within its circumscription. It was to secure the agreement of the Central Consistory before being made mandatory by the different prefects in their respective departments.

Nothing in the second decree was not a direct consequence of the first: it was intended only to make possible its practical application. Nevertheless it gave signs of the same spirit of confusion which surrounded all the Emperor's thinking, as he had been unable to decide whether the administration of Judaism was a matter for the Ministry of the Interior or the Ministry of Cults, whether Jews should be treated, even in purely religious matters, as Frenchmen of the Jewish persuasion, or as Jews on the verge of being granted French citizenship together with the civil rights this implied.

The third decree, which occupied the Council of State for a lengthy period, dealt with the rights and duties of the Jews; that is, with their economic activities, their rights of residence and their military duties. Its provisions were to remain in effect for the next ten years, in the hope that at the end of this period and with the help of the new measures taken, there would be no difference left between the Jews and other citizens of the Empire. If this hope were to be deceived, the interval would be extended. This was tantamount to declaring that the Jews would remain on probation until they had proved worthy of a citizenship which they had received nearly seventeen years before, and of the benefits of which they would now be partially deprived. In more than one way the new legislation re-enacted many of the provisions of the 1784 Letters Patent which had been granted to the Jews of Alsace, and had been repealed by the French Revolution.[14] It is therefore not surprising that it was designated later on as the *infamous decree*, and that it greatly diminished the admiration most Jews had hitherto felt for Napoleon.

The decree lifted the suspension of the repayment of the debts due to the Jews from the very day of its publication: this suspension had therefore been in force nearly two years. It was nevertheless immediately added that there would be conditions to this liberal decision. All the liabilities entered into because of a loan by minors unauthorised by their trustees, by a wife unauthorised by her husband, by a soldier unauthorised by his captain, and by an officer unauthorised by his commanding officer would be nullified. The courts would give no help to the lender in such cases. No letter of exchange, no bill payable to order, no debenture, no promissory note would be paid by a Gentile to a Jew until the latter had been able to prove that its value had been drawn in full. Debts bearing an interest higher than 5 per cent would be reduced. If it was higher than 10 per cent the debt was to be annulled as usurious. As for the legitimate and non-usurious debts, the courts would be empowered to grant debtors an extension for their repayment. These measures applied to the past and could have but one result: to bring about the suppression of most debts due to Jews and the ruin of the latter. This was effectively the case, as the courts constantly took the debtor's side and asked the Jews to give proofs of their good faith, and to show that the debtors had indeed received the whole sum mentioned in the deed. This was very often impossible, as the loan had been given a long time before, and because the court took into consideration complaints which had never been lodged before and which its interpretation of the law now made possible.[15]

For the future, the decree imposed a condition on the right of the Jew to enter commerce: he would be able to do so only after he had obtained a *patente* – that is, a licence to do so. This would be handled by the prefect of his department, after an enquiry had been made and a recommendation received from the municipal council of his city or village certifying that he had not entered into any illicit commerce, and another from the consistory of his circumscription which would testify to his good conduct and honesty. This licence would have to be renewed every year by the attorney-general, but could also be revoked by the courts if it became known that the licensed Jew had practised usury or entered some illegal trade. Any commercial deal made by a non-licensed Jew would be void. The same would be true of any mortgage given to him as the result of some commercial venture or for a bill of exchange. The courts would be empowered to confirm the validity of other contracts or debentures if convinced that they did not result from any commercial activities. Nevertheless the debtor would always be allowed to bring proof that there had been some usurious practices, and the courts would then have to act accordingly. On the other hand, the creditor could always be asked to prove that he had in fact handed the borrower the whole sum mentioned in their agreement.

Pledged loans were strictly regulated. They were forbidden so far as servants or hired persons were concerned. Otherwise a contract would have to be drawn up by a public notary, who would also confirm that the complete sum had been handed over in his and the witnesses' presence. The Jewish lenders were also forbidden to receive as pledges instruments, utensils, tools, or clothes belonging to servants or hired hands.

All these measures were in the spirit of the 1784 Letters Patent which had already requested that there should be some form of legal control over the dealings of the Jews of Alsace, or that the leaders of the communities should serve as witnesses for their contracts. The influence of these long-abolished regulations was even more evident in that part of the decree which dealt with the Jews' residence. No Jew, unless he was already a resident of the Upper and Lower Rhine departments, would be allowed to settle there. No Jew, who was not yet a resident of the Empire, could settle in other parts of the Empire unless he intended to devote himself to agriculture. This last provision was intended to limit Jewish immigration into France. The 1784 Letters had already threatened with expulsion from France the Jews found in Alsace who were not known to be residents of this province. They also controlled very severely the settlement of foreign Jews in France. The new decree nevertheless took into account the possibility of granting exemptions.

The freedom of the Jewish population was further limited when the decree took away a faculty the Jews had hitherto shared with the rest of the French population: the possibility of conscripts providing a replacement for military service. From the publication of the decree, the Jews of France would have to serve in person in the army. Obviously the Emperor attributed great virtues to the prolonged presence of the Jews in the army.

The last provision of the decree granted complete exemption from the decree's provisions to all the Portuguese Jews from south-west France: they would not be bound by the regulations applying in general to the Jews of France. This was clearly a consequence of the good reputation they had acquired in the commissioner's opinion during the meetings of the Assembly. They had asked, with some Avignon deputies, in a printed petition received by the council on 13 June 1807, to be set apart, as had always been the case, from the other Jews.[16] They felt that their past conduct justified their demand. Whatever the reason, the request of the Portuguese Jews – not those of Avignon – was granted by the Emperor's decree.

A few months later, on 20 July 1808, another decree completed Napoleon's legislative work on the Jews: the Jews were requested to adopt private and family names. It had already been noted that although many Jews had a first and a family name, they were not very conscious of the importance of the family name and attached greater importance to their and their father's first name, and preferred to be known as 'X son of Y' in their religious life. This had given rise to many errors and misunderstandings, as quite often father and son would use different family names. All

Jews were now requested to choose a *nomen* and a *cognomen* within three months and to have them recorded in the place of their residence. Foreign Jews settling in France would have to do the same within three months after their arrival. The use of names from the Hebrew Bible or hinting at a city was prohibited. The consistories would of course have to check whether everybody had complied with the decree, and to report those who had not done so. The restrictions on the choice of names did not apply to those Jews who already had well-known first and family names. Lack of compliance could cause the expulsion of the offenders. They could also be punished if they chose names which were not acceptable.[17]

The application of this last decree did not involve many difficulties, as everybody had already recognised the need for this reform. Many Jews retained their former names, and met few difficulties in recording them, although in at least one locality of Alsace, the Jewish inhabitants were compelled to take names not of their choice, which were occasionally rather ridiculous. In several localities the Jews kept Jewish names, and shunned the so-called French or Italian names.[18]

Things were quite different when it came to the application of the infamous decree. The wording of the law was so loose that it invited endless litigation. The greater part of the economic life of the Jews of the Empire would now take place in court. Jewish lenders were asked to provide evidence that the whole sum mentioned in the deeds had indeed been handed over to the borrower. This was of course very often impossible. The Jewish leaders felt that the ruin of all the lenders was near, even where their dealings had remained completely within the framework of the law. Nevertheless the local courts very often chose to extend it in ways which had never been intended. Although it is difficult to give an exact appraisal of what happened, it seems that at least one-half, if not three-fourths, of the debts due to the Jews were never paid back. Without any doubt, the infamous decree contributed greatly to the deterioration of the economic status of the Jews.[19]

The licence which the decree had provided for was not always granted as easily as should have been the case. Some municipalities made no difficulty in giving the Jews the recommendations requested by the law, but many others delayed doing so as long as they could. In the end most of the Jews who applied for licences eventually received them.[20] The problem of their residence in Alsace proved more complicated: very probably a number of the civil servants in Alsace remembered the provision of the 1784 Letters Patent which had made the marriages of Jews conditional upon the government's agreement. Then, just as now, the aim was to prevent the natural growth of the Jewish population in Alsace. It is not very surprising therefore that an attempt should have been made to prevent Jews from Lower Rhine marrying Jewesses from other departments, as this would have meant – so the civil servants maintained – that the law which prohibited the settlement of non-Alsatian Jews in Alsace was disregarded. The Minister of the Interior had to reject this excessive interpretation of the law. He remarked that this specific provision applied to Jews, but not to Jewesses, who were allowed to marry without any geographical limitation.[21] It is rather remarkable to note how this obstinacy of the public authorities prevented the mingling of the different elements of French Jewry, each of which remained as isolated as before. The very division of France into a number of regional consistorial circum-scriptions also contributed to the preservation of the different nations which had existed before the Revolution, as the circum-scriptions more or less corresponded to the old geographical areas of the *nations*.

The decree had mentioned the possibility of exemptions. It had hardly been published when many groups or individuals decided that they wished to enjoy the same benefits which had already been granted to the Portuguese Jews of the Gironde and Landes departments. On 6 April 1808, less than three weeks after the publication of the infamous decree, the Minister of the Interior inquired into the Emperor's intentions regarding the Seine department; that is, the Paris Jews. The Minister affirmed that the first exemption granted to the Portuguese Jews was based on the absence of complaints lodged against them. He had asked for an enquiry to be made on the activities of the Paris Jews. Only 4 of the 2,543 Parisian Jews had been accused of entering usurious practices, and then only in a fairly mild way. They had never taken part in extremist movements and more than 150 of them were serving in the army, many with distinction. The Paris deputies had very actively supported the Emperor's views in the Assembly and the Sanhedrin. The Emperor's answer was positive, and the Paris Jews were soon exempted from the decree's provisions.[22]

Once this precedent was established, other departments were quick to follow. Most of the southern and Italian departments eventually benefited from the exemption. The northern ones, and especially those of Alsace, did not apply, as they were quite convinced that they stood not the least chance of being heeded.[23]

One of the decrees of 1808 had provided for the establishment of a new religious organisation for the Jews of France. The whole system was organised in a hierarchy headed by the Central Consistory, which had to be appointed first, in order to allow for the implementation of the Emperor's decree. The Central Consistory was to contain three chief rabbis and two lay members, but who was to appoint its ecclesiastical members? After all, the bishops, even when the agreement of the French government was necessary, were appointed by a religious authority, and not by the state. Who, then, should appoint the chief rabbis? The Emperor's advisers reminded him that before the Revolution the rabbis had also been appointed by the public authorities, but forgot to tell him that this was done only after the Jewish communities concerned had agreed on a candidate. The ministry now turned to the commissioners to bring forward a recommendation. They suggested a choice from amongst the following rabbis: David Sintzheim, the former chairman of the Sanhedrin, who was at the time the rabbi of Strasbourg, and was looked upon as the best qualified candidate; Salvator Segré, the rabbi of Vercelli (Italy); Abraham Cologna, the rabbi of Mantua, who had both served as vice-chairmen of the Sanhedrin, and three other candidates. The former officers of the Sanhedrin were finally appointed to serve on the Central Consistory. It was not by accident that there was only one German rabbi among them, although the great majority of the Jews of the Empire belonged to the German nation. The commissioners, and the Minister of the Interior, felt that the Italian rabbis would be more understanding. The first two lay members chosen were Baruch Cerf Berr, the great Cerf Berr's son and Sintzheim's nephew, and Jacob Lazard, the Paris jeweller who had taken such a large part in the Assembly's discussions. These two lay delegates had been chosen in order to counter-balance rabbinic influence. It is obvious that in view of the rabbinic predominance and Sintzheim's authority in his family and outside it, this fear was not completely unfounded.[24]

The members of the Central Consistory were officially appointed on 19 October and could then begin organising the Jewish religion in France. They took the oath of loyalty to the Emperor which was requested from them, as it had been from all other civil servants or bishops, and promised to report anything they heard, which might be detrimental to the interests of the state: they had now officially become a part of the organised Empire, although they were never recognised as such by the state itself. It would be false to think that the members of the consistory were unaware of the scarcely disguised hostility of the Emperor against them, and of its repercussions among the higher civil servants. Nevertheless they decided to do their work as effectively as they could. Their first important task was to prepare the list of the proposed regional consistories, which had been called 'consistorial synagogues' in the Emperor's decree. Before that, they had settled with the Minister the status of the chief rabbis who were not requested to give up the rabbinic position they had held before being called to the Central Consistory. As their new functions were not to be permanent, they were allowed to have a replacement appointed in their stead for the duration of their service in Paris.[25]

The Ministry of the Interior and the prefects had meanwhile prepared a list of proposed consistorial synagogues, some of which covered only one department, while others included many departments. The Central Consistory agreed to their suggestion, and the Emperor decreed their establishment on 11 December

1808. The seats of these synagogues were to be set up in Paris, Strasbourg, Wintzenheim (later Colmar), Mainz, Metz, Nancy, Trier, Coblenz, Crefeld, Bordeaux, Marseilles, Turin and Cassel. Later on, as the results of the extension of the Empire's borders, other consistorial synagogues were established in Leghorn and Florence (8 March 1810), Rome (5 June 1810), Amsterdam, Zwolle, Rotterdam, Leeuwarden, Emden and Hamburg (14 July 1812). This territorial framework, which was intended to renew the organisation of French Jewry, in fact re-created its former divisions: there were now German, Portuguese and Italian consistories, just as before the Revolution there had been German, Portuguese and Italian *nations*. The sole exception was Paris, where the different elements mingled. In the other consistories, the former leadership, which was generally identical with the financial élite, was recalled to power, as the prefects generally chose from among its members the board of notables which was to elect the regional consistory. By the month of February 1809, all the notables of the different consistorial circumscriptions had been chosen, thanks to the persistent efforts of the Central Consistory which was fully convinced of the need to move as quickly as possible. It had not always accepted the prefect's recommendations, very often preferring to rely on its own sources of information. In May 1809, all the regional consistories had finally been set up and their members appointed. It is remarkable that none of the boards of notables had seen fit to elect more than one rabbi to the departmental consistory, although Napoleon's decree had provided for such a possibility. Some had elected in his stead a fourth lay member, which was obviously illegal and was declared so. This was a portent of future problems and difficulties, when rabbis and lay people would fight for leadership within the Jewish community.[26]

As a matter of fact the fight started in Paris in the most unlikely place: between Sintzheim and the local Paris consistory which was dominated by the 'philosophical' clan and whose chief rabbi was without any influence. On 10 October 1810 it sent a complaint against Sintzheim to the Central Consistory whose president was Sintzheim himself: during his sermon on the Sabbath before the Day of Atonement, he had devoted much time and attention to the details and minutiae of the holy day but had 'neglected to speak to them of the much more essential duties which religion teaches them'. Although the decree on the organisation of the Jewish religion requested rabbis to teach the decisions of the Sanhedrin and the duties of morality, he had taught only what they called 'accessories of religion'. They felt that this was opposed to the spirit of the Sanhedrin's decision, and that they were compelled by law to put a stop to this way of thinking. They expected that the Central Consistory would look into this matter, and that they would be spared the unpleasantness of having to report to the superior authority the wrong which chief rabbi Sintzheim would bring about, if he were to continue to preach 'a doctrine which can but obscure the eternal truths of religion while replacing them with external practices which speak only to the senses'. On 28 October they answered the letter with which the Central Consistory had forcefully reacted to their criticism. They felt they had been misunderstood, and although they had not been present during Sintzheim's sermon, renewed their criticism: they reproached Sintzheim for having told his congregation of the duty to dress in white for Yom Kippur, to maintain the practice of *Kapparot*, and the obligation to abstain from drinking non-kosher wine. These were incidental practices that ignorance and superstition wished to maintain, and which the chief rabbis and the consistories should help to eradicate. As for themselves they insisted on their duty to prevent the preaching in their synagogues of teachings which would tend to weaken the good social relations which should exist between Jews and Gentiles. They were quite positive that if Napoleon's decree had instructed the rabbis to teach the Jewish religion, it had also asked the consistories to check up on what they were saying. Not surprisingly, their letter was annotated: *sans réponse*, not to be answered.[27]

This did not prevent the controversy reviving two years later, when Sintzheim had already passed away. The Portuguese congregation had decided to set up a choir, and the Paris consistory, which had approved of this endeavour, had asked parents to send their children on the Sabbath to the Portuguese synagogue for training. With only one exception – the son of the new chief rabbi Deutz – no 'German' child had registered for this. When they tried to find out why this had happened, the administrator of the German community had answered that parents did not want their children to be brought up in a different religion from their own! This turned immediately into an argument between the liberals and the so-called fanatics. The Paris consistory asked for the Central Consistory's help in its fight for educational reforms. The answer of the Central Consistory is not known.[28]

A few months later, the Minister of Cults sent the Central Consistory the manuscript of a book of religious instruction written in the form of a catechism, which was intended for young Jews of both sexes desirous of celebrating their 'first communion' at the age of thirteen. This book was the work of Joseph Johlson, a Jewish teacher from Creuznach in the Rhine and Moselle department. His request to have the book approved by the Minister was not surprising in itself, as this was the only way to have it published. But now that the Jewish religion had an official organisation, the Minister turned this manuscript over to the Central Consistory, which could not avoid passing judgment on a book which was obviously inspired by the manuals used for the benefit of Christian youth. In its lengthy report it defined the official doctrine of the central body of the Empire's Jewish organisation, which can be described as a resolute rejection of reform, although it replied to the Minister that the proposed book was very learned, and that with a number of additions and corrections it would be of great use to the Jewish schools. It is precisely the list of these additions and corrections which reveals the nature of the Central Consistory's religious policy.[29]

Johlson had included in the first part of his book a discussion of the different religions, which the Central Consistory felt was out of place for children. They thought that it was dangerous to render a child philosophic before making him religious. This approach could produce some form of indifference to specific religions, as it was absurd to teach a child that the plurality of religion was 'a harmonious variation, which could but please the

Lord.' Such teachings could only confuse a child, despite Judaism's well-known spirit of tolerance.

Thus they reproached the author for reducing the number of the articles of faith, as he had declared that the belief in one God, the immortality of the soul and reward in eternal life were principles which could be demonstrated by reason alone. He had also omitted in his list the resurrection of the dead, and the advent of the Messiah.

Furthermore, in explaining the festival of Passover, the author had omitted to describe the practices connected with it. The same omission occurred with the New Year, as Johlson had failed to mention that it fell on the day of the creation of the world, and had not indicated the meaning of the *shofar*. He had not even mentioned the duty of fasting during the Day of Atonement. He had likewise omitted any mention of the four species* when discussing the Feast of Tabernacles. In general, the Jewish calendar had been neglected.

The members of the Central Consistory felt also that Johlson had erred in his description of the rabbis' power. If he was to be believed, the rabbis could institute laws according to circumstances, and change the existing ones. They claimed that nothing in Scripture allowed a rabbi or a consistory to introduce the smallest reform or changes in the religious laws of Judaism, and stated very clearly: 'in one word nothing is more opposed to our dogmas than this spirit of reform which is always fatal and pernicious to religious societies which stray from the accepted rules . . .'[30]

They then proceeded to reject his views on the sacrifices, which had not only a propaedeutic aim, but were the word of God. They reproached Johlson for having forgotten the duty of daily prayer and not even having mentioned circumcision. He had also neglected to mention the duty to establish houses of worship wherever there were ten adult Jews, and to maintain in them a Scroll of the Law. He did not mention the duties of the wearing of the prayer-shawl and the phylacteries. Although the book was

---

* The *etrog* or citron, palm, myrtle and willow used for the celebration of the festival of Tabernacles (Sukkoth).

supposed to help prepare young Jews for their first religious duties at the age of thirteen, he had not explained the duties that the thirteen-year-old boy would have to take upon himself. The obligation of studying the law had likewise been omitted, and the regulations concerning dietary laws had hardly been mentioned. Most of the fastdays, and the holidays of Purim and Chanukah, had failed to find their way into his presentation.

In conclusion, the members of the Central Consistory, rabbis and lay members, felt that the proposed book could eventually be adopted for the religious instruction of the Jewish children of the Empire on condition that its omissions be rectified, mistakes corrected, and the over-philosophic tone adapted to the capacities of the pupils. This was tantamount to a general rejection of the proposed text, which would have to be rewritten if its author still wanted to obtain the Central Consistory's recommendation. It is interesting to note that they had required the elimination of 'those principles which we have described in our remarks as non-orthodox'![31] In the argument between philosophers and the traditionalists, the Napoleonic consistory had very firmly stated where it stood.

The Central Consistory also took some positive steps in the field of education. The leaders of the French community had insisted in the report sent to the Minister of Cults in 1805 at his request, before the project of a meeting of a Jewish Assembly had even been thought of, that it was indispensable to set up seminaries for young men who wanted to enter the rabbinate. They called these schools faculties of theology, although they were probably thinking of a modernised kind of *yeshivah*. On 16 October 1809 the Central Consistory wrote to the Grand Maître de l'Université to ask that schools of first instruction, i.e. primary schools, be opened wherever necessary and that two schools of theology – one in the north and one in the south of the Empire – be created. The Grand Maître (that is, the Minister of Education) asked for the Minister of Cults' opinion. The latter thereupon turned to the Central Consistory in order to obtain the necessary information. The consistory had therefore to state precisely what its educational policies would be.

It defined the study of theology as the perfect knowledge of the Bible and its classic commentators, of the Mishnah, the Talmud and the rabbinic codes of Maimonides and Joseph Caro. In view of the changes in the status of the Jews and their involvement in French society, the curriculum should also include the study of the French language, Latin and Greek literatures and languages, logic and rhetoric. It was also requested, contrary to ancient usage, that only members of the Faculty of the Seminaries to be established should have the right to examine the students and grant them their rabbinical diplomas.

As for the primary schools, they recommended reading and writing in Hebrew – in order to enable the children to study the Bible and the prayerbook – reading and writing in French, arithmetic and grammar. The establishment of the necessary schools was particularly urgent in the north, as too often Christian primary-school teachers refused to accept Jewish pupils in their schools, and thus left them deprived of education.

After a short exchange of letters, the Minister of Cults finally replied on 4 January 1812 to the effect that he saw no need for the establishment of Jewish seminaries as he felt that the number of rabbis would never be great enough to make the opening of such an institution indispensable. He remarked that although, according to law, every consistory could include one chief rabbi and one other rabbi, the notables had elected only the chief rabbi, and did not bother about the second rabbi, which proved that they did not feel that his services were indispensable. Therefore, they could make do with the domestic system of rabbinic training, whereby each rabbi who chose to do so would instruct the young student in his home by means of private lessons. Thus the consistory's wish met with a blunt refusal. It would not be until 1829 that a rabbinic seminary would be opened in France.

In the same letter, the Minister also turned to the problem of primary instruction. He remarked that the existing primary schools had been set up by welfare and religious organisations. The Jewish community could do the same, and rabbis would be able to teach religion classes in the new primary schools. The Ministry of Cults even recommended that the Central Consistory act in this direction, and stated that it would be ready to have the necessary sums included in the budget of the different consistories. This did not in the least mean that the state would take over part of these expenses, but that it would allow the different consistories to raise the necessary funds among the Jewish tax-payers! Although the Central Consistory decided to act accordingly, progress was very slow. It was only after Napoleon's fall that Jewish primary schools became a fact.[32]

Despite these difficulties, the Central Consistory felt that it should regulate the activities of the rabbinate, perhaps in the hope that these very rules would convince the Minister of Cults of the need to institutionalise the training of rabbis. On 6 July 1810 it published instructions to the rabbis, asking them to preach every Saturday and holiday morning in order to remind the congregation of its religious, civil and moral duties. The sermons should deal exclusively with the duties of man toward his Creator, his fellow-men and his fatherland, compliance with religious teachings and the laws of the state, and with the love of the ruler. They would of course have to teach the decisions of the Sanhedrin. The synagogue administrators were asked to report to their consistories on the rabbis' submission to these instructions.[33]

Most of the Central Consistory's work did not deal with such ambitious subjects. It devoted much time to answering the letters of the regional consistories, and approving their budgets before transmitting them to the Ministry of Cults for final approval. It also tried to explain the details of those decrees which were doubtful in meaning. In general its activity was of an administrative nature, but that did not prevent it from setting standards for the authorised interpretation of Jewish religious injunctions.

There can be no doubt that the personal influence of its members, and especially that of the chief rabbi, played a very important role in the formulation of these standards. Another very important part of their work was to persuade the regional consistories to send their contribution to the Central Consistory's budget. Their reluctance to do so very often created great difficulties, as it was impossible to pay the chief rabbis' salaries. Sintzheim, for instance, did not receive his salary for a very long period, although its amount had been settled in Napoleon's decree. After his death, long litigation brought his successors into conflict with the Central Consistory, as they claimed the sums which had been so long overdue![34]

The regional consistories, which were under the control of the Central Consistory, dealt with the daily life of the local communities. Napoleon's decree had granted them almost absolute authority in their circumscriptions, where they were the only intermediaries with the public authorities, which refused to deal with the lower levels. They had to cope first of all with the problem of the *Chevroth*, or religious brotherhoods, which had concentrated in their hands practically all the charitable activities of the communities, and managed to raise considerable sums, which of course escaped control by any extraneous organisation. In Paris there existed nine such *Chevroth* at the time of the creation of the Consistory, which very soon decided to reduce their number. Only the three oldest were retained, and the others were required to merge. As this proved unsatisfactory, it was resolved to suppress them and establish in their stead a Society of Encouragement and Mutual Aid, the ancestor of the welfare board, which was to take care of the sick poor, to attend to funerals, to ensure the daily *minyan*, and to take care of the cleansing and burial of the dead. It would employ a physician. Very soon it began distributing relief to the needy, and supporting a number of young people entering apprenticeships. Thus, side by side with every consistory, there appeared a Comité de Bienfaisance israélite, which, although parallel with the consistorial organisation, was nevertheless entirely controlled by it, and entrusted with such tasks as were not of a purely religious nature.[35]

The administration of the synagogues was to become the major care of the all-powerful consistories. These insisted that all Jewish public worship take place in the synagogues. They did not want to know of any private prayer-meetings, and were extremely active in suppressing them. They were thus following the established policy of the former *nations*, which held that all prayer-meetings must be controlled and authorised by the *nation*, and that any private organisation or meeting could weaken the community, and must therefore be resisted. This of course occasionally brought the consistories into conflict with the *Chevroth*, which had often set up their own *minyanim*. As for the authorised prayer-houses or prayer-meetings, the consistory appointed *commissaires surveillants* in each of the departments belonging to the consistorial circumscription. These would make sure that nothing would be done which would be contrary to the Assembly's and the Sanhedrin's decisions, and that, except in the case of a circumcision, illness and mourning, there would be no private prayer-meeting. They would have to inform their consistory of the number, age, profession and families of the Jews of their department, and provide them with a list of the prospective conscripts. They were also to verify if every Jew had adopted a family name, and give a financial report to the consistory. They would be responsible for the collection of the taxes due to the consistory. Should there also be synagogues in other cities of the department, the *commissaire surveillant* was empowered to appoint in each of then a sub-delegate who would exercise the same functions.[36]

This largely Parisian-inspired organisation was imitated elsewhere, and the consistorial organisation was soon established all over the Empire, the sole difference being the number of synagogues in each circumscription. The Napoleonic organisational ideal reinforced the influence of the leadership and concentrated all power in the hands of a religious and lay hierarchy which could very easily be controlled by the prefects. Contrary to the Catholic and Protestant organisations, it involved the state in no expense, as the Jewish communities had to pay for everything. On the other hand, it allowed for the re-establishment of a stable Jewish organisation as the communities had recovered the right of taxation, albeit controlled by the prefects, and could impose their authority on all the Jews who had not left Judaism. The regional consistories also made it possible to prevent possible rivalries or clashes between the different sections of the community.

What was the attitude of the consistorial leaders toward the imperial régime? It is obvious that they avoided everything which might hint at dissatisfaction with the Emperor's policies, or opposition to them. All France was careful not to engage on such a course, and the Jewish community and its leaders were no less careful. In all probability they could not avoid taking cognisance of a number of indications of the Emperor's decided hostility towards them.

The Assembly of Notables and the Sanhedrin, being official state-established bodies, had not hesitated to use the imprint of the imperial eagle on their stationery, as befitted every governmental body. The central and regional consistories had of course done likewise, and the imperial eagle holding the two tables of the law decorated all their documents. Nevertheless on 26 June 1809, the Council of the Seal of Titles, which was empowered to decide who could use the Empire's official symbol, issued an order forbidding its use to the Jewish consistories, and so informed the Central Consistory, which passed it over to the regional consistories. On the printed letterheads, it was covered by a disc of paper bearing the inscription: *patrie religion*![37]

The Assembly of Notables had long asked to be received by the Emperor on an official visit. Despite many promises, but partly because of the Emperor's constant moves, this was never done. Finally, the new Central Consistory was presented to him, as was the custom with all other central bodies, on 12 December 1809. After a short address by J. Lazard, the following conversation took place, which was dutifully recorded, and reported to the Jewish consistories of the Empire:[38]

> Your name? – Lazard, Sire. – And you?. – Cologna. – A rabbi, no doubt? – Chief Rabbi, Sire. (*The Emperor to Lazard*): Are you one of the principals? Are you from Paris? – I am from Paris, Sire, and a member of the Central Consistory. – From Paris proper? – Yes, Sire, from Paris. – Well, how are things going? – We are organising, Sire. – Are you beginning to correct the evil ones? – They will soon all deserve to be Your Majesty's subjects. – Well ... well ..., do as those from Bordeaux, as the Portuguese.

The historic and only meeting ended this way and the members of the Central Consistory left. The Emperor, who had not only shown considerable rudeness, also prohibited any mention of the audience in the official newspaper of the Empire. The detail did not escape the attention of his visitors, who dared not say anything about it. Only after Napoleon's fall did they comment on this added, and gratuitous, show of hostility.[39]

The recognition of Judaism as a religion did not solve three problems: despite all efforts, it was not possible to ensure that the rabbis' salaries were paid by the state. The problem of the Jewish debts was not solved, and the Jews of Alsace, Metz and the Comtat communities had to maintain during the Empire, and into the middle of the nineteenth century, a special organisation which would handle the debts and ensure their repayment.[40] Therefore many of them remained for a very long time subject to double taxation: for the needs of their present organisation, and for the repayment of these debts. The state showed very little interest in easing their burden.

The different consistories also failed in their fight for the abolition of the Jewish oath. They had felt that emancipation, and the proclamation of legal equality, would have been sufficient to put an end to a practice which applied only to Jews, but they were soon proved wrong. The court of Colmar codified the oath in a decision rendered on 10 February 1809 and the Cour de cassation, the highest court of appeal, on 12 July 1810, rejected the appeal which had been lodged against it. Here, too, it would take more than thirty years finally to abolish this practice.[41]

In these circumstances, it is hardly surprising that the consistories showed no great regrets at the fall of Napoleon. When the Bourbons returned, the Central Consistory felt no great pangs of conscience in telling the regional consistories of the lack of recognition which had been its lot during the Empire. This was furthered by the rather cordial response of the new régime: the king and his brother very soon received the Central Consistory in audience, showing that a change of attitude toward Judaism was forthcoming, and that the future of the new Jewish organisation was not in danger.

CHAPTER VII

In the Empire

When the Assembly of Notables first met, the French authorities might have hoped that its proceedings would arouse great interest in the European Jewish communities. If the new borders of the French zone of influence are borne in mind, this hope was not completely unfounded. There is no doubt that directly or indirectly the events which took place in Paris had many repercussions in those countries which had accepted French influence. The Assembly, very probably at the instigation of the commissioners, had sent an appeal to all Jewish communities in Europe in order to inform them of the Sanhedrin's forthcoming meetings and to invite them to send delegates.[1] Nevertheless the Assembly of Notables was visited by only two delegations, one from Frankfurt on Main and the other from Amsterdam.

On 15 December 1806, a letter signed by 205 Frankfurt Jews was read before the Assembly. It expressed the high hopes its meeting had raised, and the admiration felt for the answers it had given to the Emperor's questions. It commended Napoleon for having decided 'to purify religion and reform abuses' and having deemed it necessary to call a meeting with the Jews' representatives in order to consult with them and to prevent any harm to their religion. On behalf of the Assembly, Furtado, its president, prepared an answer which was read before its plenary session on 27 December. He expressed the Assembly's thanks for the good wishes which had been sent to it and added, 'We have done what the circumstances allowed.' More could have been done quicker if it had taken place twenty-five years earlier. He hoped neverthe-less that the impulse given by France, aided by its great influence in Europe, would encourage a number of states to follow its example. He hoped that the present discussions would help to bring about changes in the Jews' professions: fewer merchants and bankers, more landowners, artisans, farmers and soldiers.[2]

It would seem that the Frankfurt community had decided to take a more active part in the Assembly's meetings. At the end of 1806 or at the beginning of 1807, an appeal was sent by its leaders to its members in which they described the new Assembly and expressed their admiration for Napoleon's affectionate interest in the Jews. They were of the opinion that the Frankfurt Jews should send deputies to the Sanhedrin meetings: had they not twice been requested to do so? Two such delegates had been chosen and should now be sent to Paris. In order to cover their expenses, a committee of six was appointed to gather the necessary funds.[3] On 22 February they sent a letter of thanks to the Assembly for its understanding. They added that it was because of the great advance of culture in France in general that the French Jews had been recognised as equal citizens, but the other sovereigns of Europe had not yet been fully inspired by the principles of philosophy. They had therefore encountered great difficulties on the way to their regeneration. Later the two delegates, Salomon Treves and Isaac Hildesheimer, arrived in Paris. On 9 March 1807 they appeared before the Sanhedrin. Hildesheimer made a speech in which he informed the Sanhedrin that his electors had instructed him to communicate with the Sanhedrin and to report that they had decided to accept and recognise the Sanhedrin's decisions. He hoped that the Jews of Frankfurt would also one day obtain an improvement in their legal status.[4] On 25 March 1807 they appeared before the Assembly of Notables and declared that they had sent its decisions and those of the Sanhedrin to their electors, who had very carefully examined them, and that[5]

far from having found in them the least attack on religion, they had recognised that everything in it was consistent, true, just,

decent, beneficial and laudable; that if they enjoyed, like the
Jews of France and of the kingdom of Italy, civil rights, and if the
laws of their country would allow them to fulfil its duties, they
would feel bound by religion to neglect none; and that while
giving their full and complete assent to the Sanhedrin's results,
they make it conditional upon their sovereign's agreement, whose
slightest wishes they will always respect.

On 12 February 1807 a delegation of Dutch Jews sent by the
Amsterdam congregation Adath Jeshurun was received by the
Sanhedrin. In two speeches, one in German, and the other in
Hebrew, they expressed their gratitude for the convening of the
Sanhedrin, and their attachment to the Emperor who had
ordered it. They proclaimed their attachment to their ruler, and
their esteem for the present meeting. Later, on 9 March, they
announced their agreement with the Sanhedrin's decisions.[6]

These were the only delegations which bothered to attend the
meetings of the Assembly and of the Sanhedrin, although a
number of enthusiastic messages had been sent to its leader.[7] One
may therefore be justified in asking why they had come at all, and
how representative they were. It is quite clear that the Dutch
delegates represented only the new moderately reformed congregation which had been set up as a direct consequence of the
discussions and tensions which split the Amsterdam community
after the proclamation of the emancipation of the Dutch Jews, and
the end of their communal autonomy. It could therefore not
aspire or claim to represent the Jewish community of Holland.[8]
As for Frankfurt, the initiators of the appeal to the Assembly of
Notables were the founders of a local 'Society of Frankfurt Jews
which aims to contribute to the welfare of the Israelites'. They
managed to impress upon the board of their community, which
probably chose the delegates, the need to send them to Paris, and
to pay their expenses.[9] As has been seen, these delegates reported
to Frankfurt, and asked for instructions. They were therefore the
only bona fide delegates, who were citizens neither of France nor
of the kingdom of Italy, to take part in the Assembly's and the
Sanhedrin's proceedings. It would seem that Napoleon's efforts
and the whole Sanhedrin were an utter failure, an ambitious plan

which was disregarded by the great majority of the Jews of Europe, and remained without any serious influence on the fate of Judaism. Such a view is not supported by the turn of events which began at that time, and left its mark on all European Jewish communities.

Napoleon's policies toward the Jews cannot be isolated either from the reactions and hopes of the different Jewish communities, or from the growing influence which his military successes had brought him in Europe. France itself included in 1811 no less than 130 departments which, apart from France proper, stretched from Rome to Hamburg. Belgium and Holland and a considerable part of Italy belonged to it directly. At the same time Napoleon, represented by his son-in-law, reigned in the kingdom of Italy. A governor administered in his name the Illyrian provinces, which had been taken from Venice and Austria. Napoleon's brother Jerome had ruled the kingdom of Westphalia since 1807. Another brother, Louis, had ruled Holland from 1806 to 1811 until it was integrated into France. Louis' young son was the nominal ruler of the Grand Duchy of Berg. Another brother, Joseph, had successively ruled the kingdoms of Naples and Spain where there were practically no Jews. Tuscany was ruled by Elisa, Napoleon's sister. No less than thirty-six states in central and southern Germany – including the kingdom of Westphalia and the Grand Duchy of Berg – were organised in the Confederation of the Rhine, the protector of which was none other than Napoleon himself. He was also the Mediator of the Swiss Confederation. Even the new Grand Duchy of Warsaw had French administrators, even though it was theoretically dependent on the King of Saxony. Only Great Britain, Prussia, and the Austrian and the Russian Empires did not form part of the French political sphere – which does not mean that they were indifferent to what was happening there. In all the areas of French influence, a certain spirit of religious toleration had become the rule, and the principles of civic equality had become generally recognised. This fact, and the prestige which was normally attached to what was happening in Paris, had obviously prepared the ground for a certain Jewish effervescence, which was already beginning to stir.

In the departments which were included in the French Empire, such as those of Holland, Northern Germany, Illyria and Italy, the consistorial system, as defined in the decree of 1808, was immediately introduced, and the local Jews at once became French citizens. Their major problem was to obtain an exemption from the application of the Infamous Decree, and this they often succeeded in achieving. In the other areas of French influence, the local Jewish communities had an uphill struggle in order to achieve the same status. The fact that there were already a number of accepted precedents considerably facilitated their efforts.

The Assembly of Notables had hardly begun meeting when the Brunswick Court Jew, Israel Jacobson, published in French a pamphlet entitled *The First Steps of the Jewish Nation toward Happiness under the Auspices of the Great Monarch Napoleon.*[10] In this publication he described his efforts and success in the establishment of a Jewish school in the city of Seesen, where he had tried to prepare a new generation of Jews for their entrance into modern society, while giving up the traditional Jewish occupations in favour of the trades from which they had hitherto been excluded. He felt that this effort toward Jewish regeneration could be greatly extended, as Napoleon himself now took such a great interest in it. He regretted he was not a French citizen. He belonged to the unfortunate Jewish nation against which ignorance and superstition had allied in order to bring about its degradation. But God had chosen Napoleon to improve the welfare of the world of which the Jews were a part. For a thousand years they had been unable to find compassion and humanity among the princes. Now at last a saviour had appeared in the person of Napoleon. Jacobson, for his part, had tried for a number of years to help his people and to civilise them. He had succeeded in having the special toll on Jews removed, and had set up an educational institution in which twenty young Christian pupils studied alongside the Jewish pupils. He asked the Emperor also to show his interest in the Jews who lived outside France. To allow a difference to be instituted between French and other Jews would make even commercial relations between them nearly impossible. A French Jew would even hesitate to marry a German Jewess in such conditions!

The German princes, Jacobson added, would not be opposed to the regeneration of the Jews. As for the German Jew, he would be overjoyed if he were allowed to earn his bread in an honest way and to enjoy the rights of citizenship. He would agree to give his religion a form and content, which, without deviating from the law, would be harmonised with the exercise of civic obligations. Jacobson then suggested that a Supreme Jewish Council be set up, under the chairmanship of a patriarch, which would have its seat in France. All the Jewish communities should be organised on a regional basis, and should be subordinated to a synod to be established under the auspices of the French government and the Supreme Jewish Council. The synods would be empowered to deal with all the problems of Jewish worship and to appoint the rabbis. The Supreme Council would be authorised to grant dispensations from the performance of some religious duties in so far as this was necessary to enable the petititioners to perform their duty as citizens. Jacobson felt that this indispensable organisation would free the Jews from political and spiritual enslavement. Then the Jews would, as in Palestine in former times, devote themselves to agriculture and to the arts and crafts.

It has been suggested that Jacobson's plan was not without influence on the decision to set up a Sanhedrin.[11] Although this is not impossible, it is highly unlikely that Napoleon could have read Jacobson's pamphlet. It is more probable that the whole idea emerged in the discussions between his commissioners and the rabbinic leadership of the Assembly. Nevertheless, Jacobson had managed to give a résumé of the political theory of emancipation. The Jews had prepared themselves for it and believed that they could become citizens of their country without having to renounce, or to distort, their religious beliefs. Therefore the different governments should grant them the citizenship they deserved. The Jews, on their side, would be willing to make the temporary arrangements necessary to enable them to fulfil their duties toward the state. This was very probably an allusion to the necessity to ease the observance of the dietary laws and of the Sabbath and holidays for civil servants and soldiers.

Jacobson's activity in France proper did not go further than the statement he sent to Napoleon. Things were quite different in Germany, where this typical Court Jew was able to use his influence and his personal position in order to further the aims he had nurtured for Judaism. The establishment of the kingdom of Westphalia under Jerome Bonaparte's rule in August 1807 gave him a new opportunity to act. In Cassel, where he had settled by that time, he did his best to emulate the French example in this new French-dominated kingdom. Jerome's sympathy toward the Jews, for which he was strongly rebuked by his brother,[12] greatly encouraged the change which was now to take place in their condition. On 27 January 1808, that is, only six weeks after Jerome had taken over his new kingdom, a decree was published which granted equal rights to the Jews of Westphalia.[13] Jacobson's dream of emancipation had come sooner than he had expected, because of the inner dynamics of the French influence. The obvious thing to do now was to adopt a constitution for Westphalian Jewry which would emulate what was projected at the time for the French Jews; i.e. the consistorial system. Although the decree organising the French consistories had not been published, it is evident that Jacobson and his friends had heard about the discussions and suggestions of the Committee of Nine, which had for so long awaited enactment by Napoleon.

A meeting of the notables of Westphalian Jewry was therefore called on 8 February 1808. Jacobson had already by that time acquired a predominant position in Westphalian Jewry. He thus became the major influence in the proceedings of the new assembly. By the strength of his personality he was able to give the Westphalian assembly a direction very different from that which had been adopted in Paris. Whereas in Paris the rabbinic element had progressively assumed greater influence during the debates until it finally dominated them under the guidance of David Sintzheim, the opposite occurred in Cassel, where Jacobson, the lay leader, was in complete charge. It is also true that in Paris the intervention of the government was much more conspicuous than in Westphalia, where the general lines of the Emperor's plan, which was not even under consideration when the Paris Assembly had first met, were already known. The peculiar recognition given in Germany to the Court Jews had, without any discussion or dissension, brought Jacobson to the forefront, whereas in France the administration and the commissioners had been unable to exert great influence in the formation of the Assembly's leadership.

It would nevertheless be mistaken to deduce from Jacobson's almost absolute leadership that his ideas were shared by the mass of Westphalian Jewry. It would seem that the Jewish population, long used to the Court Jew's leadership, had chosen not only not to oppose him publicly, but also to avoid any public manifestation which could be construed as a limited form of acquiescence in the reformist ideas. It remains the case nevertheless, that the leadership became more and more detached from the local communities, and thus very often represented ideas which were its own, and not those of its constituents. In order to avoid dangerous tensions at this meeting, the aim of which was to teach the new Westphalian citizens of the Jewish faith how to use their newly-won rights without giving up their religion, it was decided that no part of Mosaic law, in all probability biblical law, would be modified or even touched. However, customs could be changed in order to facilitate a rapprochement between Jews and Christians: the assembly would have to choose those specific customs which were not essential to the Jewish faith and which could therefore be altered.

Earlier, on 9 February, King Jerome had received the Jewish delegates and had given them the support which his brother had always refused to grant them in France. Jacobson addressed the king in the name of his colleagues and told him that the emancipation of the Jews would now allow them to become soldiers, farmers and merchants. When the meeting resumed, he had a committee appointed to study the definition of a satisfactory religious service. The problem of the synagogue had become very important with the recognition of Judaism as one of the state religions. This was not only because the impression made upon Gentiles had acquired great importance as a consequence of the more frequent contacts between Jews and Gentiles, but also because the newly emancipated Jews, who now knew more about the decorum and the ceremonies of Christian religious services, often looked at them with the envious admiration of those who had at last been accepted by their fellow-citizens as equals. Christianity, so long feared or despised, seemed now to have acquired suddenly many religious values, which had not hitherto seemed indispensable for Judaism, the ceremonies and services of which did not require the solemnity of a church service.

As another concession to Christian influence, the new Westphalian consistory was asked to prepare a catechism: the Jewish teachers would be required to teach only in accordance with this catechism. The state authorities would of course be asked to approve it before it was published. It is quite probable that it was with this intention that Johlson had sent his proposed catechism to Paris to have it officially approved there. One of the results of this approach was a rehabilitation of theology in Judaism.

In order to solve the problem of possible opposition between Jewish and civil law, it was decided to draw inspiration from the example of the other faiths and to drop Jewish laws which contradicted civil law wherever other religions had done the same. This would of course make it possible to retain the obligation to solemnise religious weddings and divorces after the civil ceremonies. Jacobson himself had also reported on the work of the committee which dealt with the religious responsibilities of the projected consistory. It had distinguished three kinds of commandment in Judaism: the fundamental principles, the moral laws and the various commands and prohibitions. Only the latter could be modified by the consistory. This distinction was to be the theological basis and justification of the intended reforms, about which the future consistory would always have to communicate with the Westphalian government before enacting them. This last promise seems to have been given in the hope of enlisting the government's aid in pushing through these reforms against the will of the mass of the Jewish people.[14]

Once the Westphalian authorities had been informed of the assembly's wishes, things moved rather quickly. On 31 March 1808, King Jerome instituted the consistorial system in

151

Westphalia, only two weeks after Napoleon had established it in France. He justified it by the need to give the Jewish religion a constitution, just as all other state-recognised religions had received: now that the Jews had ceased to be a separate body in the state, they should be enabled, as the communicants of other religions, to merge in the common nation.

The consistorial system, which had been devised in large measure to facilitate state control of the Jews, was a strongly centralised and hierarchical organisation. It might then become the ideal instrument with the help of which a strong personality such as Jacobson could try to impose his ideas. Contrary to what was the case in France, the Westphalian consistory was presided over not by a rabbi, but by Jacobson himself. As in France, the state did not take part in the financing of the consistory's activities, and it was left to the Jewish communities to collect the necessary funds. This of course only reinforced the influence of the richer elements among the Jews, and that of Jacobson himself.

The duties of the rabbis were defined as in France: they would have to teach respect for the state laws and the sacred nature of military duty. As for the consistory, it felt that its major duty was to explain Judaism as a religion and to make the necessary adjustments to enable it to develop in this direction. This course might have led the consistory towards extreme reform. But this was not to happen because of the very nature of the consistorial system, which always attempted to encompass the whole of the Jewish community. The possibility of schism or dissidence was alien to the consistorial system, the politics of which were always based on the necessity for moderation. The movement towards reform had therefore to be slow, and its pace moderate. Nevertheless, it was all-important to bring about a change in Judaism as it was unfortunately too obvious that the Jews had a long way to go in order to regenerate themselves, although they could hardly be blamed for the laws which had provoked this sad and regrettable state of affairs. The consistory should show the way by which this aim might be reached. This justified some steps it would have to take, which contradicted its stated aim. The religious organisation of Judaism would not hesitate to give advice on matters which were not exactly related to religious duties, such as encouraging Jewish youngsters to enter those crafts which had up to now been closed to them. It also encouraged the establishment of schools and of a seminary for teachers and rabbis, which introduced a general curriculum besides the traditional Jewish studies.[15]

The new consistorial school which was set up at the time gives an interesting illustration of Jacobson's practical plans for the regeneration of Judaism: of fifty boys who were to be educated free of charge alongside paying pupils, twenty-five were to be taught trades, fifteen the sciences and business and ten were to continue their studies at the seminary in order to become rabbis or teachers. Jacobson intended to transform Westphalian Jewry's social structure as well as its way of thinking. The problem of liturgy was also very prominent in his thoughts. In Seesen, where he had founded his first school, he also set up a Temple, having thus abandoned the traditional name of the synagogue. In this showpiece of Judaism, as he understood it, neither the bell-tower nor the clock was missing. Jacobson, who himself led the first prayer service in the Temple, did not hesitate to wear Protestant clerical garb. The rabbinate had been definitely pushed aside, not only because of the fear of lack of co-operation on its side or because of its rather unsatisfactory knowledge of German which would also have unfitted it to take a proper part in the proceedings: it would seem that Jacobson was also intent upon replacing the rabbinic tradition and the authority of its bearers by the consensus of the community. These were services which could be attended by Gentiles, without the Jews fearing any hostile reaction on their side. Their decorum, the discipline which reigned among its participants, the use of the German language would arouse nothing but admiration and understanding. Jacobson therefore did not hesitate to invite Christians to attend these services and the visitors were duly impressed. This somewhat pathetic attempt to make Judaism acceptable by borrowing many Christian usages should not be construed as a deliberate step on the road to Christianity. Jacobson, and most probably the great majority of his supporters, would not have thought of it. Whatever its success, their effort had only one goal: to allow Jews to remain faithful to their Jewish faith in the modern world. They were ready to compromise to achieve this aim, but it would be malicious to accuse them of having had other plans. The fact that conversions were to be numerous in their circle cannot be ascribed to their deliberate religious policies: they most certainly had not desired this result.

In their slow progress on the way to regeneration, the necessity of which they had never doubted, the members of the new Westphalian consistory dealt with matters which should clearly have been left to the rabbinate. In 1810, for instance, they attempted to regulate and give uniformity to the laws concerning Jewish marriage. Only rabbis were supposed to perform them. Every detail of the ceremony was carefully determined, and many old customs, such as breaking the glass, the showering of wheat grain on the bride, etc., were prohibited. The sermon in German became imperative. Judaism was to be detached more and more from popular tradition and to become intellectually purified.[16]

The same process took place in the synagogue, which was now put under the authority of the syndicus, the local synagogue administrator. These administrators were instructed how to preserve decorum during services. The rabbis' sermons were to deal exclusively with moral and religious instructions. Some of the *piyyutim* were suppressed. Everything which had a vague kabbalistic flavour was suppressed. Many popular customs, e.g. the processions on The Rejoicing of the Law, or the *Haman-klopfen* which accompanied with much noise every mention of Haman's name in the Purim scroll, were strictly forbidden. Every synagogue which did not heed these instructions could be closed by consistorial fiat. This was rather in the nature of a threat than of practical policy, although its authoritarian slant could not be mistaken.[17]

The control of the synagogues became even more effective with the promulgation of a royal decree on 5 July 1811, which severely forbade private religious meetings. Such a measure had also been taken in France, but there the aim had been completely different: the large communities were endangered by the centrifugal tendencies of many small groups. In Westphalia the aim was to create a captive audience for the services organised according to Jacobson's theories. It would seem that many worshippers had preferred to set up small prayer-meetings in order to avoid attending the new services, and the decree was to encourage them to return.

It would seem that in view of the lack of any strong opposition from the rabbinate, Jacobson, well established in the chairmanship of the consistory and assured of the king's more or less benevolent neutrality, felt that he was slowly winning the understanding of the people, and that, given sufficient time, his ideas would become accepted by all of Westphalian Jewry. He was not at all aware of the mistrust he was creating. When his consistory issued certain dispensations from various Passover observances, even the Paris Central Consistory felt it had to write to him to express its utter surprise at the step he had taken without any consultation with other Jewish religious organisations. Very soon Jerome Bonaparte also became dissatisfied with Jacobson's methods, as he feared that instead of bringing about a unified Jewish community within the consistorial system, he was creating strong opposition and endangering the very unity which had been aimed for. Protests became more and more numerous, and the public authorities were in no mood to compel the reluctant majority to comply with all of Jacobson's ideas. He was now becoming a cause of dissension in the very community he had wanted to unify. He still wanted to continue ruling from his entrenched position as head of the consistory, without understanding in the least that he could not do so without enjoying a measure of popularity amongst the rabbinate and the people whom his despotic ways had in fact alienated.[18]

There is therefore no reason for surprise at the joy which greeted the end of the consistorial system with the fall of Westphalia at the end of 1813. Once Jerome and his French administration had left Cassel, nothing remained of the autocratic system Jacobson had so long and so forcefully wished to build. The historic leadership of the Jewish community re-emerged at once, supported by the near-unanimity of the Jewish people. A disappointed man, Jacobson soon left Cassel and settled in Berlin.[19]

During his Westphalian activities, Jacobson had taken an important part in the debate on the emancipation of the Jews of Frankfurt on Main. The French influence had made itself felt there. On 15 September 1806 the prince primate, Karl Dalberg, had deemed it necessary to write to Bishop (formerly Abbé) Grégoire that the Frankfurt Jews would have no cause to complain against him on account of the measures he intended to take concerning their organisation. He had already removed a personal tax which was required from them, and most German rulers had done likewise.[20] This was then an enlightened prince, anxious to improve the Jews' lot and aware of the changes the French Revolution had brought about. The greater, then, the deception of the Frankfurt community when, towards the end of 1807, Dalberg finally published his new constitution for the Frankfurt Jews.[21]

The new regulations bore witness to such a condescending attitude to the Jews who had to be regenerated that Jacobson, although not a Frankfurt citizen, could not refrain from writing to Dalberg to protest against the measures he had taken.[22] In very strong words he told him that a religion which was based on beliefs would not be subjected to orders: changes could occur in it only as a result of the action of reason. And even then, changes would take place only very slowly. Judaism, properly treated, would show that it was endowed with all the qualities the state could reasonably require from any religion. It must be allowed to take the necessary measures to reform itself, and not be submitted to useless external coercion.[23]

How, then, could the community of Frankfurt be asked to submit a list of three candidates for the function of rabbi or rabbinic judge, and to agree that the Lutheran consistory examine them in order to recommend to the sovereign which candidate should be appointed? Did the Protestant consistory and the sovereign have the necessary qualities which would enable them to choose a rabbi for the Jews? How could the Jewish community have any confidence in rabbis appointed in such a way?

Jacobson asked the same question about the proposed supervision of the Jewish schools, which was to be entrusted to Protestant inspectors who knew nothing about Jewish youth: why was it impossible to entrust this function to the most learned members of the Jewish faith? The constitution also limited the number of Jewish families tolerated in the city to five hundred and maintained the old conditions which limited their right to marriage. Young men would not be allowed to marry before the age of twenty-five, and girls before eighteen. Non-residents of Frankfurt who wished to marry there could do so only if they brought a respectable dowry! The constitution intended to put an end to the special taxes imposed on the local Jews, but made this conditional upon the demise of those who at present received these payments. All this meant that the Jews of Frankfurt paid considerable sums far in excess of what was required from their Christian neighbours. They were even compelled to pay property taxes on those of their houses which had been burnt down in the conflagration which had almost destroyed the local Jewish quarter in 1796! Their trade was very strictly limited, as they could employ only Jewish workers in their factories. As in the past, they could open shops in only two streets. Almost all the pre-revolutionary restrictions on their economic activities were maintained.

The Jews of Frankfurt, no less than Jacobson, could hardly conceal their disappointment. It was only in 1810 with the creation of the Grand Duchy of Frankfurt in that year that the prince primate eventually granted equal political and civil rights to the Jews, on condition that they redeem at twenty times their face value the taxes they had traditionally paid. The Jews complied with this demand and raised the sum of 440,000 gulden, and were finally emancipated on 28 December 1811. The ghetto of Frankfurt was then formally suppressed, although most of the local Jews continued to live there.[24] Officially all laws discriminating against Jews, or limiting their right to marry, had disappeared. A new Jewish organisation was established, which was influenced in very large measure by the French consistories. The responsibilities were divided between an executive board which

157

was to be elected by the Jewish community – although the first one was appointed – and a council of fifteen notables who were appointed, and whose functions were to suggest replacements for the executive board when there was a vacancy, and to present a list of three acceptable candidates for the chief rabbinate or the rabbinate, when the need occurred. The organised community became, as in France, a part of government, and in practice accepted all the decisions of the Sanhedrin.[25]

Its reign was very short, as Frankfurt was conquered in November 1813 by the anti-Napoleon coalition. As part of the reaction against French rule, the laws concerning the status of the Jews were abrogated. The Jews had again lost their civic rights.

In the north of Germany, Hamburg became a part of France at the end of 1810. As a consequence, the decrees concerning the organisation of the consistories automatically applied to the city, and a regional consistory was duly established. As much as the local Jews may have enjoyed this newly-won equality of rights, they were also concerned at the thought that the infamous decree concerning the debts due to the Jews might also apply there. They therefore did their best to secure an exemption, which they seem to have obtained. In March 1813, with the entrance of the Russian troops, their new status was abolished, although it was to be renewed with the return of the French troops in May, and maintained for a further year. By that time, it had already become evident that the whole question of Jewish emancipation would be reopened after the departure of the French forces, and so it was.

In other regions of Germany which were also subjected to French influence, the old tradition remained stronger, and there was no great enthusiasm for the new French legislation. Saxony was very reluctant to change anything in its attitude to the Jews, although it was eventually compelled to abolish discriminatory measures against French or Westphalian Jews who happened to visit the state.[26] When Mecklenburg decided upon the emancipation of its Jews, it asked them to pay the price in advance, and to give up many practices such as the dietary laws, or the Sabbath observance, and to allow only one child in every family to enter commerce. This was tantamount to making emancipation impossible. It was only in 1813 that it was finally decided to recognise as citizens those Jews whose families had been officially tolerated in the duchy. This measure did not mean that the Jews had received complete equality with their fellow Christian citizens, although it conclusively recognised their right to live in the duchy.[27]

The pressure of the French influence was even felt in Bavaria. The personal tax was abolished, but the new status of the Jewish religion published in 1813 was very far from satisfactory. All the Jewish families which had lawfully settled in the new kingdom received a licence which could be handed over only to the oldest son: he alone would have the right to establish a new family in the state. His younger brothers would have to wait until a licence became vacant as a result of death or emigration before being allowed to marry. The granting of a new licence was conditional upon the payment of a substantial sum. The aim was obvious: to prevent any increase in the number of authorised Jews. The fate of the happy few thus licensed became of course quite acceptable, but it remained a privilege, and was not the recognition of any Jewish equality. The cage had just become gilded.[28] In Baden, any improvement in the Jewish status was made conditional upon the Jews bringing proof that their means of existence resembled those of the Christians. This meant that they would have to give up at once the practice of usury and peddling. In 1809 the Jewish community was finally granted the status of a religious community, although it was made clear that individual Jews would have to do their best to emulate the Christian way of life in order to receive their full citizens' rights. On the model of the French consistories, a supreme Council of the Israelites was to be set up, to be composed of eight rabbis and lay leaders appointed by the Grand Duke. It was instructed to work out a constitution for the different Jewish communities. This form of control did not seem tight enough to the authorities, who decided in 1812 that from now on a government commissioner would have to approve all their decisions before they could become effective.[29]

It is clear that all these changes were not because of any desire to improve the condition of the German Jews, but were rather consequences of French pressure. From 1808 on, this had become rather ambivalent, as the very hostile implications of the Infamous Decree had become well known in the whole area subjected to French influence. The rulers, who felt they could avoid taking decisions on the Jews' status, felt at the same time that nobody would reproach them were they to use the French precedent and insist on the need to bring about a revolution in the Jews' habits and professions. A classical example of this ambiguous policy came from the Grand Duchy of Warsaw.

After his defeat of Prussia, Napoleon detached from it the province of Great Poland and turned it into the Duchy of Warsaw, which was to be ruled by the king of Saxony, himself a grandson of the last Polish king of the Saxon dynasty (1807). Two years later, after his victory over Austria, he also joined a part of Austrian Poland to the Duchy, which thus became a rather important state. Nominally independent, it was in fact under French influence. It accepted the Code Napoléon which had proclaimed the equality of all citizens, and should therefore have granted automatic emancipation to its Jews. The new Duchy contained in 1810 about 400,000 inhabitants of the Jewish faith, and could therefore not avoid dealing with their specific problems. These Jews joyfully greeted the French victories. Hebrew poems were written in praise of Napoleon as well as of the new Duke.[30]

At the beginning of 1808 they had already submitted a petition claiming their civic rights. The elections to the Sejm were imminent and it became necessary to decide who should be allowed a vote. By that time the memories of the Assembly of the Notables and of the Sanhedrin were already fading, but the decision to publish the Infamous Decree was already known. A report could therefore be brought before the Grand Duke which pointed out the danger of granting full civil rights to the Jews, as this people 'cherishes a national spirit alien to the country',[31] and had engaged in unproductive trades. The Polish Finance Minister felt that, according to the constitution, the Jews should have no communities, courts of justice, oaths, peculiar dress, uses and prejudices, no private schools or instruction: 'they should not set up a particular tribe through special marriage laws.' It was argued that inasmuch as Napoleon had managed to suspend for ten years the granting of full citizenship to the Jews of his Empire, it was no more imperative to comply with the Jews' demands in Poland right away. Negotiations were undertaken with the French authorities in order to clarify this point, and as a result, a decree was published on 17 October 1808, which closely followed the French precedent in ordering that the inhabitants of the Duchy of Warsaw professing the Mosaic religion be barred for ten years from enjoying the political rights which were due to them 'in the hope that during this interval they may eradicate their distinguishing characteristics, which mark them off so strongly from the rest of the population.' Nevertheless the decree provided for individual exceptions in favour of those Jews who should prove worthy of them. In this respect, the Polish authorities were at variance with the accepted policy in France which refused to grant individual exemptions, but was willing to exempt whole departments from the law's limitations.[32]

The decree which mentioned only political disabilities also applied to civil rights. In November 1808 the Duchy's Jews were forbidden to acquire patrimonial estates which had belonged to the Polish nobility. The next year practically all the laws which had limited the right of Jewish residence in the capital were renewed. Only a few bankers, businessmen, physicians and artists were allowed to take up residence in the main streets of Warsaw. The new era which the French troops had brought to Poland seemed to be disappearing very rapidly.[33]

At that time there existed already in Warsaw a not inconsiderable concentration of enlightened Jews who were not ready to give up the rights of citizenship which they felt were their due. In January 1809 seventeen of these Jews who thought that they had done what was necessary to come closer to the Christian population asked for the exemption for which the decree had provided. The Minister of Justice replied that the fact that the constitution had proclaimed the principle of equality was not sufficient to turn all the state's inhabitants into fully fledged citizens: how can those who follow the laws of Moses look upon

Poland as their fatherland? Do they not wish to return to the land of their ancestors? They look upon themselves as part of a separate nation. The mere abandonment of traditional Jewish dress could not turn them into Polish citizens. It would seem that the Minister of Justice had declared in this way that Jewish particularism was rooted in Jewish religion, and could be rooted out only by a profound change in their religion.

Other members of the Warsaw community did not accept this answer and turned to the senate: they wrote that thousands of members of the Polish nation of the Jewish persuasion, whose family had lived in Poland for centuries, felt they were entitled to consider this country as their fatherland. They could not understand why they were persecuted, and why laws of exception applied to them, in utter contradiction to Napoleon's decrees. The senate answered that the Jews could blame only themselves for their difficulties, and that a committee should be set up in order to look into methods of reforming the Jews. This was of course tantamount to delaying any useful solution of the Jews' pressing problem.[34]

It is interesting to note that at that time the Jewish soldier Berek Yosselovich, who had taken an illustrious part in the last battles for Polish independence in 1794 and later joined the Polish legion in Napoleon's wars, returned to Poland and received a commission in the new Polish army, where a sizeable number of Jews was by now serving. He was killed in the battle of Kotzk in 1809, fought between Polish and Austrian forces. His son, Joseph Berkovitch, who participated in the same battle, went on to serve in Poland and France until the fall of Napoleon. Whatever their personal merits and their devotion to the Polish national ideal, their example was of no help to their co-religionists, who had by then already lost a great part of their enthusiasm for the new régime, which wished to enlist them into its army, while at the same time refusing to recognise them as citizens. Here again Napoleon's policies had greatly influenced the Polish legislators who followed him in deciding that the army would be the best influence in turning the Jews into proper Polish citizens, in as much as it would also estrange them, even if only temporarily, from many Jewish practices. A movement of civil resistance broke out, and the prospective Jewish recruits did their best to avoid being drafted into the army. This movement met with such success that the Minister of War Poniatowski finally proposed the exemption of all Jews from military duty: this seemed to him all the more justified since the Jews had been excluded from the benefits of citizenship for a period of ten years. In 1812 the government of the Duchy agreed to his suggestion, and the Jews were excused from service in return for the yearly payment of a sum of 700,000 zlotys. This prevented them from having to take part in Napoleon's Russian expedition.[35]

It is remarkable that the French army's difficulties did not divert the attention of the Warsaw government from the Jews' affairs. As late as October 1812 it decreed that within two years the Polish Jews would be forbidden to sell liquor or manage taverns! Such was the unjustified confidence in Napoleon's eventual victory against Russia. In 1813 the French troops evacuated Poland, and thus the Grand Duchy came to an end. The remains of French influence were obliterated, and the greater part of the former Duchy now became united with Russia, under the guise of a puppet kingdom of Poland. The Polish Jews had now become for all practical purposes Russian Jews.

Thus ended the chequered history of French influence on the Jews in Western, Central and Eastern Europe in Napoleon's time. Most of the reforms it had brought about in the Jews' status disappeared with Napoleon wherever they had been imposed on a reluctant state. In the aftermath of the European reaction, Napoleon's policies seemed almost liberal when compared with the new régime imposed on the Jews after 1815. The Jewish struggle for emancipation was therefore to gain great intensity, as it was strengthened by the memory of what had been lost. The French Revolution had created standards for Jewish emancipation, which did not suffer too much from Napoleon's strictures; these were in any case described as temporary. A new nostalgia remained after the Empire's fall which would strengthen the reformist tendencies of those who were willing to pay the price they felt was required to regain the rights they had lost.

CHAPTER VIII

In Non-French Europe

Echoes from the meetings of the Assembly of Notables and the Sanhedrin were distinctly heard beyond the borders of France, even in those countries which were fighting increasing French influence and trying to avoid subjection to it. The transactions of the Paris meetings were very soon translated into English, as the interest was great at 'the novelty of a Jewish assembly deliberating on the national interests of a people which had so long ceased to be numbered among nations.'[1] As there was no need for the English translator to pay his respects to Napoleon, he felt free to expatiate on the Emperor's real intentions which were not yet known at the time his book was published (1807). He had kind words for the policies of the Ancien Régime concerning Jews which 'happily united tolerance and even encouragement with circumspection'! He felt that the change in the Jews' condition was ineluctable and that Napoleon had only tried to take the credit for what would have happened anyway: what could indeed be added to the decree of the National Assembly which had granted the Jews full citizenship? In view of the small number of Jews in France and Italy, what purpose was served by the insistence on the Jews' duty to protect their fatherland, which the law had already imposed upon them as it had on all other French citizens? Even the pretext of the need to fight the Jewish practice of usury was not very plausible, as the Jews were not the only people who could be accused of indulging in usury. Probably, the translator felt, Napoleon had not entirely given up his old plan of re-establishing a Jewish state on the banks of the Jordan![2] He dismissed the whole proceedings in Paris as a demonstration of the politico-religious conceptions of the French government, which looked upon religion as a convenient means to control the French population. Perhaps he even thought of using his hold on the French Jewish community to exert his influence on other Jewish groups which had relations with the French Jews. The whole Napoleonic system could only bring about greater separation between the Jews and the French nation as they would now have separate elective assemblies and would pay separate contributions and there would now be separate police powers at the disposal of the rabbis who would be empowered to control the Jews for military, statistical and other purposes. The translator felt that the Jews might have shown greater strength in opposing Napoleon's demands, but admitted that it was not likely that any assembly meeting under Napoleon's auspices could have shown great independence.[3]

A few pamphlets were also written at that time by English Jews and Christians alike.[4] It would be difficult to attribute to them much more than a passing importance. English Jews were not very numerous at the time, and being largely free from discrimination, were not really concerned by what was happening on the Continent. They identified themselves with the accepted British policies and seem to have been convinced that their lot would improve even without the help of external intervention.

The same equanimity did not prevail in the large Austrian Empire which enjoyed a common frontier with the French zone of influence, and which was to be the scene of several military visits by Napoleon and his army.[5] Already in August 1806, the Vienna court's representative in Venice had reported to the Ministry of Police that he had heard from reliable sources that the Assembly of the Notables of France and Italy had been called at the suggestion of a Bordeaux rabbi – was there a confusion with Furtado? – and aimed at the realisation of far-reaching plans and 'even to the gathering of the Jews in a particular kingdom'.[6] It was therefore very important to check whether Jews of other countries could exert any direct influence on the debates in Paris, and what influence these proceedings could have on the Jews of Austria. The report, with its recommendations, was immediately brought to the attention of the Minister of Foreign Affairs, who was asked to inform the Ministry of Police of any relevant communication it might receive in this connection. It was obviously feared that through the Assembly of the Notables, Napoleon's influence could grow among the Jews of the Austrian Empire, and this was of course unacceptable. The Austrian ambassador in Paris, who was none other than Metternich, was alerted at once and requested to report on the meetings.

On 24 September 1806 he sent in a first report in which he commented on Napoleon's purposes as he interpreted them:[7]

> The impulse has been given: the Israelites of all the lands have their eyes turned to the Messiah who seems to free them from the yoke under which they find themselves; the aim of so many sentences (as it is only that much) is not at all to give full licence to the citizens professing this religion in the lands submitted to French rule, but the desire to prove to the whole nation that its real fatherland is France.

Metternich had obviously been led to this conclusion by the Napoleon-inspired invitation sent to the Jewish communities of Europe asking them to send delegates to Paris. He was not convinced that the convocation of the Sanhedrin had been planned to coincide with Napoleon's renewed campaigns, but he was nevertheless certain that the Emperor would not hesitate to use it in order to present himself not only as the liberator of Poland, but also as the messiah to its numerous Jewish population. Thus the meeting of the Assembly of Notables and of the Sanhedrin could become a threat to the integrity of the Austrian Empire. It was therefore of the utmost importance to prevent any participation by Austrian Jews in the discussions taking place in Paris, and to limit as much as possible the dissemination of information which might cause agitation among the Jews themselves. The fear of such a ferment had become all the greater as the police had heard that a personal invitation to Paris had been sent to one of the foremost members of the Vienna Jewish community, the financier Baron Eskeles. This fact was sufficient to strengthen the fears of the Austrian government.[8]

Despite the strong censorship which had been introduced, the invitation sent by the Paris Assembly to all the Jewish communities of Europe had now become a known fact. The Austrian Emperor therefore asked for a study of the trend of opinion among Austrian Jews, and for a report of the impression made on them by events in Paris. Measures were to be taken to prevent any Austrian Jew from going to Paris during the meetings of the Sanhedrin, and to exercise very strict supervision over foreign Jews who were travelling through the Empire. Interestingly enough, instructions were given to keep watch on the Jewish notables in general, and particularly on 'those who distinguish themselves by their high culture and their situation and separate themselves from orthodoxy'.[9] This would indicate that the Austrian government felt that the danger of French influence would be felt mostly among the philosophers, the enlightened Jews, and not among the ordinary people, and that the group which supported the reformist ideas would be more likely to fall prey to French propaganda. In view of the fact that the first meeting of the Sanhedrin was imminent – nobody expected at the time that it would be delayed so long – it was imperative to act immediately in order to prevent any Austrian participation in the Paris meetings. Metternich himself was asked to report on any eventual Austrian-Jewish participation in the Paris meetings, which meant that the participants would be taken into custody upon their return home.[10]

It was soon reported that the Viennese Jews had shown no great interest or confidence in Napoleon's plans, although there were reports that in Germany proper some Jews had been influenced by the progress in their civil status which the French presence had brought about in some of the occupied regions. Later on, the Austrian police heard of a French spy network which employed a number of Jewish spies all the way from Vienna to Russia: it concluded at once that there was a connection between this activity and what was happening at the time in

Paris on the French government's initiative. It would seem that the Austrian authorities were particularly afraid of eventual difficulties in the southern provinces of the Empire, which were close to the centres of the newly emancipated Italian Jews.[11]

As the Jews of Bohemia and Moravia had enjoyed, since 1797, a status much more favourable than their brethren of the other parts of the Austrian Empire, it was feared that they would be more likely to be won over by French influence. The enlightenment had met much greater success in this part of the Empire than anywhere else. The respective governors were therefore ordered to check on the attitude of the local Jews. They first tried to find out whether these had received any formal invitation to attend the Sanhedrin meetings, but could find no trace of it. They found that Austrian Jews had occasionally received information about the Assembly of Notables and the Sanhedrin's proceedings, but these were in the nature of private letters sent to members of the same family who happened to live in the Austrian territories and in France. It was discovered that rabbis corresponded, and this is how the censorship was able to intercept a letter sent by David Sintzheim to the rabbi of Prague in which he told him his difficulties with the Notables who wanted to overturn all Jewish religious legislation. He had finally managed to have the questions of the Emperor brought before a rabbinic forum, which would meet as a Sanhedrin. This letter was later transmitted to its addressee, as it was not possible to discover anything obnoxious in it.[12] As a matter of fact, the governor agreed that in general the Jewish communities did not wish to associate themselves with the Paris meetings, as they feared that these would result in an alteration of the talmudic teachings and an attack on Jewish religion. Some accused the Paris delegates of having been influenced by Frankist heretical doctrines. A very small number of Bohemian and Moravian Jews expected that the Paris proceedings would exert a positive influence on the evolution of Judaism. Others went as far as declaring that the granting of citizens' rights in exchange for the abandonment of the Talmud would be tantamount in their eyes to a conversion to Christianity. It would seem that very soon rumours had begun to circulate concerning Napoleon's plans to limit the civic and economic rights of the French Jews: the last hopes for a strengthening of French influence were thus definitely condemned.[13]

The Jews of Trieste nevertheless seem to have remained rather enthusiastic about the projected meetings in Paris. It is likely that their long-lasting relationship with the Jewish communities of Italy had convinced them that they belonged more to the Judaism of the peninsula than to the great community of the Austrian Empire. Whatever may have been the case, they were subjected to very strict supervision on behalf of the Austrian government. Some local Jews, who had been suspected of wanting to attend the Paris meetings, were especially watched. It would seem that the Vienna government's fears were not unjustified, as the Illyrian departments, including that of Trieste, were later annexed by France. The Code Napoléon was of course introduced. As a logical consequence of French law, the Jews of this region were organised within the consistorial system, as all other Jewish communities within the French Empire. This was to last as long as the Empire survived.[14]

As for Galicia, its Austrian governor had no difficulty reporting that the local Jews had shown practically no interest in what was going on in Paris: he wrote to the Minister of Police that 'the orthodox as well as the Chasidim are absolutely stupid and bound to the Torah and the Talmud.' They felt that the Sanhedrin constituted a grave threat to Judaism. Only a few enlightened Jews from Brody had shown some interest in the events in Paris, and had had to be cautioned. In general, the governor felt that the Polish Christian populace were much more likely to be influenced by Napoleon's policies, which aimed at the re-establishment of Polish independence, than the Galician Jews, who were rather frightened by the whole affair.[15]

The Austrian government had over-estimated the possible repercussions of the Sanhedrin's meetings on the major European Jewish communities. Its nervousness contrasts with the composure of the Jewish populace. Very probably, it had been over-impressed by the vocal claims of the enlightened elements of the community and had not assessed the narrow limits of their influence. It is true that fear of Napoleon's ambitions and the general demand for greater civic rights which followed the French Revolution had compelled it to show greater caution than ever before in its treatment of such problems. One fact remains nevertheless clear: because of, or perhaps despite, the government's fears, no Austrian Jew took part in any of the proceedings at Paris.

This does not mean in the least that the Jewish leadership was unaware of what was going on. As has already been shown, Moses Schreiber, better known as *Chatham Sofer*, who was then the rabbi of Pressburg, and already the undisputed leader of the orthodox camp in its fight against reform, kept in touch with David Sintzheim whom he had known in his youth, probably in Frankfurt. He showed great admiration for the latter's handling of the Paris meetings, and applauded him for not having yielded to the demands of the Emperor. Very probably he must have approved of the way in which Sintzheim always succeeded in rooting in rabbinic tradition the answers which were to be given to the twelve questions. It is a fact that after Sintzheim's death he made a point, despite the considerable distance and the aversion of the Austrian government from any show of sympathy for what was happening in Paris, of publicly pronouncing a eulogy as soon as he heard of his death. This would prove that the attitude of orthodox circles toward the Paris meeting was less uniform than had been reported by the different provincial governors.[16]

Less surprisingly, Aaron Chorin, the rabbi of Arad, who was a strong supporter of changes within the Jewish tradition and who had always felt that a rabbinical synod would be empowered to decree such changes, wrote to Abraham Furtado on 9 September 1806, expressing his joy at hearing of the meeting of the Paris assembly, and at the Emperor's fatherly advice to the Jews to take up useful crafts. He was certain that the Assembly would not hesitate to purify the Jewish religion and he felt that the Paris meeting would merit the opportunity it was offered, and would prove a guiding light for the other Jewish communities of the world.[17]

It is difficult to find a better illustration of the contradictory reactions to which the Paris meeting gave rise: the head of the orthodox party and one of the first reformers approved of them for opposing reasons. Each found in them reasons for satisfaction, either because the integrity of the Jewish heritage had been preserved, or because they promised great changes in a purified Jewish tradition.

Prussia, in north-eastern Germany, despite its bitter defeat at the hands of Napoleon, had managed to remain outside the French zone of influence. Considerably diminished by the Peace of Tilsit, it finally resolved to enact those reforms which had now become indispensable in order to create a new feeling of national unity. The aim was to give the populace a feeling of participation in the nation without losing the support of the nobility. A moderate revolution was to take place, which would have to be visible enough to enlist popular support without alienating the established ruling classes. This also applied to the Jewish population of Prussia which was eager to take part in the rebuilding of the country. Already in 1808 the tolerated Jewish inhabitants of the Prussian cities had received municipal rights, and could thereby vote or be elected to office in municipal elections. This did not mean that they received the same rights on the national scene. It nevertheless encouraged them to ask for full emancipation, although it must be remembered that by that time Napoleon's Infamous Decree had already been published and that what could have been construed as the irresistible social and legal progress of the Jews towards full emancipation seemed now less assured than had been thought before. Nevertheless the influence of Paris was still to be strongly felt in this respect.

The promoters of the new measures felt that any advancement in the condition of the Jews would automatically bring with it a weakening of the communal and national ties which so strongly united the Jews, and that this in itself was a desirable end. If there had been hitherto an inescapable connection between the lowly state of the Jews and their religion, what would happen if this status were to be transformed in a favourable sense? If baptism was to remain an indispensable condition for the marriage of a

Jew and a Christian, there could be no possibility of a change in Jewish separatism and their entry into modern society would be delayed. It was thereupon decided that a change in the Jews' status was imperative, and that civic rights should be granted to them. They would be requested to accept at once all the civic duties which were incumbent on Prussian citizens, such as the obligation to perform military service. The Jews should stop perpetuating themselves as a nation within the nation. As in France, however, there was a difference of opinion whether equality of rights should come as a recognition of the Jews' efforts to conform to the ways of the dominant Christian society, or as an inducement to do so: very often positions were taken up on this problem not as the consequence of any serious study, but according to established prejudice for or against the Jews.

After protracted discussions, the edict regulating the Jews' civic rights in the Prussian state was finally published on 11 March 1812. It proclaimed the citizenship of all legal Jewish inhabitants of the kingdom. All restrictions concerning their freedom of movement and the trades, arts and crafts they would want to enter were lifted. They could now assume municipal or academic functions or dignities, although the problem of their entrance into the Prussian state's civil service was set aside for further study. As far as duties were concerned, the Jews were proclaimed the equals of their fellow-citizens. They would now have to serve in the army. The use of Hebrew or Yiddish in business documents was prohibited. Within six months all Prussian Jews would have to adopt family names, and to inform the public authorities of their choice. The settlement of foreign Jews in Prussia remained forbidden, and they could only stay in the country temporarily for business purposes.[18]

All these measures showed a strong nationalist tendency. Expulsion and persecution of the Jews having become in practice impossible in the modern era, the state must deal with them as if they were either a temporary, or a permanent but downtrodden, element in the state. This being so, it became important to prevent a great increase in the size of the Jewish population, which would have to be maintained at a low percentage of the general population. This made measures limiting the immigration of Jews mandatory. Thus the principle of discrimination was maintained, although an attempt was made to make the life of the local Jews more tolerable. The autonomous organisation of the Jewish community was dismembered in order to turn it into a purely religious system. This of course would eventually involve the abandonment of these characteristics of the Jewish religion which could be construed as separatist, such as the prayers for the return to Zion, or the use of Hebrew, as well as the setting up of a school system where Jewish and general studies would be combined. The universal use of the German language became imperative as well as the constant expression of love and devotion to the German fatherland. This was a price many enlightened Jews felt was not exorbitant. They were ready to pay it, and did not hesitate to say so. It is difficult to know what the populace really felt: in Prussia, as in the other great Jewish communities of Europe, they could hardly express themselves, even when they felt that enlightened spokesmen or authors barely represented them. It is nevertheless a fact that a sizeable number of Jews volunteered for service in the Prussian army and thus expressed their approval for the policies of their government. Still their emancipation was not complete: Prussia had chosen to make its fulfilment conditional on their assimilation into the German nation. This most probably did not mean that they were expected to become Christians, but that everything would be done to induce the Jews to resemble Christians as much as possible.

This was then an indirect consequence of the French Revolution and of Napoleon's policies. The spirit of the time had not left the Prussian authorities at liberty to choose their own independent path to a solution of their national Jewish problem: everything they did was done in the shadow of the French Emperor, even when they felt that they had to oppose some of the measures he had taken. It is nevertheless interesting to see how this new mood was used in accordance with the needs of resurgent Prussian nationalism.

The Russian, no more than the Prussian, government could afford to ignore the new current of ideas which had emerged in

Paris in 1806. No less than the Austrian government it was considerably perturbed by what was happening at the Great Sanhedrin's meetings in Paris. It was precisely at that time that Napoleon's disquieting proximity began to be feared in Eastern Europe: he had appeared on the Lithuanian border and taken the threatening step of re-creating Polish independence in the guise of the Duchy of Warsaw. He was now too close to Russia's borders to be easily dismissed. The very fact that a general invitation had been addressed to non-French European Jewish communities to attend the Paris meetings only served to increase and sharpen Russian suspicion: was not Napoleon planning to influence in his favour the great Jewish population of Eastern Europe? It therefore became urgent to take appropriate measures in order to ensure the Jews' loyalty, or at least their neutrality, toward the Russian fatherland.[19]

A law enacted in 1804 had prepared the resettlement of a considerable part of Russian Jewry in a number of regions: this step was looked upon with great dismay by the numerous Jews whose means of existence and ways of life would be endangered by this enforced migration. In the opinion of a number of civil servants, such a step would only throw the Jews into the arms of Napoleon: the timing of this far-reaching measure was definitely dangerous, and should therefore be changed. Representative meetings of the Jews of the different regions concerned were summoned in the provincial capitals in order to consider the best means of enforcing the 1804 law. This was an invitation to delay, as the collecting of opinions and their discussion would take time. The Russian government was ready for this, and the projected transfer of population was duly delayed.

At the same time, the Russian government ordered that any contact between the Russian Jews and the Paris Sanhedrin be prevented, as this could constitute a future threat to Russia. It is remarkable that the Russian government chose to impress on the Jews that the Paris proceedings were a threat to the integrity of Judaism, the tenets of which it was rumoured it intended to modify. The Holy Synod issued circulars to the clergy in order to inform the Russian people that Napoleon was an enemy of Christianity and a friend of the Jews: he had assembled the Jewish synagogue in Paris to put the Church to shame. He had not hesitated to revive the Sanhedrin, that is, the body which had ordered, according to traditional church teaching, the crucifixion of Jesus. Now he planned to unite all the Jews, whom the Almighty had seen fit to scatter all over the earth, in order to undermine and overthrow the Church, and to have himself proclaimed as the Messiah. Thus the meeting of the Sanhedrin could be interpreted, according to need, as a way to improve the lot of the Jews, or to weaken their faith through the imposition of reforms.

These measures, inspired by the fear of Napoleon, seemed to announce a softening of official Russian policy toward the Jews, whom it had become necessary to save from Napoleon's influence. The signing of the Peace of Tilsit in July 1807 was to change this course of events, as the Tsar was convinced that a clash between France and Russia had been avoided and that Napoleon would now recognise the integrity of the Russian zone of influence. The fears relating to the Jews had now become out of place. As early as 19 October 1807, the Tsar stated that the circumstances which had complicated, and caused a suspension of, the transfer of the Jews had ceased to prevail. The original policy could now be resumed in order to have the re-settlement of the Jews completed by 1810. The brutality of the decision was such that it had again to be suspended at the end of 1808 pending new Imperial instructions. All of this was decided with complete disregard for the general trend of opinion in Western and Central Europe, which aimed at the complete integration of Jews, even where there was debate whether the Jews already deserved the improvement of their condition or not. But soon the danger of a French invasion was to reappear, and the Russian government decided to concentrate more on the strengthening of national unity than on pursuing its discriminatory policy against the Jews. The re-settlement scheme was once more temporarily shelved.

Most of the fighting and skirmishing during the French invasion of Russia took place in that part of Russia which was densely inhabited by the Jews, who could not abstain from taking up one position or another. The treatment they were suffering at the time at the hands of the Russians should have made them more than receptive to the French influence. It is nevertheless a fact that this was not the case. The leaders of Russian Jewry with very few exceptions took up a position hostile to Napoleon. Rabbi Shneur Zalman from Ladi, the founder of Lubavitch Chasidism, wrote to Moses Meisels, one of his supporters, a letter in which he recounted an apparition, in which he had been told:[20]

> If Bonaparte wins, wealth will increase in Israel, and the glory of Israel will be raised, but the heart of Israel will be separated and estranged from their Father in Heaven. But if our Lord Alexander should win, even though poverty will increase in Israel, and its glory be lowered, the hearts of Israel will be bound, fastened and tied to their Father in Heaven. This shall be the sign: soon the longing of your heart shall be taken away. Soon some of our brethren, the children of Israel, shall be drafted into the army ...

This rather cryptic prophecy which seems to have been written in the autumn of 1811 leaves nevertheless no room for doubt. In Shneur Zalman's view the only important value in life was complete and utter devotion to Judaism and to the fulfilment of its teachings. Any other consideration was of secondary importance. Any advancement in the Jewish condition could be judged by this sole standard: did it threaten, directly or indirectly, the integrity of Jewish belief and observance? If it did so, a régime of discrimination and bitter poverty was infinitely preferable to any change. Shneur Zalman had very clear views about Napoleon's policies, and condemned therefore any form of support of the French invaders, who brought with them opinions which were definitely dangerous for the orthodox Russian Jewish community. This is a far cry from the Russian patriotism which has occasionally been held responsible for Jewish resistance to Napoleon and his army!

During the pursuit of Napoleon's retreating troops, two Jews, Sundel Sonnenberg from Grodno and Eliezer Dillon of Nezwitz, very often stayed at the Russian army's headquarters. It would seem that this was due to their function as suppliers of the Russian forces, and to their usefulness as go-betweens linking headquarters and the Jewish communities. As happened so often in the past, these two functions were somewhat mixed, the representatives of the Jews using their commercial and economic activity to enhance the cause of their brethren, and the businessmen using their Jewish connections to find the necessary supplies. Anyway, they communicated with the army and informed it of the wishes of the various Jewish communities. On the other hand, the government found it convenient to use them in order to convince the Jews not to succumb to French influence. The needs of the large Russian army in its advance through Europe justified this new leniency toward the Jewish communities, which seemed to proclaim a general if limited change for the better in the Tsar's policies. It is quite possible that he had intended to introduce such a change, but had to abandon his plan as a result of the great changes which were to take place in post-Napoleonic Europe.

The quasi-unanimous opposition of Russian Jewry to Napoleon, although it had no reason at all to feel any loyalty toward a ruler and a country which had so greatly contributed to their debasement, is rather surprising. The question may well be asked why this happened, and in what light Russian Jewry saw the French Emperor. Their attitude differed considerably from that of the leadership of the Polish Jews. This was probably due to the fact that Russian Jewry had not yet been touched by the Enlightenment. Nobody was really asking for civic and political rights. Religious dissension did not separate the enlightened from the orthodox, but the Chasidim from their opponents. They did not yet conceive of the possibility of obtaining improvement in their status through the influence of the new philosophic trends. On the other hand, the quest for a revolution, as a substitute for the disappointment resulting from thwarted social improvements, did not yet exist.

If their major fear was that the whole structure of Jewish communal life ran the danger of being disrupted and destroyed, the Russian Jews could certainly not have accused Napoleon of pursuing this aim: just the opposite. A great part of his legislative action aimed to re-create these communal and even national structures, through the national and regional consistories, which imposed a common organisation on all the Jews of a given region or country, and recognised the pre-eminent role of the rabbinate. The religious organisation had thus become the only recognised mouthpiece of the community, and was immune to dissident manoeuvres or tendencies. These the central government could only frown upon, as it did not countenance any schism in a recognised community. Napoleon's policies should therefore have met with at least a small measure of approval.

It would seem then, that Napoleon appeared in the East, not so much as the reorganiser, although a rather hostile one, of the Jewish community, but as the bearer of the ideals of the French Revolution, which, in the opinion of the Russian Jewish leadership, could only spell the decline of Russian Jewry. They had heard of incipient anarchy in the German-Jewish community, where centrifugal forces had been set free and could only attribute this to French influence. It thus happened that the French-Jewish leaders, who had fought for the preservation of the integrity of the Jewish faith, were accused, by an ironic twist, of having condoned the very changes Sintzheim and his rabbinic friends had opposed. It was not the Sanhedrin as such which aroused opposition, but all those changes which were taking place at this time in Western and Central Europe. The opposition to Napoleon thus became an aspect of the opposition to Enlightenment and to the philosophers' ideas, but with no specific reference to what had been decided in Paris.[21]

CHAPTER IX

The Results

Whatever his real intentions may have been, and despite his undoubted aversion to the Jews, Napoleon's systematic regulation of Jewish life must be looked upon as a turning-point in the long history of Judaism. Detached from the religious, political and economic reasons which were the determining factors which brought it about and which were soon to fade away, these far-reaching decisions were to mould the life of most Western Jewish communities during the nineteenth and twentieth centuries. As such, they deserve to be examined, apart from the resolutions of the Assembly of Notables and the Sanhedrin as independent decisions, which were to stand in many ways the test of time, even when isolated from the personality of their initiator.

The sudden irruption of French Jewry into the modern world for which it was completely unprepared, the fact that the Revolution of 1789 had chosen to declare the irrevocable unity of mankind, the helplessness of the Jewish populace suddenly extricated from the traditional bonds of autonomy, the compulsion to become a part of the modern state, the general advance of religious scepticism, were some of the reasons which compelled French Jewry to consider possible modes of existence in the modern free world. Granted equality, it could no longer escape the obligation to define itself alongside the dominant

Christian religions. A new definition of Judaism was inescapable, inasmuch as a return to Jewish autonomy was impossible as a consequence of Christian, or rather French, opposition to the ways of the *ancien régime* which were construed as anti-revolutionary, and as the result of Jewish reluctance to return to an abhorred past, which it had no reason to regret. There was no possibility, and, most probably, no intention, of reviving the past. That is why a new approach to Judaism had become indispensable.

The very personality of Napoleon, which overshadowed all the changes which took place in his time, may have been the reason for the optical illusion which attributed to him the whole merit, or demerit, of the new organisation of Judaism. The fact that in 1815, at the Congress of Vienna, the reaction against his policies was so violent, and finally brought about a radical change in the condition of the Jews of many countries who were suddenly deprived of all the benefits of citizenship, helped to reinforce this error: if Napoleon's policies toward the Jews were reversed after his fall, would this not be clear proof that whatever had been achieved in his lifetime was due to his personal action, and must therefore decay and disappear with his own exit from the world scene? This view ignores the fact that the consistorial system was not only maintained, but even prospered, in France after the Emperor's fall. It was condemned in those countries where it had been imposed by force of arms. Wherever the progress in the Jews' status had been reached without the intervention of Napoleon or the French army, it was generally maintained and consolidated.

In France, the progress of the consistorial system was continuous. The Infamous Decree of 1808 had been enacted for a period of ten years and it was intended to review the matter at the end of this interval. As this date approached, the Central Consistory acted in order to prevent any positive action being taken in the new Parliament. It met with considerable success in this endeavour, and the year 1818 passed without the Decree being extended, and without any hostile intervention from the Bourbon régime. As a matter of fact, the Bourbons, upon their return to France in 1814 and 1815, did not try to abolish the consistorial system, or to bring about any change in the French Jews' situation. The new régime recognised the Central Consistory as an official body, and the king gave it the public recognition of an official reception at his court, which Napoleon had always tried to avoid.[1] It was only in Alsace that there was a short-lived attempt in 1814 on the part of the local Jews to suppress the consistorial system in the wake of Napoleon's defeat: the Central Consistory reacted very quickly and showed the Alsatian Jews that any radical change would only be to its detriment.[2] This was to be the last and rather feeble attempt to suppress the consistorial system in France. It is not even certain that this attempt was intended to have the consistorial system changed and not rather to reach some accommodation over the problem of the Jewish loans.

Not until 1831 did the Jewish religion secure financial equality with the other French cults: only then was it decided to have the salaries of the rabbis paid by the state. The abolition of the oath *more judaico* was somewhat longer in coming: it was finally done away with, after considerable legal wrangling, in 1846. From then on and until 1905, when the French state finally became separated from religion, and the official status which had been granted to the recognised religions in continental France came to an end, French Jews enjoyed complete equality with the other official religions. But even after the new French Jewish community chose to keep the old titles and names: the regional consistory became the consistorial association, and the chief rabbis carried on with their duties. In those parts of France – Alsace and Lorraine – which were under German rule when separation took place in 1905, the old system was maintained after their reunion with France, and the Jews kept their consistories until today. The system had shown great resilience in France and in the new kingdom of Belgium which had also accepted it, and its popularity remained widespread. But even in those countries in Western and Central Europe which had rejected it through coercion or by free choice, its influence remained very strong for a considerable time.

There can be no doubt that the consistorial reorganisation of Jewish life, even if its more apparent cause was Napoleon's decision to regulate the working of the Jewish community, was intended to be an answer to the new problems which confronted the Jewish population as a consequence of its emancipation. Until that time there had been little place for doubt as to the importance of the Jewish community for Jewish life. Jewish identity implied membership of the Jewish community, as no Jewish existence was possible outside of it. As far as the Gentile world was concerned, the Jew existed only as a member of his community. In this way there was more than a measure of truth in the saying that they constituted a nation within the nation, or perhaps a nation alongside the nation. They had definitely succeeded in creating a Jewish cultural world, with its own standards and ideals of conduct, which recognised the standards of the Gentile world only inasmuch as they were compelled to do so. Their achievements, whether material or spiritual, were judged according to their own set of values, which attributed great weight to intellectual excellence. There can be no doubt that despite their legal and material decadence, the Jews were deeply convinced of their moral and intellectual superiority over the Gentiles. This was true as long as Judaism remained a closed world, which was not allowed to communicate with the Gentile environment, and did not even wish to do so. It had a problem of survival, but not of co-existence with other groups or faiths. With the French Revolution, this not so splendid isolation was condemned and the Jews as such were thrown into the open and democratic society into which they could not bring the traditional ways and institutions of their lost autonomous status.

The new revolutionary society had proclaimed the freedom of all French citizens and resolved, as a consequence, that there should also be full freedom of religion, on condition that its exercise did not disturb public order. Judaism was to be considered as one of the legitimate faiths allowed in the Republic, and later, in the Empire. It was therefore unavoidable that Judaism should be looked upon as a religion, and not as a nation or a closed society. The old characteristics of the pre-revolutionary Jewish communities were considered remnants of the oppressive régime under which they had suffered. Freed from the shackles of the past, Judaism would join the modern world as the equal of the other great religions. The parable of Nathan the Wise had finally become reality.

The result was to be a general trend towards the Christianisation of Judaism, which was encouraged by the representatives of the political power as well as by the new Jewish leadership. Napoleon's whole consistorial system was a definite attempt to give a Christian structure to the new Jewish organisation. A Jewish church was established side by side with the Christian church. There is no reason to believe that this was done with hostile intentions: Napoleon looked at Judaism with Christian eyes because he was unable to do otherwise. This becomes quite obvious in his thinking about the leadership of the new Jewish community.

In pre-revolutionary French Jewish communities the role of the rabbinate was of rather minor importance. The real leadership of the Jewish nation belonged to its lay leadership. Without going to the extremes of the Bordeaux community which treated its rabbis in a most cavalier fashion, there can be little doubt as to the real influence of the rabbis in the different communities. Even in Metz, a community which made a point of, and succeeded in, securing famous rabbis, rabbinic influence was limited: the rabbi was foremost a judge and a teacher, and could in no way be compared to the head of a parish, still less to a bishop. He was the foremost authority in judicial and ritual matters, and usually acted only when called upon to do so. He was estranged from the actual communal leadership, and had nothing to do with the political negotiations the community would occasionally enter upon in order to obtain a renewal or a strengthening of its privileges. Whenever he was consulted on problems of taxation, he was requested in his judicial function to ascertain whether an aggrieved taxpayer had been discriminated against or not; but even then, the community usually tried to reserve this matter to a select committee which was empowered to take a final decision. His function as a spiritual leader was of very little consequence as there were few spiritual problems in the community: crises of identity were unknown and nobody seriously put in doubt the authority of Jewish tradition. Very often he could be defined as the best expert in judicial and talmudic matters the community could hire, whose decisions it agreed to heed in these and other purely religious problems.

The real power remained therefore in the hands of the lay leadership, which took upon itself all political and financial responsibilities. By contrast with the rabbinate, which, despite the fact that there existed rabbinic families, always remained open to newcomers distinguished for their intellectual activities, this leadership was reserved to an oligarchy of wealthy businessmen and money-lenders. This somewhat secondary role of the rabbinate was inherent in its origin: after all, rabbis, contrary to Catholic ecclesiastics, had no priestly functions and could not be looked upon as real members of the clergy. They were, foremost, teachers, people who knew what the teachings of Judaism were and were able to apply them to the concrete problems they were confronted with.

This aspect of Judaism was unknown to the Christian lawyers who dealt with the Jewish problem on Napoleon's instructions. This explains the questions put to the Assembly about the functions and the training of the rabbinate: it was difficult for them to understand that there were rabbis who did not exercise any function in a synagogue or a larger community, and they wanted therefore to be reassured about their duties.

In the first draft of the consistorial regulations, Napoleon's advisers had proposed the establishment in Paris of a central committee of rabbis, which would supervise and serve as the leadership of the Jews of the Empire. This was of course consonant with the Christian point of view of Napoleon, who could not imagine any other religious leadership of a religious community than that of its ordained ministers. The commissioners, headed by Molé, who discussed the problem of the Jewish organisation with the Committee of Nine understood how mistaken this point of view was, and how much easier it would be to come to an agreement with the lay leadership composed of such people as Furtado or Lazard. They had therefore decided for 'the good of the service of His Majesty to introduce some Jews who were not rabbis into this committee.' They had felt, they added, that it could prove dangerous to leave the supervision of the synagogues exclusively to 'men who constitute among themselves a kind of corporation', and whose virtually exclusive mastery of a particular language – this was an allusion to the rabbinic Hebrew used in their writings – would enable them to evade any kind of police or administrative control in their activities within the community or in their relations with other bodies. The introduction of non-rabbinic members into this committee would annul any plots or attempts to disobey the Emperor's orders. This measure, it was noted, would prove very popular among many Jews who were afraid of rabbinic influence and were eager to counterbalance it. This was obviously an echo of the well-known tendencies of the Portuguese communities, which looked upon the rabbinate as one of the community's institutions, but not as its leadership. The commissioners added nevertheless that even the more religious, that is the more practising, Jews did not wish to fall under the exclusive authority of the rabbis. Thus they also presented the view of the north-eastern communities.[3]

Their opinion, which had been acquired during their dealings with the members of the Committee of Nine, was not accepted by the Emperor, at least as far as the central board of the proposed Jewish organisation was concerned. He had already shown in the summoning of the Sanhedrin the great importance he attached to a purely religious sanction for the Assembly's decisions. Although he accepted the addition of a number of lay members to the future Central Consistory, he finally decided that it should retain a rabbinic majority. Thus it was decided that it would be composed of three rabbinic members and two lay representatives, its chairman being its oldest member. This was tantamount to handing over permanent chairmanship to a rabbi, as age was usually an important consideration in their choice. David Sintzheim chaired, as the Ancien – this was the chairman's official title – the Central Consistory until his death in 1812. When Segré, one of his two Italian rabbinic colleagues, died in 1809, he was replaced immediately by another rabbi, Asher Lion, the son of the late rabbi of Metz, the *Shaagat Arieh*, who was then rabbi of a German community. He later changed his mind and did not come to Paris.[4] Emmanuel Deutz, then rabbi of Coblenz, was thereupon appointed rabbinic member of the Central Consistory and accepted. It is clear that Sintzheim, who had fought against the increasing influence of the enlightened lay leadership, had refused to give up the principle of rabbinic majority and authority in religious affairs: after his death a great argument broke out which was to last over a quarter of a century as to the measure of rabbinic influence in Jewish life. The lay element did whatever it could to limit and diminish it and to return to the old usage whereby one rabbi supervised the religious life of the community and a number of lay people were in charge of all its other interests. Little did they understand that in a society which would see in Judaism only a religion, this would ineluctably give the rabbi in the long run a position of dominance and reduce the lay leadership to a secondary role in the synagogue. In the regional consistories which, according to law, were to be composed of five members, three lay members and two rabbis, the matter was settled right away: the notables elected only one rabbinic member, the chief rabbi, and forgot about the second, who was later replaced by a fourth lay member. In the Central Consistory the argument was protracted. With Sintzheim's death, the rabbinic part of the Central Consistory was now reduced to two members: Cologna and Deutz who did not, or could not, decide to use their influence to have him replaced and to keep the rabbinic majority in being. It thus happened that they continued to officiate as if nothing had happened. When the Empire fell, they were both in the strange position of having been appointed to the Central Consistory from regions which were no longer a part of France. Very probably this did not help their authority.

The diminution of the Central Consistory's sphere of influence brought about very serious financial problems, as it became impossible for French Jewry alone to provide for the salaries of three or two chief rabbis of the Central Consistory. It was therefore agreed not to replace the next chief rabbi who would leave office. Thus, after 1826, when Cologna chose to return to Italy, Deutz remained the only rabbinic member of the Central Consistory. Thrift helped the lay leadership to reduce the rabbinate's influence. It is quite possible that Deutz's domestic difficulties and his resulting lack of influence played into the hands of the lay leadership.[5] Ironically enough, the result was that this establishment of a rabbinic hierarchy helped to enhance its status, as the chief rabbi, at the local and the national level, became the obvious parallel of the bishop or the archbishop. Thus another step was taken in the transformation of Judaism into a religion which was inspired by the Christian model.

It is true that the whole organisation of the rabbinate was changing very quickly, as the community itself was discarding the remnants of the ancient structures which had been in use till the French Revolution. It had given up in the wake of emancipation all the traditional forms of Jewish autonomy. Its right to raise funds through taxes was now limited to the satisfaction of its religious needs. The judicial authority of the rabbinate had disappeared with its recognition of the validity of national laws. This implied full recognition of the French courts: no Jew could be compelled any more to be judged by the Jewish court. The religious sanction of the *Herem*, the ban of excommunication, had also disappeared: in an open society it could no longer be enforced, as no Jew would now be entirely dependent upon the Jewish community for his economic and social survival. He would always be able to manage with the help of his Christian friends. The monopoly of Jewish culture and learning had been undermined also, as schools and universities had opened their doors to Jewish youth. The prestige of the old learned class suffered greatly from this revolution, as the gap between the old and the young increased, and the possibility of any understanding became scarce. In such conditions the Western rabbinate could not avoid changing its old ways in order to regain a measure of influence. It could no longer be satisfied with administering justice, but would have to try to keep in the Jewish fold those who were now beginning to leave. This danger could not be underestimated. In the best known and well-established families, conversion to Christianity was becoming a serious problem, not so much as the result of a new religious awakening, but because in the eyes of many of their sons this was the normal result of an evolution which had brought the Jews into a Christian society, or at least into a Christian-oriented open society, and thus removed from the dominating religion many of its more offensive features. It was precisely the members of those families who had felt the dangers and the occasional agony of emancipation who requested a change in the activity and the training of the rabbinate.

Thus rabbis had to become the spiritual leaders of their communities. Whereas they had been judges and the teachers of the higher classes of the *yeshivah* they would now become the expounders and vindicators of Jewish religion. A problem of communication had arisen, as young and old no longer even spoke the same language. As a result the consistories were quick to require that their rabbis command a fluent knowledge of French and receive an education which would enable them to communicate with their flock. This was of course a violent criticism of the old methods of learning. The need had arisen for special training schools for rabbis, that is, for seminaries, which would be distinct from the old *yeshivah*, professional schools. The *yeshivah* had tried to give learning, whereas the new theological school would now train rabbis. The Central Consistory did its best to set up a rabbinic seminary and repeatedly petitioned the Minister of Religion for his agreement to its opening. Despite its failure, the Consistory prepared the opening of the French rabbinic school which was inaugurated in Metz in 1829. Its opening had become all the more urgent as a consequence of another change which was taking place in the rabbinate. The new spiritual leader could not hope to have much of an influence if the rabbinate were to preserve its old structure, when there was only one rabbi to a region. He could not fulfil the new duties that devolved upon him, as these involved a personal relationship with the members of his community. On the other hand, the former Jewish settlement had lost much of its density as more and more Jews began to leave their traditional districts and take up residence in neighbourhoods and in cities which up to now had been closed to them. The combination of these two different causes necessitated a radical increase in the number of rabbis: very soon there would be a rapid evolution from the communal rabbinate to the synagogue rabbinate, as every house of prayer in the larger communities required to have its own spiritual leader. This made the need for an institutional training of the rabbis even more imperative, and made the opening of specialised seminaries urgent. All western and central Europe was to recognise this need during the whole of the nineteenth century.

Such an evolution, and the pressures which caused it, should have brought with it a decided move toward reform, as the new relationship between flock and pastor was compelling the latter to understand and try to satisfy the new needs, and deal with the new remoteness from the Jewish tradition. In France, it should also have brought about a disruption of the old rabbinic unanimity, which was content with the teachings and practice of Judaism as it had received them. It was the very consistorial system which prevented the fragmentation of French Jewry. Its centralised and hierarchical organisation, no less than its recognition by the state as the sole legitimate spokesman of the Jewish community, did not allow it to countenance, whatever the personal opinion of its leaders, the possibility of a break-up in the Jewish community. Every effort had to be made to preserve at least the semblance of unity, and the internal discipline of the community. Through all of its existence, the consistorial system remained devoted to the ideal of the integrated community. Therefore extreme orthodoxy and extreme reform were looked upon as alien to the spirit of Judaism in the modern world. Despite the dissatisfaction of many of its leaders with the situation of Jewish religion in their time, they opposed the creation of liberal congregations, which would reject fully or in part the authority of the chief rabbinate. It is not surprising to note in this connection that the first liberal congregation of French Jews was set up only *after* the consistorial system had lost its official and legal authority, after the separation of church and state which took place in 1905, nearly a hundred years after the Napoleonic enactments. There can be no doubt that the state-controlled organisation of the Jewish religion spared it the schisms which were to plague other communities, but made it pay the price of conformism. On the other hand, most of the arguments as to the adaptation of Judaism to modern society were conducted within the secret councils of the consistories, which tried to press upon the rabbinate the need to take an initiative in this matter, and attempted through its influence to reach general agreement over the changes desired. This very often put the chief rabbi in the delicate position of having to mediate between the demands of the lay membership of the consistories and the opposition of the rabbinate. Nevertheless, the general desire for unity remained supreme.

As a consequence of the end of Jewish autonomy, the community had lost many of its powers. In more than one way, the need to repay the debts of the different Jewish communities which had been contracted before the Revolution had allowed it to keep a measure of control over the descendants of their former membership, who were required to pay their share of the common debt. The communities found themselves in the odd position of having to prevent their members from slipping away, even as participation in the life of the community had become more and more voluntary. Very soon it would become possible to remain faithful to Judaism without having to become a member of any of its institutions. Even where the authority of the consistory was accepted, it hardly extended further than the obligation to pay regular dues. The consistory and the consistorial rabbinate had been deprived of the power of excommunication, and had practically no possibility of preventing a Jew who claimed to belong to the Jewish faith from joining its ranks, whatever the laxity or the scandal of his religious life. Only apostasy could be considered a good enough reason to refuse his membership, as this kind of double loyalty would have been looked upon as unacceptable to Judaism and to Christianity. Even when a case of mixed marriage was involved, it could not intervene, or even condemn it. The declaration of the Sanhedrin, which had followed the deliberations of the Assembly of Notables, and recognised the validity of civil marriages as far as the law of the country was concerned, had in no way created the problem of mixed marriages: it constituted the recognition of a new situation. Before the French Revolution and the introduction of civil marriage, mixed marriages had been an impossibility, a legal nonsense, as it was impossible to marry two persons who did not belong to the same faith: one of them would have had to convert to the other's religion in order to allow them to marry. This was not necessary any more. As a consequence, mixed marriages, which did not involve apostasy on either side, had become possible. Their number grew without any possibility of counter-action, except moral persuasion, on the part of the community.

The community was no less powerless when it came to the refusal or neglect of religious divorces. In May 1810, the Central Consistory, which was still presided over by Sintzheim, was consulted on this matter: a Jewish woman, whose husband had been jailed for some obscure reason, had obtained a civil divorce from him and was now remarrying a Jew without the benefit of a religious divorce. This of course raised a considerable scandal. The Central Consistory, which strongly deplored the fact, wrote that it could not intervene directly as it could not throw any suspicion on the validity of a civil divorce which was legal according to civil law. It recommended rabbinic persuasion in order to re-introduce respect for Jewish law, but without casting any aspersion on the validity of civil law.[6] It had thus become the prisoner of its own system, and was now destined to suffer all the disabilities of a minority religion.

There can be no doubt that this situation did not in any way increase the prestige of Judaism, which had by now been reduced to the rank of a religion comparable to all other recognised religions, while losing the authority over its members with which a long tradition of autonomy had invested it. Completely unprepared for its entry into French society, which had taken it by surprise, it was unable to resist the lure of contemporary French culture. This not only seemed richer, but its acquisition was also a guarantee of advancement in French society thanks to the recognition it gave to intellectual prowess, notably through the system of the *grandes écoles* which recruited the intellectual and technical leadership of the nation. The weakening of Jewish loyalty, combined with the attraction of general Christian-oriented culture, did not strengthen the resistance to the attraction of Christianity: conversion was soon to become a serious problem. It was now all the more dangerous as the disappearance of Jewish autonomy had also broken down the wall which had separated Judaism and Christianity, and had so long made social relations between the Jewish and apostate members of the same family practically impossible. It had become very difficult to condemn conversion in derogatory terms, as it could now involve the condemnation of another religion, the legitimacy of which was guaranteed by the state which had recognised it.

The whole ideal of the existence of different religions within the same state, the recognition of the validity of civil law, the granting of civic and political rights were all based on the conviction that not only were there no irreconcilable oppositions between the spirit of Judaism and the national civilisation, but that these were in fact absolutely compatible and even complementary. Judaism and French culture not only were not opposed, but should constitute together an almost perfect synthesis of what was best in human culture. The same would of course hold true of Judaism and German culture, or Judaism and Italian culture. Patriotism, and even chauvinism, became therefore one of the highest and most esteemed virtues. In all the Western countries which had granted recognition to Judaism, religion and patriotism were to mingle in such a way as to become nearly inseparable. The duty to one's fatherland was equated with the highest religious duty. It is not by accident that 'Patrie-Religion' became the new motto of the Central Consistory!

There can be no doubt that the acceptance of the national

geographical definition was to endanger the basic unity of the Jewish people, which was finally denied by those leaders who affirmed that Judaism was essentially a religion, the members of which were nevertheless bound by the common memories of a past of persecution. As the memories of these terrible events were to fade away, the bonds which connected the scattered communities of the Jewish diaspora would be loosened. A philanthropic duty would nevertheless remain, and the Jews of the West would have to use their newly-won freedom in order to help their downtrodden brethren from other countries to win the same freedoms that they themselves had already received. They felt that their situation was the best the Jews could dream of in the modern world, and did not hesitate to look upon themselves as a model of the modern Jew which should inspire their co-religionists and serve as their example.

The Eastern Jewish population could not understand this attitude, as they despaired of ever being able to improve their status. They felt that Jewish society as such, including its auto-nomous organisation, should not be given up. Many developed among themselves a set of values which refused the new Western definition of Judaism and insisted on the popular aspect of Judaism, even if this were to reduce it to a national minority status. Western and Eastern Judaism were to part company for some time. But it was due to the essential vitality of the religious bond and to the persistence of the feeling of a community of fate that the parting of the ways did not become permanent. The recurring persecutions, and the flight to the West which then ensued, also contributed to the preservation of the common bond, until the very possibility of the survival of Judaism reduced solely to its status as a religion was questioned in a Western world which proved less understanding of Jewish survival than had hitherto been thought.

Despite Napoleon's hostility to the Jews in general, and his Infamous Decree in particular, it cannot be denied that his reorganisation of Jewish life, which implied the definition of Judaism as a Christian-like religion, represented a remarkable attempt to solve the problem of Jewish existence in the modern world. Very probably it would have been suggested even without his intervention, as Judaism, which had become acceptable with the French Revolution, would obviously have tried to learn from Catholicism how to survive. The Christianisation of Judaism was inevitable, no less than its eventual failure, as a minority religion could not be expected to react in the same way as a majority religion, unless it were to be condemned to assimilation and to eventual extinction. There is no doubt that the attempt to force on Judaism a Catholic-like hierarchy, which would define the relations between the different Jewish communities, was a failure, and that the different national Jewries remained independent. Therefore, the relations which persisted among them, although religious, and occasionally philanthropic in nature, were always richer and more complex in content and purpose than the Napoleonic way of thinking had intended them to be. The permanence of anti-semitism, even when considered as a regrettable and temporary survival of the past, did not make it possible to have absolute and blind confidence in the new era. On the other hand, the latter was blamed for the religious indifference which accompanied this evolution and ended in not a few cases of apostasy. The new religious organisation, which was itself a result of the changing circumstances, was thus occasionally accused of having caused them.

Nevertheless, even when modern political Zionism denied the possibility of a symbiosis of Judaism and the Western world, it did not negate the new structure of Jewish society, and, although advocating a Jewish state, it rejected the old model of autonomous organisation: it admitted the existence of a rabbinate in charge of religious life and personal status in a state which removed from it the almost absolute authority which it had exerted in judicial affairs. It separated the leadership of the synagogue from the leadership of the city and of the state, thus remaining in more than one way faithful to the Napoleonic heritage in its attempt to find a balance between Judaism and the modern world.

Bibliographical Note

The major contribution to the study of Napoleon's policies towards the Jews remains Robert Anchel's *Napoléon et les Juifs*, Paris, 1928 (summarised with a few modifications in his *Les Juifs de France*, Paris, 1947, pp. 235–78). As it includes a very comprehensive bibliography (pp. xvi–xxxi), there is no need to reproduce it here. The most important publications which have been produced since 1928 are those of Zosa Szajkowski, 'Judaica-Napoleonica: a bibliography of books, pamphlets and printed documents' in *The Jews and the French Revolutions of 1789, 1830 and 1848*, New York, 1970, pp. 971–1016 (first published in Studies in Bibliography and Booklore, 1956); *Agricultural Credit and Napoleon's Anti-Jewish Decrees*, New York, 1953; *Poverty and Social Welfare among French Jews (1800–1880)*, New York, 1954; Fernand L'Huillier, *Recherches sur l'Alsace napoléonienne*, Strasbourg, 1947, pp. 519–55; R. Mahler, *History of the Jewish People in Modern Times*, vol. I, book 1, Merhavia, 1952, pp. 178–209 (Hebrew); Jacob Katz, *Exclusiveness and Tolerance*, Oxford, 1961, pp. 182–196. F. Pietri's *Napoléon et les Israélites: l'accession des Israélites à la qualité de citoyens à part entière*, Paris, 1965, is mostly remarkable for its Napoleonic fervour. The *Revue des Etudes Juives* (abbreviated *REJ*) remains an inexhaustible source for the study of French Jewry. Other publications are quoted in the notes.

It has been necessary to use three contemporary publications of the Assembly of Notables and Sanhedrin meetings: although not contradictory, they vary very much in the comprehensiveness of their reports. This is why the following have been made use of: D. Tama, *Procès verbal des séances de l'Assemblée des Députés français professant la religion Israélite*, and *Actes du Grand Sanhedrin*, Paris, 1806–7; F. D. Kirwan, trans., *Transactions of the Paris Sanhedrim* [sic]..., London, 1807; and A. Bran, *Gesammelte Aktenstücke und öffentliche Verhandlungen über die Verbesserung der Juden in Frankreich*, Hamburg, 1806–7. Many useful Hebrew texts have been reprinted in Baruch Mevorach, *Napoleon Utekufato*, Jerusalem, 1968.

The following archival sources have been used: Archives Nationales (AN) (mostly F^{19} 11000–11028 (Jewish religion) and AF IV (Council of State); Archives Départementales de la Gironde (série I); Consistoire Israélite de Paris (which includes Consistoire Central material); Library of the Jewish Theological Seminary of America (unclassified material); Houghton Library at Harvard University (Friedman collection).

The following private archives have been used: the Formiggini correspondence (he was one of the Italian deputies in Paris) now at the Biblioteca Estense in Modena, 1806, AZ 10–11 – AZ 10–12), and Abraham Furtado's papers now kept by one of his descendants, M. P. Themanlys. The Central Archives for the History of the Jewish People (CAHJP) Jerusalem has microfilms of these documents (HM 26, 445, 2/912–921).

Notes

Chapter I   The Revolution and the Jews of France

1 See Zosa Szajkowski, 'The demographic aspect of Jewish emancipation in France during the French Revolution', in *The Jews and the French Revolutions of 1789, 1830 and 1848*, New York, 1970, pp. 45–7.

2 *Nation* must be understood here as a religious community. *Allemande* or *portugaise* refer not so much to nationality as to rite and origin.

3 This was the traditional name of the four communities of Avignon, Carpentras, L'Isle sur la Sorgue and Cavaillon (in Hebrew: *mesillot*).

4 See Gilbert Cahen, 'La région lorraine', in *Histoire des Juifs en France*, ed. B. Blumenkranz, Toulouse, 1972, pp. 80–8.

5 See notably G. Cirot, *Recherches sur les Juifs espagnols et portugais à Bordeaux*, Bordeaux, 1909.

6 See H. J. de Dianoux, 'Le Sud-Est', in Blumenkranz, op. cit., pp. 193–211.

7 They were published and distributed after the meeting. For editions and translations, see Zosa Szajkowski, *Franco-Judaica*, New York, 1962, no. 481.

8 The only useful biographies are to be found in M. Ginsburger, *Cerf Berr et son époque*, Guebwiller, 1908, and R. Levylier, *Notes et documents concernant la famille Cerf-Berr recueillis par un de ses membres*, vol. 1, Paris, 1902.

9 Its first rabbi, Nehemiah Reicher, was appointed in 1737.

10 See Z. Szajkowski, 'The diaries of the delegates of the Bordeaux Jews to the Malesherbes commission (1788) and the National Assembly (1789)', *Zion*, 18, 1953, pp. 31–79; P. Grosclaude, *Malesherbes, témoin et interprète de son temps*, Vol. 2, Paris, 1961, pp. 631–49.

11 See M. Liber, 'Les Juifs et la convocation des États Généraux (1789)', *REJ*, 1912, pp. 63–4 *passim*.

12 See F. Delpech, 'La Révolution et l'Empire', in Blumenkranz, op. cit., pp. 276–8.

13 'Qu'ils puissent exercer leur culte, conserver leurs rabbins, leurs syndics, et leurs communautés', 'Motion en faveur des Juifs par M. Grégoire, curé d'Embermesnil', Paris, 1789, p. vi.

14 *Mémoire pour les Juifs de Lunéville et de Sarguemines*, Paris, 1789, p. 5.

15 Motion, pp. vi–vii.

16 Motion, p. vii.

17 Motion, pp. vii–viii.

18 Adresse présentée à l'Assemblée Nationale le 26 août 1789 par les Juifs résidans à Paris, Paris, 1789, pp. 6–7.

19 Adresse présentée à l'Assemblée Nationale le 31 août 1789 par les députés réunis des Juifs établis à Metz, dans les Trois Evêchés, en Alsace et en Lorraine, Paris, 1789, p. 18.

20 See Delpech, op. cit., p. 280.

21 This is clearly mentioned in the as yet unprinted index to their minute book which is kept in the Gironde Departmental Archives.

22 Pétition des Juifs établis en France adressée à l'Assemblée Nationale le 28 janvier 1790 sur l'ajournement du 24 décembre 1789, Paris, 1790, p. ii.

23 Très humble et très respectueuse Adresse que présente à l'Assemblée Nationale la commune toute entière de la ville de Strasbourg, Paris, 1790.

24 See Léon Kahn, *Les Juifs de Paris pendant la Révolution*, Paris, 1899, pp. 110–11.

25 See Szajkowski, *The Jews and the French Revolutions*, pp. xxxiv–xxxvi.

26 Ibid., pp. 202–19.

27 Z. Szajkowski, *Autonomy and Communal Jewish Debts during the French Revolution of 1789*, New York, 1959, pp. 36–40; see now Roland Marx, *La Révolution et les classes sociales en Basse Alsace*, Paris, 1974.

28 Ibid., pp. 37–48.

29 Ibid., pp. 73–4.

30 See Z. Szajkowski, 'The attitude of French Jacobins toward Jewish religion', in *The Jews and the French Revolutions*, pp. 399–412.

31 See Ernest Ginsburger, *Le Comité de Surveillance de Jean-Jacques Rousseau, Saint-Esprit-lès-Bayonne*, Paris, 1934.

32 Joseph David Sintzheim, *Yad David*, Offenbach, 1799, Introduction.

33 See his *Apologie des Juifs*, Paris, 1789.

34 Z. Szajkowski, 'Jewish religious observance during the French Revolution in 1789', in *The Jews and the French Revolutions*, pp. 785–808.

35 Z. Szajkowski, *Autonomy and Communal Jewish Debts . . .*, pp. 105–6.

36 AN BB³⁰ 102.

37 AN BB¹⁶ 628.

38 There is one copy in the library of the Alliance Israélite Universelle in Paris (EBr 592) and another at the Houghton Library, Harvard University.

39 E. Marco de Saint Hilaire, *Napoléon au Conseil d'État*, Vol. 1, Paris, 1843, p. 123.

40 Quoted by Anchel, *Napoléon et les Juifs*, Paris, 1928, p. 42.

Chapter II Napoleon's First Encounter with the Jewish Problem

1 First published by E. Deinard in 1915, it has been reproduced by B. Mevorach, *Napoleon Utekufato*, Jerusalem, 1968, pp. 17–36.

2 Published from the original by Noury Farhi, *La Communauté juive d'Alexandrie*, Alexandria, 1946, pp. 19–20 and then in Jacob M. Landau, *The Jews in Nineteenth-Century Egypt*, Jerusalem, 1967, p. 179.
3 The Corbet letter, which was written in French, has been published in an English translation, with a few omissions, by A. S. Yahuda, *Zion*, I(7), March 1950, pp. 29–34 and from there in Louis Hyman, *The Jews of Ireland from Earliest Times to the Year 1910*, Jewish Historical Society of England and Israel Universities Press, London and Jerusalem, 1972, pp. 237–40. The original is now to be found in the Yahuda Collection at the National and University Library in Jerusalem.
4 Franz Kobler, 'Napoleon and the restoration of the Jews to Palestine', *The New Judaea* I, 16 (12), September 1940, pp. 189–90; II, 17 (1–2), October–November 1940, pp. 18–19; III, 17 (3), December 1940, pp. 36–8; IV, 17 (5), February 1941, pp. 69–70. See now Franz Kobler, *Napoleon and the Jews*, Jerusalem, 1976.
5 The name of a Moses Aaron Halevi appears in the seventh and last place among the signatures of Jerusalem rabbis to a circular letter sent to different Italian communities in 1800 through the offices of Raphael Abraham Lev Aryeh; see n. 6.
6 See Abraham Yaari, *Sheluhei Eretz Israel*, Jerusalem, 1951, p. 564.
7 Ibid., p. 565.
8 See the Souvenirs of Issachar Hayyim Carpi in B. Mevorach, op. cit., p. 42.
9 In *Lettres inédites de Napoléon 1er (an VIII–1815)*, publiées par Léon Lecestre, vol. I, Paris, 1897, p. 159.
10 Pelet de la Lozère, *Opinions de Napoléon sur divers sujets de politique et d'administration recueillies par un membre de son Conseil d'État*, Paris, 1833, pp. 215–17.
11 In his Note particulière à Sa Majesté sur les Juifs de l'Alsace, AN AF IV, pl. 2151, no. 106.
12 AN F¹⁹ 11005; AF IV pl. 2151, no. 114; BB¹⁶ 758, dossier 5288.
13 AN BB¹⁶ 627 dossier 7109: 'Que toute opinion à leur égard soît suspendue et d'autorizer qu'il leur soît donné communication de prétendus renseignements transmis contre eux en leur fixant un terme pour éclairer la religion du gouvernement ... que celui qui pourra être ouï ne sera condamné qu'après avoir été entendu et que les coupables seuls sont dans le cas de perdre leurs droits à la protection des loix ...'
14 Although published rather later, Moureau's pamphlet may be looked upon as a very representative summary of the general attitude of the prorevolutionary tendency as far as the Jews were concerned.
15 'Sur les Juifs', *Mercure de France*, 8 February 1806, vol. 23, pp. 249–67.
16 *Quelques observations concernant les Juifs en général, et plus particulièrement ceux d'Alsace, pour fixer l'attention du Gouvernement sur la legislation des différens peuples à leur égard, sur leurs moeurs et habitudes, et sur les mesures qui pourraient être convenables d'adopter dans la circonstance actuelle*, Paris, 1806.
17 Ibid., p. iv.
18 Ibid., pp. 63–6.
19 Ibid., pp. 87–8.

20 Ibid., pp. 126–30.
21 Ibid., p. 130.
22 Ibid., pp. 135–6.
23 Ibid., p. 145.
24 Ibid., pp. 154–5.
25 See Anchel, *Napoléon et les Juifs*, Paris, 1928, p. 71.
26 Ibid., p. 43.
27 Quoted in ibid., p. 47.
28 The remains of their correspondence are in AN F^{19} 11014. The commissioners' suggestion was: 'les autoriser à reprimer les contraventions qui pourroient se commettre par une peine pécuniaire qui sera par vous fixée, applicable par moitié aux hospices civiles de la commune de Metz et l'autre à l'hospice des Juifs.'
29 This letter was annotated: 'vérifier s'il existe une première pétition.'
30 The project was entitled: 'Projet de réglement pour le culte judaïque.'
31 The prefect had written: '. . . je prie votre Excellence de vouloir bien se faire représenter les projets dont il s'agit et de proposer un Décret Impérial qui retablira l'ordre dans la synagogue.'
32 The original of this project is in AN F^{19} 11014. A copy is to be found in AN AD Bas Rhin, V. 510.

Chapter III   The Calling of the Assembly of Notables

1 See for instance Pelet de la Lozère, *Opinions de Napoléon* . . ., Paris, 1833, pp. 211–14 and *Souvenirs du Baron de Barante, publiés par son petit fils Claude de Barante*, Vol. 1, Paris, 1890, p. 149. See also Marquis de Noailles, *Le Comte Molé, 1781–1855; sa vie, ses mémoires*, Vol. I, Paris, 1922, p. 90, and *Mémoires du Chancelier Pasquier, publiés par M. le Duc d'Audiffret-Pasquier*, vol. 1, Paris, 1893, p. 270.
2 In his letter to the Minister of Justice, Councillor of State Treilhard, after having mentioned the reasons which had prevented the enactment of a law on the legal definition of interest, asked – and answered his own question: 'Les circonstances depuis cette époque sont-elles assez changées pour qu'on s'occupe aujourd'hui d'une loi sur le taux de l'interêt conventionnel? La section ne le pense pas' (19 Floréal of Year XIII). AN BB^{16} 758, dossier 5288.
3 'L'on ajouta que l'interêt conventionnel devait être fixé par écrit. On pensa que la pudeur retiendrait jusqu'à un certain point les hommes qui en ont le moins, et la section croit encore qu'à quelques exceptions près cette disposition produit l'effet que l'on avait cru devoir en attendre.' Ibid.
4 He suggested entrusting the matter to the joint sections of legislation and of the interior; ibid.
5 De Noailles, op. cit., pp. 90–2.
6 Barante, op. cit., pp. 149–50.
7 De Noailles, op. cit., p. 90. It must be kept in mind that Molé consistently tried to whitewash the activities of his youth, and his collaboration with the Napoleonic régime in the memoirs which he wrote much later.

8 Pasquier, op. cit., p. 271.
9 M. Liber, 'Napoléon et les Juifs', *REJ*, 72, 1921, pp. 149–58.
10 Ibid., pp. 158–9.
11 De Noailles, op. cit., pp. 94–5.
12 Pelet de la Lozère, op. cit., pp. 213–15.
13 De Noailles, op. cit., p. 95. Cf. Barante, op. cit., p. 151.
14 De Noailles, op. cit., pp. 96–8.
15 Pelet de la Lozère, op. cit., pp. 215–17.
16 M. Liber, 'Les Juifs et Napoléon', *REJ*, 72, 1921, pp. 160–2.
17 See Pelet de la Lozère, op. cit., p. 218.
18 The text of the decree itself has been published many times. As it has been largely corrected by Napoleon himself, it has also been included in his *Correspondance*, vol. 12, Paris, 1863, pp. 502–4, no. 10291.
19 The prefect of the Upper Rhine complained about this very soon. See AN F¹⁹ 11005.
20 See on this problem, Anchel, *Napoléon et les Juifs*, Paris, 1928, pp. 103–6.
21 Ibid., pp. 128–38.
22 The Hebrew name, which appears on its appeal to European Jewish communities, was Assefat ha-Pekidim.
23 See Anchel, op. cit., pp. 137–56. The whole file AN F¹⁹ 11006 deals with this problem.
24 Molé's letter to the Minister, 24 July 1806; AN F¹⁹ 11005.
25 'puisque c'est des croyances des Juifs que naissent toutes les difficultés qui les empêchent d'être citoyens comme les autres sujets de Votre Majesté . . .'; AN AF IV, pl. 2151.
26 *Correspondance*, vol. 12, pp. 700–71, no. 10537.
27 It was sent by the Minister of Cults, Portalis senior; AN AF IV, pl. 2151.
28 *Correspondance*, vol. 12, pp. 701–2, no. 10538.
29 Alexander Bran, *Gesammelte Aktentücke und öffentliche Verhandlungen über die Verbesserung der Juden in Frankreich*, vol. 1, Hamburg, 1807, p. 77. See also Anchel, op. cit., p. 159.
30 Bran, op. cit., p. 79.
31 Cf. Anchel, op. cit., pp. 160–1.
32 Pasquier, op. cit., p. 276.
33 See *Lettere del Rabbino Maggiore Jacob Israel Carmi . . .*, Reggio nell' Emilia, 1905, p. 39. In the Themanlys archives there is a fragment of the Assembly's report with Furtado's corrections, which, in this case, appear to be mostly stylistic (CAHJP microfilm). Another one is kept in the AD Gironde Série I (non classé).
34 *Transactions of the Parisian Sanhedrim . . .*, trans. F. D. Kirwan, London, 1807, pp. 161–4.
35 Pasquier, op. cit., p. 275.
36 D. Tama, *Procès verbal des séances de l'Assemblée des députés français professant la religion juive*, Paris, 1806, p. 18. Two biographies of David Sintzheim have recently been published as introductions to his manuscript *Min'hat Ani*, by A. Deutsch, pp. iii–x (French) and N. R. Auerbach, pp. 11–27 (Hebrew), Jerusalem, 1974.

Chapter IV   The Meetings of the Assembly of Notables

1 Anchel, *Napoléon et les Juifs*, Paris, 1928, p. 163.
2 *Mémoires du Chancelier Pasquier* ..., vol. 1, Paris, 1893, p. 276.
3 Ibid., pp. 276–7.
4 De Noailles, *Le Comte Molé, 1781–1855* ..., vol. 1, Paris, 1922, pp. 105–6.
5 In their report of 2 September 1806, for instance (AN F^{19} 11005).
6 D. Tama, *Procès verbal* ..., Paris, 1806, pp. 8–9.
7 'le rabbin allemand Sindzheimer désigné comme le principal soutien de l'orthodoxie'; AN F^{19} 11005.
8 From a letter sent to an Alsatian cantor in Bohemia by his Haguenau family; N. M. Gelber, 'La police autrichienne et le Sanhedrin de Napoléon', *REJ*, 83, 1927, p. 142.
9 Ibid., pp. 138–40.
10 See pp. 115–16 about his correspondence with Moses Sofer.
11 See Gelber, op. cit., p. 139.
12 In their letters to Lazard's friend, Mosé Formiggini, which are now kept with his correspondence concerning the meeting of Napoleon's Sanhedrin in the Epistolario Formiggini at the Biblioteca Estense at Modena. See, on these letters, Sergio I. Sierra, 'Aspetti del'opinione pubblica ebraica in Italia sul Sinedrio napoleonico', in *Miscellanea di studi in memoria di Dario Disegni*, Turin, 1969, pp. 239–53. Lazard wrote to him in his letter of 22 June 1806 that he hoped to see him in Paris with a few other enlightened Jews from the Kingdom of Italy. The Paris delegate, Olry Hayem Worms, wrote to him also the next day that it was his duty to come to Paris with other enlightened and learned persons from Italy. See also Formiggini's answer to Furtado on 28 October 1806.
13 Ibid., Lazard's letters of 6 June and 7 July 1806.
14 See Gelber, op. cit., p. 142.
15 See A. Bran, *Gesammelte Aktenstücke und öffentliche Verhandlungen über die Verbesserung der Juden in Frankreich*, Hamburg, 1806–7, p. 239.
16 See Sintzheim's letter in Gelber, op. cit., p. 139: '... die bewussten 12 Fragen, die ich beantwortet habe.' The commissioners themselves were aware of this fact; see chapter V n. 9.
17 Tama, op. cit., pp. 18–29.
18 On the general problem of *Dina d'Malkhuta Dina*, see the survey of Leo Landman, *Jewish Law in the Diaspora: Confrontation and Accommodation*, Philadelphia, 1968; and Samuel Shilo, *Dina d'Malkhuta Dina*, Jerusalem, 1974.
19 Tama, op. cit., p. 30.
20 See the commissioners' report on the first three answers to the Minister on 5 August 1806, where they ask: '... de quel principe partent-ils pour distinguer dans leurs livres sacrés ou doctrinaux ce qui est purement religieux d'avec ce qui est purement politique ou civil, les loix de Moyse étant un code entier indivisible par son essence et tendant à former un peuple plutôt qu'à établir une religion?'; AN F^{19} 11005.
21 Ibid.: '... les Juifs sont obligés de recourir à la doctrine et à l'autorité des rabbins pour pallier la faculté que leur laisse la Loi de Moyse de pratiquer

la polygamie. Sur d'autres questions, on les verra invoquer la Loi de Moyse pour condamner les Rabbins dont les doctrines pourroient compromettre leur état dans la société.'

22 The commissioners added that the Jews themselves had asked that the rabbis be forbidden to perform a religious divorce before the civil ceremony (ibid.).

23 Tama, op. cit., pp. 21–8.

24 Ibid., p. 36.

25 The commissioners (AN F[19] 11005) reported to the Minister on this matter: 'Mais les commissaires sont fondés à croire que l'opinion présentée comme celle des rabbins est véritablement celle de l'Assemblée.'

26 Tama, op. cit., pp. 37–8.

27 Ibid., pp. 38–40, 44–6.

28 In their report to the Minister on the Assembly's answers to the last nine questions which they wrote on 11 August 1806. They explained the question in this way: 'Le but de la question était celui-ci: les Juifs se considèrent-ils comme une famille, une tribu, un seul peuple? Il n'y a point été répondu'; AN F[19] 11005.

29 Tama, op. cit., p. 47.

30 'On pense qu'ici l'Assemblée a pris le fait pour le droit et qu'elle s'est moins attachée à l'espèce d'éloignement que pouvoit inspirer à ses membres la diversité des cultes qu'à l'orgueil dont les remplit justement le bonheur d'être les sujets de Sa Majesté et les enfants adoptifs de son glorieux Empire'; AN F[19] 11005.

31 Tama, op. cit., pp. 41, 47–9.

32 Ibid., pp. 41–3, 49. The commissioners remark: 'Sur la septième question la réponse n'est pas complète. Il est résulté de la conférence qu'ont eu les commissaires de Sa Majesté avec le bureau de l'Assemblée que les rabbins pour être aptes à remplir les fonctions des docteurs et des casuistes nommés par une communauté de Juifs devoient justifier d'un certificat de capacité délivré par un rabbin déjà en exercice'; AN F[19] 11005.

33 Tama, op. cit., pp. 61–3.

34 Ibid., pp. 63–4.

35 Ibid., p. 64.

36 Ibid., pp. 52–6, 64–8. The commissioners refused to recognise the Assembly's answer, and wrote: '... il est plus probable au contraire que Moyse a permis le prêt envers l'étranger comme un moyen d'enrichir sa nation aux dépens des peuples voisins'; AN F[19] 11005.

37 On the general problem of Jewish loans to Gentiles, see Judah Rosenthal, 'Ribit min Ha-Nokhri', in his *Mehqarim*, vol. 1, Jerusalem, 1967, pp. 253–323.

38 Tama, op. cit., pp. 69–75.

39 'Nonobstant la réponse à la douzième question il demeure constant que la Loi de Moyse établit relativement au prêt des règles différentes sur les relations des Juifs entre eux et avec ceux qui ne sont pas Juifs'; AN F[19] 11005.

40 'Elle [l'Assemblée] est composée de trois partis, l'un moins nombreux et plus attaché à la Loi qui n'est disposé à aucune concession; l'autre, composé de la majorité de l'Assemblée qui désire concilier les intérêts de la religion

avec la jouissance des droits civils, le troisième, qui est en petit nombre mais qui a tout conduit parce qu'il renferme les hommes les plus riches, les plus polis et les plus adroits et qui tiennent très peu à la religion et n'en conservent le nom et les apparences que par principe d'honneur'; AN F¹⁹ 11005.

41 See p. 65 above.

42 AN F¹⁹ 11005, AF IV pl. 2151.

43 '... ils ont fait, je crois, pour remplir les intentions de votre Majesté, tout ce qu'il leur était possible de faire ...'; AN AF IV pl. 2151.

44 After having stated that, for the Jews, the Christians do not belong to the nations which Moses had cursed, the Minister added: 'Ces observations répondent à celles des commissaires. Nul doute que Moïse ne supposât l'existence de sa nation comme nation quand il leur donnait des loix et que les loix civiles ne tendissent à resserer les liens qui en unissoient tous les membres. Mais il n'avait point préscrit de précepte pour une hypothèse qu'il n'avait pu ou voulu prévoir, et lorsque, par la dispersion, cette hypothèse s'est réalisée, les rabbins ont dû suppléer à son silence; ils l'ont fait. Qu'on ne blâme donc pas l'Assemblée d'avoir cité ici les rabbins au lieu de Moise'; ibid.

45 'Les consequences naturelles des rapprochemens que je viens d'établir entre les questions proposées à l'Assemblée et ses réponses sont: 1° que l'Assemblée a pu répondre ainsi avec sincerité; 2° qu'elle n'auroit pu donner des réponses plus positives sans déroger aux principes regardés comme sacrés par les Juifs rigoristes 3° enfin qu'en adoptant la sevérité des opinions même les plus rigoristes parmi les Juifs, on ne sauroit trouver dans la loi qu'ils suivent un précepte qui prescrive de faire ce que le Code français interdit, ou qui interdise ce que le Code français aurait prescrit'; ibid.

46 See pp. 118–19 below.

47 They are printed at length in Napoleon's *Correspondance*, vol. 13, Paris, 1863, no. 10686, pp. 122–6.

48 Pasquier, op. cit., pp. 277–8.

49 See n. 16.

50 'pour leur faire trouver Jerusalem en France'; *Correspondance*, vol. 13, no. 10686, p. 126.

51 The whole report is in AN F¹⁹ 11005.

52 'Tous les membres également jaloux de répondre aux intentions de S.M. n'ont pas dès l'origine des choses bien saisi le sens de ces intentions. Il en est qui ont pensé qu'il ne fallait travailler qu'à effacer les différences qui séparent les Juifs des autres hommes et qui peu touchés part des considéra-tions religieuses voyoient exclusivement dans tout ce qui se feroit leurs interêts civils et politiques. Cette classe a paru ne pas comprendre la néces-sité de la mesure vaste et vraiment regénératrice que S.M. se propose de prendre. Elle ne s'occupe que de ses propres interêts et circonscrit dans la sphère étroite de ses affections personnelles le bien que l'Empereur projette et dont il veut faire jouir tous les sectateurs de Moyse. Elle ne voit dans les réponses faites à S.M. qu'un moyen d'attirer individuellement à ses membres une consistance sociale plus grande et s'en repose sur le temps et les progrès de l'indifférence religieuse pour diminuer le nombre des Juifs croyants. Elle n'a pas saisi avec empressement les ouvertures qui lui ont été faites et

les Commissaires de S.M. outre ces motifs généraux ont bientôt découvert à cette opposition d'autres motifs qui seront detaillés plus bas. Au contraire les véritables Juifs de l'Assemblée qui sont au sentiment des Commissaires de S.M. les représentants de la majorité des Juifs, ou plutôt les seuls représentants des Juifs qui sont Juifs, et sur lesquels l'Empereur se propose d'agir, pleins d'une joye vive, touchés même jusqu'aux larmes de ce qui leur a été annoncé au nom de S.M. qu'elle entendoit les laisser jouir de la plénitude de leur croyance et leur assurer le complet exercice de leur culte ont applaudi à l'idée lumineuse et bienfaisante qui leur a été communiquée'; ibid.

53 'Ils ont développé avec force l'avantage que l'État en particulier et la civilisation en général retireroient de l'éspèce de législation nouvelle qui seroit promulguée par une assemblée religieuse. Ils ont insisté sur l'autorité qu'obtiendroient par ce moyen les maximes déjà reconnues par l'Assembléé et qui interviendroient en forme de canon théologique. Ils ont assuré qu'aucun des Juifs d'Occident ne pourroient y refuser son assentiment sans erreur et presque sans rebellion. Mais ils ont fait observer aux Commissaires de S.M. qu'en matière de doctrine il y avoit un depôt et une tradition qui reposoient en des mains choisies, que chaque religion avoit ses docteurs auxquels il appartenoit d'expliquer la Loi et qui seuls le pouvoient avec autorité, que tous les synodes tenus depuis la destruction de Jerusalem avoient été exclusivement composés de rabbins, que si dans l'ancien Sanhedrin on admettoit des laïques, c'étoient les plus recommandables d'entre le peuple par leur science et par leur piété, et qu'enfin pour composer actuellement un Sanhedrin, il faudroit que les rabbins ou docteurs composâssent au moins les deux tiers de l'Assembléé si l'on vouloit qu'elle obtînt autorité et croyance tant dans l'intérieur qu'à l'étranger.

'La nature de ces informations a fait connaître aux Commissaires de S.M. une nouvelle cause de la répugnance manifestée par le parti philosophique pour la formation de l'Assemblée en Grand Sanhedrin. Les Commissaires se sont aperçus que ce parti craignait de perdre tout à coup l'influence qu'il a exercée jusqu'ici. Ils ont en effet recueilli de leurs communications successives avec un grand nombre de députés que le parti philosophique toléroit à peine même l'existence nominale des rabbins, tendoit à la destruction de leur ministère pour arriver à l'oubli de toute doctrine religieuse et n'avoit négligé aucune occasion de les éloigner des deliberations et de la préparation des travaux qui devenoient l'objet des délibérations de l'Assemblée. Mais d'un autre côté ils ont reçu des membres de ce parti même l'aveu que les rabbins seuls avoient autorité en matière de doctrine et que toute notification officielle qui pourroit être faite aux synagogues de France, d'Italie et d'Allemagne des décisions déjà prises par l'Assemblée présente ne pouvoit l'être exclusivement que par les rabbins actuellement membres de l'Assembléé'; ibid.

54 *Correspondance*, vol. 13, pp. 158–60, no. 10725.

55 'Ces membres sont les bases de l'opération puisque ce sont eux qui ont fait les réponses. Ainsi l'on quitterait le certain pour l'incertain'; ibid., p. 158.,

56 'le danger d'un refus dont la suite serait l'expulsion du peuple juif'; ibid., p. 159.

57 'Il serait en effet fort ridicule de faire venir à grands frais trente nouveaux

rabbins pour déclarer que les Juifs ne sont pas les frères des Français';
ibid., pp. 159–60.

58 'nous nous engageons à concourir à ce changement de tous nos moyens et
de toutes nos lumières, en nous renfermant toute fois dans le sens positif
qu'elles expriment'; AN F¹⁹ 11005.

59 Tama, op. cit., pp. 236–46.

Chapter V   The Great Sanhedrin

1 In Molé's letter of 2 September 1806 to the Minister of the Interior (AN
F¹⁹ 11005). For the election see D. Tama, *Actes du Grand Sanhedrin*, Paris,
1806–7, pp. 91–9.

2 Ibid., pp. 99–100.

3 Ibid., pp. 112–13. In their report, the commissioners wrote: 'Les commissaires de Sa Majesté ne doivent cependant pas dissimuler à Son Excellence
le Ministre de l'Intérieur que le parti religieux de l'Assemblée se plaint de
voir parmi les vingt cinq députés élus plusieurs individus qui à cause de leur
ignorance religieuse ou de leur irréligion notoire sont aux yeux des croyants
zélés un sujet de scandale et de murmure. Mais ils doivent ajouter que cet
inconvénient était inévitable, puisque le Bureau de l'Assemblée et plusieurs
de ses membres les plus influents encourent les mêmes reproches'; AN F¹⁹
11005. See also Nathan Levy's letter of 11 January 1807 in ibid.

4 See Lazard's letter to Formiggini of 4 (or 14) October 1806 in the
Formiggini Archives.

5 Tama, op. cit., pp. 105–9. For the different editions, see Z. Szajkowski,
'Judaica-Napoleonica . . .', in *The Jews and the French Revolutions of 1789,
1830 and 1848*, New York, 1970, nos 79–82.

6 See, on this problem, Anchel, *Napoléon et les Juifs*, Paris, 1928, pp. 139–56.

7 In his letter to Formiggini of 4 (or 14) October 1806, in the Formiggini
Archives.

8 AN F¹⁹ 11005.

9 'Après avoir mûrement réfléchi au choix du chef du Grand Sanhedrin, nous
nous sommes déterminés à présenter à Son Excellence pour remplir ce poste
le nommé David Sintzheim, Grand Rabbin de Strasbourg. Le but de tout ce
qui passe à l'égard des Juifs étant d'influer sur l'esprit et la doctrine de
ceux dont on se plaint, c'est à dire de ceux du Nord, il nous a paru qu'il
convenoit de donner l'un d'entre eux pour chef à l'Assemblée qui doit
les réformer. Il ne faut pas d'ailleurs oublier qu'ils ne reconnoissent pas
l'orthodoxie des Juifs du midi. Le Rabbin Sintzheim convient encore au
poste qu'on lui destine par son grand âge. Il est considéré de tous ses coreligionnaires. Il étoit de la première Assemblée et a concouru à la rédaction de
ses réponses.

'Les Rabbins Segré et Cologna sont les seuls que nous puissions présenter
à Son Excellence pour les deux places d'assesseurs. C'est peut-être de tous
les membres de l'Assemblée ceux dont les lumières et l'influence nous ont
été le plus utile'; AN F¹⁹ 11005.

10 In the same letter; Cambacérès had informed Napoleon on 3 February

that the Sanhedrin would meet on the 11th. See his *Lettres inédites à Napoléon* ... *Presentation et notes par Jean Tulard*, Paris, 1973, vol. 1, p. 442.

11 D. Tama, *Actes du Grand Sanhedrin*, pp. 1–22.

12 Furtado's letter to Formiggini of 19 October 1806, in the Formiggini Archives.

13 Tama, *Actes* ..., p. 42.

14 Ibid., pp. 92–4.

15 Ibid., pp. 95–6.

16 Ibid., p. 104.

17 Ibid., p. 101.

18 Ibid., pp. 89–92.

19 Ibid., p. 25. On Sintzheim and Cerf Berr's family, see Kellerman's report to the Emperor of 23 July 1806; AN AF IV, pl. 2151.

20 Tama, *Actes* ..., pp. 55–60.

21 Ibid., pp. 61–76.

22 Ibid., p. 78.

23 'Vous avez reconnu la validité de certains actes civils; mais vous avez avoué leur incohérence religieuse'; ibid., p. 82.

24 'La protection du Souverain et le salut de l'État vous faisoient un devoir de les accorder'; ibid., p. 82.

25 Ibid., p. 83.

26 Ibid., pp. 87–8.

27 Ibid., p. 78.

28 See Napoleon, *Correspondance*, vol. 13, Paris, 1863, pp. 715–19, no. 11320. Anchel has shown that they did not arrive at the end of November 1806, but in the middle of February 1807; Anchel, *Napoléon et les Juifs*, Paris, 1928, p. 210 n.1.

29 AN F^{19} 11005.

30 *Correspondance*, vol. 13, pp. 717–19.

31 'Actuellement je vais hâter les décisions religieuses demandées au Grand Sanhedrin et je ne lui ferai pas entrevoir toute l'étendue des vues de Votre Majesté qui pourront effaroucher quelques rabbins trop servilement attachés à leurs anciennes pratiques'; AN AF IV, pl. 2150.

32 'et je tâcherai d'obtenir d'elle d'inviter l'autorité publique à prescrire et à faire exécuter ce qu'elle ne pourroit, tout au plus, que conseiller'; ibid.

33 'Je tiens beaucoup à ce que l'Assemblée Générale en exprimant ses desirs pour la régénération de ses coreligionnaires, en reconnaissant l'insuffisance de ses moyens pour l'opérer supplie l'autorité publique pour intervenir pour completter cet ouvrage ...'; AN AF^{19} 11005.

34 The report is in AN AF IV pl. 2151.

35 D. Tama, *Procès verbal* ..., Paris, 1806, pp. 114–18.

36 Later, the Central Consistory would have to explain the precise meaning of each of these terms in its *Solution donnée par le Consistoire Central des Israélites de l'Empire à diverses questions qui lui ont été proposées par la Synagogue de Coblentz* ..., Paris, 1809.

37 Tama, *Procès verbal*, pp. 120–36.

38 Ibid., pp. 136–41.

39 Ibid., pp. 144–5.

40 Ibid., p. 147.
41 Ibid., p. 148.
42 Ibid., p. 153.
43 Ibid., pp. 141–2, 154–64.
44 Ibid., pp. 165–6.
45 Ibid., pp. 169–84.
46 Ibid., pp. 185–200.
47 Ibid., pp. 201–6.
48 Ibid., pp. 206–15.
49 Ibid., pp. 217–30.

Chapter VI The Duped

1 For the full text of the letter, see N. Gelber, 'La police autrichienne et le Sanhedrin de Napoléon', *REJ*, 83, 1927, pp. 138–40.
2 'Sefer Chatam Sofer', *Derashot*, vol. 1, Cluj, 1929, pp. 80b–82a. (Now republished in Sintzheim's *Min'hat Ani* as well as a manuscript eulogy by Rabbi Karlburg from Krefeld (ibid., pp. 33–8).)
3 His answers were first published by J. Rosenthal in *Talpiyot*, 4 (3–4), 1950, pp. 565–81 and later in his *Mehqarim*, vol. 2, Jerusalem, 1967, pp. 513–32, and in Mevorach, *Napoleon Utekufato*, Jerusalem, 1968, pp. 104–20.
4 AN AF IV, pl. 2151.
5 'Elever ainsi à toute la dignité de français ceux qui en sont véritablement dignes en s'efforçant de corriger ou d'éloigner ceux qui ne sauroient le mériter'; ibid.
6 'Le premier [remède] consisterait à rédiger une formule de déclaration ou de serment qui leverait d'une manière authentique pour tous les Juifs résidant ou réuni en France le doute qui pu s'élever par rapport aux obligations civiles ... Cette déclaration serait exigée individuellement de tout Juif qui résiderait en France ou qui y serait admis à l'avenir comme de la condition à laquelle il jouissait des droits de français'; ibid.
7 'Il serait extrêmement à désirer que les enfants des Juifs fussent tenus d'aller également aux écoles publiques sans y être assujettis à déroger à leur culte ...'; ibid.
8 'Les mesures nécéssaires pour arrêter ces abus, pour opérer cette réforme, ne porteront point l'empreinte de l'arbitraire, puisqu'elles sont sollicitées par ceux là même auxquels elles doivent s'appliquer'; AN AF IV pl. 2151.
9 In a letter of 1 June 1807; AN AF[19] 11005, Cambacérès wrote to Napoleon on 14 June that the Council of State had completed the discussions on the Jews the day before; *Lettres inédites à Napoléon ...*, Paris, 1973, vol. 1, p. 550.
10 Furtado's passport is still to be found in the Themanlys Archives. Cambacérès informed Napoleon on 19 June of Furtado's plan, and that he had told him to secure permission for his intentions from the Minister of the Interior; *Lettres ...*, vol. 1, p. 552.
11 Mémoire sur les projets de décrets presentés au Conseil d'État concernant les Israélites, Paris, no date (in the AD Gironde, Série I, copy, the manuscript date is 1807). Cambacérès (*Lettres ...*, vol. 1, p. 534) wrote to the Emperor

on 28 May to remind him that the one-year moratorium on Jewish debts was about to expire. He added the following (Furtado-inspired?) remark: 'de l'avis même des Israélites de bonne foi, il y aurait de l'inconvénient à le faire cesser avant que les affaires des Juifs soient réglées.'

12 Quoted by H. Léon, *Histoire des Juifs de Bayonne*, Paris 1893, p. 192. A letter protesting against the proposed decrees seems to have been sent to the Emperor some time before by a number of Jewish notables, including Furtado. It has been published by G. Moyse, a descendant of Furtado, under the title: 'Supplique à Napoléon 1er concernant les Israélites d'Alsace et de Lorraine en 1808 (probablement)', *Revue juive de Lorraine*, 4(41), November 1928, pp. 228–30. A draft of a letter of protest by Furtado dated 17 April 1808 is to be found in AD Gironde, Série I, Papiers concernant les Juifs . . ., which contains also a number of other documents pertaining to this controversy.

13 For the editions, see Z. Szajkowski, 'Judaica-Napoleonica . . .', in *The Jews and the French Revolutions of 1789, 1830 and 1848*, New York, 1970, nos 127–8.

14 See Anchel's study, 'Les Lettres-patentes du 10 juillet 1784 pour les Juifs d'Alsace', in his *Les Juifs de France*, Paris, 1946, pp. 214–33.

15 See Anchel, *Napoléon et les Juifs*, Paris, 1928, pp. 285–304.

16 It is signed, among others, by Furtado; AN F^{19} 11008.

17 Anchel, *Napoléon et les Juifs*, Paris, 1928, pp. 433–44.

18 Ibid., pp. 447–52.

19 See, on this matter, Z. Szajkowski, *Agricultural Credit and Napoleon's anti-Jewish Decrees*, New York, 1953.

20 Anchel, *Napoléon et les Juifs*, pp. 304–36.

21 Ibid., pp. 304–36.

22 Ibid., pp. 353–67.

23 Anchel, ibid., pp. 371–3, gives a table of the decisions concerning the different departments in this connection.

24 Ibid., pp. 462–8.

25 Ibid., pp. 466, 474.

26 Ibid., pp. 479–86.

27 The correspondence is kept in the Archives of the Paris Consistory, 1^{cc}33, liasse 2.

28 Paris Consistory Archives, 1^{cc}33, liasse 3.

29 The manuscript of Johlson and the Central Consistory's report are in AN AF^{19} 11028.

30 'Rien n'est plus contraire à nos dogmes que cet esprit de réforme toujours fatal et pernicieux aux sociétés religieuses qui s'écartant des règles adoptées livre les institutions sacrées aux caprices des hommes et les subordonne à la versatilité de leurs penchants et de leur passion'; ibid.

31 'Supprimer les principes que nous avons signalés dans nos observations comme non orthodoxes'; ibid.

32 The whole matter is analysed in a dossier on Jewish public instruction; AN AF^{19} 11028.

33 Anchel, *Napoléon et les Juifs*, p. 492.

34 See my analysis of the correspondence of the Central Consistory with the

Italian Consistories, 'Les communautés italiennes et le Consistoire Central (1808–1815)', *Michael*, I, Tel Aviv, 1972, pp. 109–62.

35 See Léon Kahn, *Le Comité de Bienfaisance*, Paris, 1886, *passim*.

36 All these regulations are to be found in AN AF^{19} 11034.

37 Paris Consistory Archives, I^{cc}33, liasse 1.

38 S. Schwarzfuchs, 'Les communautés italiennes . . .', p. 125.

39 Anchel, *Napoléon et les Juifs*, p. 468.

40 See Z. Szajkowski, *Autonomy and Jewish Communal Debts during the French Revolution of 1789*, New York, 1959, pp. 91–135.

41 For the text of the judgment: T. Hallez, *Des Juifs en France: de leur état moral et politique*, Paris, 1845, pp. 352–65.

Chapter VII In the Empire

1 D. Tama, *Procès verbal des séances de l'Assemblée des Deputés français professant la religion israélite*, Paris, 1806–7, pp. 105–9. See also Z. Szajkowski, 'Judaica-Napoleonica . . .', in *The Jews and the French Revolutions of 1789, 1830 and 1848*, New York, 1970, nos 79–82.

2 Tama, op. cit., pp. 149–52, 166–9. The Hebrew original of the Frankfurt letter is in the Themanlys Archives (CAHJP microfilm). According to I. Kracauer, *Geschichte der Juden in Frankfurt am Main (1150–1824)*, vol. 2, 1927, p. 358, there were 250 signatures.

3 See E. Klibansky, 'Les Juifs de Francfort et le Grand Sanhédrin', *REJ*, 84, 1927, pp. 97–9.

4 D. Tama, *Actes du Grand Sanhedrin*, Paris, 1806–7, pp. 76–7. The letter is in the Themanlys Archives.

5 D. Tama, *Procès verbal . . .*, p. 205.

6 D. Tama, *Actes du Grand Sanhedrin*, pp. 35–6, 77.

7 Some are to be found in the Themanlys Archives. See ibid., p. 36. Nevertheless the great Amsterdam community wrote that it would not be represented at the Paris meeting; *Lettere del rabbino maggiore Jacob Israele Carmi . . .*, Reggio nell'Emila, 1905, pp. 100–1.

8 Furtado was aware of this fact, as Asser, one of the Dutch delegates, had handed him a memorandum on the situation of the Dutch communities (AD Gironde, Série I).

9 See Kracauer, op. cit., p. 358.

10 Israel Jacobson, *Les premiers Pas de la nation juive vers le bonheur sous les auspices du grand monarque Napoléon*, Paris, 1806. I have had to use the summary in Jacob R. Marcus, *Israel Jacobson, the Founder of the Reform Movement in Judaism*, Cincinnati, 1972, pp. 39–42, and the German translation of the address to Napoleon published in A. Bran, *Gesammelte Aktenstücke und öffentliche Verhandlungen über die Verbesserung der Juden in Frankreich*, Hamburg, 1806–7, pp. 109–12.

11 Marcus, op. cit., p. 42 (after Graetz, *Geschichte der Juden*, vol. 11, Leipzig, 1870, pp. 273–4).

12 See chapter II n. 9.

13 See S. Dubnow, *Die Weltgeschichte des jüdischen Volkes*, vol. 8, 2nd ed., Berlin, 1928, pp. 229–36.

14 Marcus, op. cit., pp. 82–3.

15 Ibid., pp. 84–6.

16 Ibid., pp. 87–92.

17 Ibid., pp. 93–4.

18 Ibid., pp. 95–9.

19 Ibid., pp. 102–4.

20 A copy of this letter is to be found in the Themanlys Archives.

21 See Kracauer, op. cit., pp. 377–82.

22 In his Très humble remontrance adressée à Son Altesse Eminentissime le Prince primat de la Confédération du Rhin sur la nouvelle constitution des habitans Juifs établis à Frankfort, Brunswig, 1808.

23 Ibid., pp. 5–6.

24 Kracauer, op. cit., pp. 414–17.

25 Ibid., pp. 421–6.

26 Dubnow, op. cit., p. 244.

27 Ibid., pp. 245–7.

28 Ibid., pp. 248–50

29 Ibid., pp. 250–3.

30 Reprinted as appendices to A. N. Frank, *Yehudei Polin bimei Milhamot Napoleon*, Warsaw, 1913.

31 Dubnow, *History of the Jews in Russia and Poland*, vol. 1, Philadelphia, 1946, 2nd ed., p. 299.

32 Ibid., pp. 299–300.

33 Ibid., p. 300.

34 Ibid., pp. 302–3.

35 Ibid., pp. 302–4. See also Dubnow's *Die Weltgeschichte des jüdischen Volkes*, vol. 8, 2nd ed., Berlin, 1928, pp. 335–44.

Chapter VIII   In Non-French Europe

1 *Transactions of the Parisian Sanhedrim or Acts of the Assembly of Israelitish Deputies of France and Italy* . . ., trans. F. D. Kirwan, London, 1807, p. iii.

2 Ibid., pp. iv–ix.

3 Ibid., pp. x–xvi.

4 See the list in Z. Szajkowski, 'Judaica-Napoleonica . . .', in *The Jews and the French Revolutions of 1789, 1830 and 1848*, New York, 1970, nos 23, 37, 46, 50 and 52.

5 See in particular N. M. Gelber, 'La police autrichienne et le Sanhedrin de Napoléon', *REJ*, 83, 1927, pp. 1–21, 113–45.

6 Ibid., pp. 5–6.

7 Ibid., pp. 6–7, 136–7.

8 Ibid., pp. 11–12.

9 Ibid., pp. 10–14.

10 Ibid., p. 11. Metternich reported on 8 February 1807 on the arrival of the Frankfurt delegates, and those of a few German cities; ibid., pp. 137–8.

11 Ibid., pp. 14–20.
12 Ibid., pp. 113–20.
13 Ibid., pp. 121–4
14 Ibid., pp. 127–30.
15 Ibid., pp. 131–3.
16 See chapter VII n. 15.
17 His letter in Hebrew is kept in the Themanlys Archives.
18 On the Jews of Prussia see Ismar Freund, *Die Emanzipation der Juden in Preussen unter besonderer Berücksichtigung des Gesetzes vom 11. Marz 1812*, vol. 1, Berlin, 1912, pp. 103–226, and S. Dubnow, *History of the Jews in Russia and Poland*, vol. 1, 2nd ed., Philadelphia, 1946, pp. 218–29.
19 On the Jews of Russia see Dubnow, op. cit., pp. 345–59 and his *Die Weltgeschichte des jüdischen Volkes*, vol. 8, 2nd ed., Berlin, 1928, pp. 360–77.
20 Republished in Mevorach, *Napoleon Utekufato*, Jerusalem, 1968, pp. 182–3.
21 See nevertheless Z. S. Pipe, 'Napoleon in Jewish folklore', in *Yidn in Frankraikh*, vol. 1, New York, 1942, pp. 153–89 (Yiddish).

Chapter IX   The Results

1 According to a still unclassified letter kept at the Jewish Theological Seminary of America library (similar letters were probably sent to all other consistories), the Central Consistory felt at the beginning of 1816 that Judaism had finally achieved full governmental recognition:

'Paris le 9 janvier 1816

Le Consistoire Central des Israélites à Messieurs les membres du Consistoire de Marseille,

Messieurs,

Vous aurez sans doute appris par la voie du *Moniteur* que nous avons eu l'honneur d'être présentés au Roi, et de lui offrir en corps nos hommages au même temps que les autres corps religieux à l'occasion du renouvellement de l'année. Nous nous faisons un plaisir de vous informer que notre réception a été on ne peut plus satisfaisante. Notre Président ayant adressé à S.M. des paroles exprimant les sentiments de notre hommage et nos voeux pour la conservation des jours précieux du Monarque et pour sa plus grande prospérité, le Roi a daigné les accueillir avec bonté et nous en a remerciés de la manière la plus gracieuse. Nous avons également eu l'honneur d'être présentés à Madame, et ensuite à Monsieur Frère du Roi qui a répondu par ces paroles: "Je vois avec plaisir Messieurs du Consistoire Central des Israélites, les bons et fidèles sujets de Sa Majesté."

La lettre d'admission que nous a adressée S.Exc. le Grand Maître des Cérémonies d'après les ordres du Roi est placée dans nos archives comme un monument de la bonté de Sa Majesté et comme une pièce qui consacre le principe de notre admission de même que les autres corps religieux.

Nous avons l'honneur de vous saluer avec une considération distinguée,

Les membres du Consistoire Central.'

2 The Jewish Theological Seminary of America keeps another unclassified draft of a letter sent by the Central Consistory to Chief Rabbi Jacob Mayer in his capacity of Ancien of the Lower Rhine Consistory. Dated 17 October 1814, it contains more than an echo of this anti-consistorial mood:

'. . . Nous sommes affligés, Monsieur l'Ancien, des détails que vous nous donnez sur l'esprit d'insubordination qui règne parmi les administrés de votre circonscription consistoriale et de leur abrutissement en désirant la suppression des établissements consistoriaux. Ces hommes égarés dont les vues se fixent uniquement sur l'interêt pécuniaire, quelque faible qu'il soît, ne refléchissent pas à quels malheurs et à quel avilissement ils se trouveraient bientôt livrés, dans vos contrées surtout, s'ils avaient le malheur de perdre une administration dont l'institution spéciale est de les regénérer et de leur conserver la jouissance intacte des droits civils et politiques, mais, heureusement pour eux, leurs voeux indiscrets ne seront pas accomplis . . .'

3 AN F¹⁹ 11005: 'Les instructions portaient qu'il y aurait à Paris un Comité Central de rabbins qui seraient les surveillants et les supérieurs de tous les Juifs de l'Empire. Les commissaires de l'Empereur ont cru nécéssaire au bien du service de Sa Majesté d'introduire quelques Juifs non rabbins dans ce Comité. Il leur a semblé qu'il pouvait, sous certains rapports, devenir dangereux d'abandonner la surveillance exclusive des synagogues à des hommes qui forment entr'eux une sorte de corporation et qui, étant en possession presque exclusive d'une langue particulière, pourraient échapper dans les communications intérieures et leur correspondance habituelle, à la surveillance de la police et de l'administration . . . cette mesure sera très populaire parmi les Juifs, dont une partie redoute l'influence rabbinique et qui verront avec plaisir qu'on lui donne un contrepoids . . .'

4 In a letter kept at the Harvard University Houghton Library (*57JM-53) he wrote to an unknown friend that he was overjoyed at his forthcoming return to France. The date – which was added in another hand – seems to be mistaken (21 Adar 5569 = 9 March 1809).

5 His son, who converted to Christianity and later returned to Judaism, had taken an active part in the arrest of the Duchess of Berry. His son-in-law, David Drach, also converted, and was very active in missionary endeavours for the conversion of the Jews.

6 See S. Schwarzfuchs, 'Les communautés italiennes et le Consistoire Central (1808–1815)', *Michael*, 1, Tel Aviv, 1972, pp. 129–30.

Index

Aaron, son of Levi, 25, 26
Aleppo, 24, 26
Alexander, I, Tsar, 175–7
Alsace, 1–3, 5–8, 10, 12–14, 19, 27, 28,
   30, 33, 34, 49, 50, 52, 65, 89, 96, 118,
   125–30, 142, 181
Amsterdam, 132, 143, 145
Ancona, 22, 23
Andrade, Abraham, 63, 66
Asser, 210
Austria, 26, 146, 160, 166
Avigdor, Samuel, 60, 110
Avignon, 1, 5, 10, 14, 32, 65, 127, 197

Baden, 159
Barras, Paul, 24, 25
Basel, 8
Bavaria, 159
Bayonne, 6, 63, 66; see also Saint
   Esprit
Belgium, 146, 181
Berg, Grand Duchy of, 146
Berlin, 156
Berkovitch, Joseph, 162
Berr, Berr-Isaac, 7, 60, 63, 65, 88
Berr, Michel, 63
Berry, Duchess of, 213
Beugnot, Jacques Claude, 47–9
Bohemia, 168

Bonald, Louis de, 33–4
Bonaparte, Elisa, 146
Bonaparte, Jerome, 27, 146, 149–51,
   155
Bonaparte, Joseph, 146
Bonaparte, Louis, 146
Bonaparte, Napoleon, see Napoleon
Bordeaux, 1, 4, 6, 7, 10, 19, 60, 132,
   141, 165, 183
Bourbons, 142, 180
Brancas family, 8, 14
Brody, 169
Brunswick, 147
Buonaparte, 26

Cahen, Goudchaux Mayer, 7
Cairo, 23
Cambacérès, Jean-Jacques Régis de,
   49, 208, 209
Carmi, J. I., 201
Caro, Joseph, 137
Carpi, I. H., 199
Carpentras, 4, 197
Cassel, 132, 149, 155, 156
Cavaillon, 4, 197
Cerf Berr, 2, 3–7, 10, 18, 19, 42, 53,
   59, 63, 94, 131, 207
Cerf Berr, Baruch, 53, 63, 131
Cerf Berr, Lippman, 53, 61

Cerf Berr, Théodore, 5, 53, 60
Champagny, Jean Baptiste, 77–81, 101, 102, 118, 120
Chatam Sofer, see Schreiber, Moses
Chorin, Aaron, of Arad, 170
Coblenz, 132, 186
Colmar, 2, 60, 142
Cologna, Abraham de, 90, 130, 141, 186, 187
Comtat (Comtat Venaissin), 1, 4, 5, 65, 142
Constantinople, 24
Corbet, Thomas, 24, 25
Cracovia, 92
Crefeld, 132
Creuznach, 134

Dalberg, Karl, 156
Deutz, Emmanuel, 134, 186, 187
Dillon, Eliezer, 176
Drach, David, 213

Edom, 22
Egypt, 23, 25–7
Emden, 132
Ensheim, Moses, 90
Eskeles, Baron, 167

Formiggini, 205–7
Frankfurt am Main, 143, 144, 145, 156–8, 170, 211
Furtado, Abraham, 6, 59–62, 64, 65, 71, 87, 88, 90, 92–7, 101, 110–13, 120–3, 143, 165, 170, 185, 202, 207–10

Galicia, 169
Gerando, Joseph-Marie de, 96
Germany, 31, 52, 85, 146, 147, 150, 158, 167, 171
Gershom, Rabenu, 69
Gironde, 53, 129
Great Britain, 146
Grégoire (abbé, then bishop), 8, 156
Grodno, 176

Haguenau, 16
Haman, 154
Hamburg, 132, 146, 158
Hell, François, 13
Hertz of Medelsheim, see Cerf Berr
Hildesheimer, Isaac, 144
Holland, 145–7
Hourwitz, Zalkind, 19, 90

Illyria, Illyrian provinces, 146, 147, 169
Ishmael ben Abraham Isaac ha-Cohen, 116, 117
Isle sur la Sorgue, 4, 197
Israel, 25, 27, 93, 176
Italy, 22, 23, 53, 74, 85, 89, 93, 104–6, 113, 116, 130, 145–7, 164, 165, 169, 187

Jacobins, 16
Jacobson, Israel, 147–53, 155–7
Jean-Jacques Rousseau Committee, 17
Jeiteles, B. B., 115
Jerusalem, 24–6, 82, 83, 199
Johlson, Joseph, 134, 135, 151, 209
Jordan, 165

Kellerman, François Christophe, 30, 207
Kobler, Fr., 199
Kotzk, 162

Ladi, 176
Landes, 129
Lazard, Jacob, 60, 63, 66, 88, 90, 131, 141, 185, 202, 206, 207
Leeuwarden, 132
Leghorn, 132
Lev Aryeh, Raphael Abraham, 26, 199
Levy, Moise, 71
Lipman, Solomon, 60
Lion, Asher, 186
Lorraine, 1, 4–8, 10, 89, 181

Louis XVI, 3
Lozère, Pelet de la, 49
Lubavitch, 176
Lucca and Piombino, Prince of, 109
Lunéville, 8

Maimonides, 76, 137
Malesherbes, Chrétien Guillaume de, 6, 59
Mantua, 130
Marengo, 27
Marseille, 5, 14, 132, 212
Marx, Mayer, 7
Mayer, Jacob, 213
Mecklenburg, 158
Meisels, Moses, 176
Messiah, 135, 166, 175
Metternich, C. W. L., 166, 167, 211
Metz, 1, 4–9, 12, 14–17, 37–9, 52, 78, 89, 118, 132, 142, 183, 188
Milan, 23
Modena, 116
Molé, Louis-Matthieu, 46–50, 54–5, 62, 65, 81, 86, 88, 90, 94, 98, 101, 184
Mont Tonnerre, 52
Moravia, 168
Moselle, 38, 39, 41, 52
Moses, 67–8, 76–83, 87, 99, 100, 161
Moses Aaron ha-Levi, 199
Moureau, Agricol, 31, 32
Mulhouse, 8

Nancy, 12, 71, 89, 120, 132
Naples, 146
Napoleon, 6, 21, 22, 23, 26, 45, 46, 49, 50, 52, 55, 59, 61, 68, 80–2, 93, 97, 116, 122, 125, 127, 133, 138, 139, 141, 142, 144–9, 152, 158, 160–7, 169–71, 173–84, 193
Nathan the Wise, 183
Nezwitz, 176
Nidernai, 5

Palestine, 24, 26, 95, 100, 148

Pasquier, Etienne Denis, 47, 55, 62, 64, 65, 80
Pharaoh, 115
Poland, 100, 161–3, 166
Poniatowski, J. A., 163
Portalis, Jean Etienne, 37–40
Portalis, Joseph Marie, 55, 62
Portugal, 4, 85
Poujol, 34–7
Prague, 25, 66, 115, 168
Pressburg, 115, 170
Prussia, 146, 171–3

Ratisbonne, Auguste, 53
Reicher, Nehemiah, 197
Rhine, Confederation of, 146
Rhine, Lower, 2, 28, 30, 34, 52, 126, 129
Rhine, Upper, 2, 30, 52, 61, 126
Rhine and Moselle, 52, 134
Rodrigues junior, 60
Roer, 52
Rome, 132, 146
Rotterdam, 132
Russia, 163, 167, 174, 175

Saint-Angély, Regnault de, 46, 47, 49, 50, 51, 61
Saint Cloud, 49
Saint Esprit, 1, 7, 17; see also Bayonne
Sarre, 52
Sarreguemines, 8
Saverne, 29
Saxony, 146, 158, 160
Schreiber, Moses, 115, 116, 170
Seesen, 147, 153
Segre, Salvator, of Vercelli, 63, 66, 90, 130, 186
Seine, 43, 48, 129
Selestat, 29
Shaagath, Arieh, 186
Shneur Zalman, 176
Sintzheim, David, 7, 18–20, 53, 63, 66, 67, 81, 88–90, 92, 94, 95, 115, 116, 130–3, 138, 149, 168, 170, 178, 185, 186, 191, 201, 202, 206, 207

Sonnenberg, Sundel, 176
Spain, 4, 85, 146
Strasbourg, 2, 3, 11, 12, 14, 16, 17, 20, 28, 29, 45, 77, 90, 130, 132
Sundgau, 8, 13
Swiss Confederation, 146
Syria, 24, 26

Tilsit, 120, 171, 175
Treilhard, 200
Treves, Solomon, 144
Trier, 132
Trieste, 169
Turin, 66, 132
Tuscany, 118, 146

Valence, 13
Vaucluse, 31
Venice, 92, 146, 165, 167
Vienna, 25, 165, 167, 169, 180

Vitta, Emilio, 60
Voltaire, 60, 65
Vosges, 52

Warsaw (city), 161–3
Warsaw (Duchy), 146, 160, 161, 174
Westphalia, 146, 149, 152, 155
Wintzenheim (Colmar), 132
Wittersheim, Seligman, 7
Wolf, Louis, 7
Worms, 66, 69
Worms, Olry Hayem, 60, 202

Yosselovich, Berek, 162

Zinsheimer, *see* Sintzheim
Zion, 18, 173
Zwolle, 132